Consuming Culture

By the same author

TO KILL A BIRD WITH TWO STONES:
A HISTORY OF VANUATU

Consuming Culture

Jeremy MacClancy

CHAPMANS

Chapmans Publishers Ltd
141–143 Drury Lane
London WC2B 5TB

First published by Chapmans 1992

ISBN 1–85592–522–2

A CIP catalogue record for this book is
available from the British Library

Photoset in Meridien by
Ace Filmsetting Ltd, Frome, Somerset
Printed and bound in Great Britain by
Butler & Tanner Ltd, Frome and London

To My Mother and Father

Acknowledgements

Vicks Hayward first suggested the idea of this book to me and Bill Hamilton realized its potential. Chris McDonaugh, David Zeitlyn, Marcus Banks, Jonathan Webber, Mike Gilsenan, and my mother all provided useful ethnographic data. Rosalind Coward directed me to references on the Alternative Health Movement, Rodney Needham introduced me to the unappetizing world of scatology, and Peter Riviere gave me the low-down on dirt-eating and passed on reports of farting. Hilary Callan, John L. Cox, Lynette Hunter, Alison James, Gerald Mars, Sharon McDonald, and Anne Murcott kindly sent off-prints. The Henley Centre and A. C. Nielsen & Co. generously supplied survey data. Tina King and Vera Ryhajlo of the Upper Reading Room in the Bodleian Library, Oxford, managed to put up with my repeated demands with surprisingly good humour. Elaine Genders constructively criticized the section on women. Nick Fiddes gave me a diskette of his thesis and commented on the section dealing with meat-eating. Vicks read much of the manuscript; sometimes I followed her suggestions.

My thanks also to John Murray for permitting publication of John Betjeman's 'How to Get on in Society' and to Peters Fraser & Dunlop for the excerpt from Evelyn Waugh's *Brideshead Revisited*; and for illustrations, my thanks to Routledge for 'The naming of parts. The edible dog as a Peugeot 404 station wagon', to Trefoil for 'manandwomanatmidnight' from Marinetti's *The Futurist Cookbook*, translated by Suzanne Brill and published by Trefoil Publications, and to Centre d'Etudes et de Documentation du Sucre for the illustration of Etienne Tholoniat, the great French sugar-baker.

I am grateful to all the above. The usual disclaimers apply. If you have any complaints direct them to

Jeremy MacClancy

Contents

Illustrations
Between pages 118 and 119

Jain food offerings (*Marcus Banks*)

George Bush on broccoli (*The Hulton Deutsch Collection*)

The Rt. Hon. Margaret Thatcher, food technologist
(*The Hulton Deutsch Collection*)

Priapic Primo? The dictator and a load of old bull
(*The Hulton Deutsch Collection*)

The last of the Milesians (*The Hulton Deutsch Collection*)

'manandwomanatmidnight' (*Trefoil Publications*)

The Kitchen Army (*The Food Magazine*)

The naming of parts (*Routledge and Peter U. Idika*)

The wolf-girl of Midnapore (*The Revd J. A. L. Singh*)

Nineteenth-century 'evidence' of cannibalism
(*Oxford University Press*)

Mid-morning meal in Nepal (*Christian McDonaugh*)

Sugar-daddy (*CEDUS*)

Mambila porridge (*David Zeitlyn*)

A yam for all seasons (*Jeremy MacClancy*)

'Pepper No. 30' (*Edward Weston*)

Introduction

William Buckland, the geologist and gastronome, thought mole the worst thing he had ever tasted – until the day he tried a bluebottle.

Whatever food you can think of, no matter how disgusting or nasty, the chances are someone, somewhere is eating it. Whether it is flamingo tongues, elk droppings, the foetuses of rodents, rat *à la bordelaise*, the stomach contents of seals, or dancing prawns that tickle your gums as you crunch them live, some humans in some part of the globe have tried it or still eat it regularly.

For good or for bad, that bizarre list does not exhaust the outer limits of the edible, for some groups of people on this planet have a very singular definition of 'food': among the people living along the banks of the Bajo Urubambu river in the Amazon, some of the children eat earth, while some of the adults consume cigarette ash, matches, aspirins and camphor; the Aghori ascetics of Benares survive on alms, excrement and even the occasional putrid corpse; and in one country the natives cook a mixture of cows' lungs, intestines, pancreas, liver and heart churned up with onions, suet, and oatmeal, all stuffed together into a sheep's stomach. The Scots call it a haggis.

Despite this unsavoury evidence of human variety in taste, we do not eat randomly. Within any one society, all its members eat more or less the same foods. Though some may have their individual likes and dislikes, the great majority learn to agree on what are the most flavoursome dishes and what are the least. Each culture has its own culinary guidelines of acceptability. The sorts of food they eat, the sorts they actively prohibit, and the way they time and structure their meals say something about them as a group. Their particular cuisine becomes a statement of their identity, of their distinctiveness as a culture. And, in a complex society like ours, the food we choose to eat and cook reveals our class as well. We can quickly and usually accurately gauge

1

people's social position simply by looking at what is on their plates. In this sense the food we consume is a way of asserting, both for our sake and for that of others, that we are different; we don't eat like *them*. Try asking a Geordie if he has ever tasted the sweet belly of a toasted sugar ant, and you will get my point.

It is all very simple. Without food we die. But, for some people, food does not merely provide sustenance, it is also the very substance and fibre of their bodies. They believe they are physically made up of the staple they eat, whether it be maize, rice or cassava. And in the myths of many cultures, the first humans were born of these sorts of foods too. For these groups of people, their original ancestors were edible plants, and their own bodies are transformed plants. They are walking food.

Humans feed on symbols and myths as much as on fats, proteins, and carbohydrates. Food is both nutrition and a mode of thought. We use food words as metaphors, as ways of talking about something else: he's a nut; your car is a lemon; my daughter is the apple of my eye; and that man just blew you a raspberry. There are so many of these figures of speech in English that we can mention a wide range of feelings, attitudes, and occurrences by reference to different foods. Thanks to food we can express ourselves. In some cultures, the plant and culinary metaphors are so extensive that it is difficult for people to talk to one another without using them. People understand the world in terms of these metaphors. In other words, as Lévi-Strauss said, 'Food is not only good to eat, but also good to think with.'

Sex is food for the body, the mind – and the foetus. In certain cultures, it is believed that the sexes nurture one another and the future child through coupling. Among some groups, a meal together is seen as a form of sex, and it is intended that eating should lead to intercourse. Particular foods can symbolize parts of the male and female genitalia while food terms may act as euphemisms for various kinds of copulation. Saying you are hungry may just be a way of telling people that you crave sex right now. Food can also be a sexual aid, stimulating one's desire for another; whether or not aphrodisiacs really do work, there are enough people who believe they do.

Food is power. Those who regulate its production, distribution, and consumption can control others. Men exploit women, women manoeuvre men, and both hold children in check – all thanks to food. Family mealtimes are a privileged occasion for parents to teach their offspring the rules and manners of their society or subculture. Adults can also use food to barter with their children, manipulating it as a system of reward and punishment in order to get the brats to obey. But boys and girls can get their own back, and they strive to become independent by making up their own gastronomic rules, and exchanging food among themselves.

Food is friendship. A cooked gift for one's relatives is a way of keeping in touch, and receiving something from them shows they have not forgotten you. Preparing a large meal and sharing it is an age-old way of making friends and allies. However, laying on a feast so lavish that it is difficult for your guests to reciprocate is also a time-honoured way of putting others down and elevating your own name. One can also sneer at people by ridiculing their food habits: 'Those bloody frogs!' Of course, a most effective and highly traditional method of overcoming or insulting your enemies is to eat one of them.

Food is religion. From the sacred cow to the host of Holy Communion, we venerate the hallowed and commune with the Lord and other spirits through the medium of food. If we break their dietary rules, we commit sin and provoke their wrath. Should we keep to their culinary edicts, only eating the correct foods at the correct times, then they will watch over our fields, protect our animals, and fulfil the promise of a bountiful life. We can communicate more directly with the supernatural and transmit our desires to them by sacrificing animals, or even vegetables, in their name. Food also links the living and the dead, making them all part of the same community. By leaving out dishes for the deceased we maintain contact with them; so long as they are still remembered and fed, they remain members of our society.

Food is magic. Some sorcerers use the leftovers from others' meals to work their evil tasks – destroying their opponents' fields, rendering them impotent or crippling them with stomach cramps. The less maliciously inclined use food for more beneficial ends: in the sixteenth century the English ate hot-cross buns on Good Friday in order to bring good fortune in the coming year and to guard the house from fire; on the feast-day of St Blas, Spanish Catholics eat *roscos* (ring-shaped pastries) as a prophylactic against throat disease. Either way, in religion or in magic, food is an intimate medium for conversing with other-worldly beings and

HOW TO MAKE BLOOD SAUSAGE
Nineteenth-Century Swedish Style

1. Kill a pig. Mix its blood with rye flour and rye grains.
   Beat the mixture and thin it somewhat with water or
   small beer. Add in cubes of pork and pieces of apple.
   Pour the mixture into cleaned pig intestine. Leave it
   three-quarters full, as the flour and grains will expand
   when it is boiled. Tie both ends, and fasten with a thorn
   from a sloe bush or a 'sausage stick' specially cut for the
   purpose.

2. Boil very slowly in a large kettle. Place a coin in the
   bottom. If the water is boiling as it should (evenly and
   quietly) then the coin should clatter lightly. Close the
   door to prevent draughts. If air bubbles form within
   the sausage, prick them with a thorn.

3. To prevent the sausage bursting while it is on the boil,
   do not talk or fart. If forced to speak, do not include the
   words 'blood' or 'blood sausage'. (It seems the locals
   thought that if the human gastro-intestinal tract let air
   escape – from either end – the sausage would follow
   suit, and so break.) It is best if only the housewife and
   one other is at the stove, and that no men are present.
   If you have to let strangers in, they must taste the
   sausage: that way, they will not be envious and try to
   spoil it.

4. Before placing the sausage into the kettle, smack it
   against the side of the stove while reciting a 'sausage
   prayer' to guard against it splitting. Traditional example: 'Hard as a stick and tough as cunt, you must hold
   and never split.' (The idea here is that the sausage
   should be as tough as a vagina can be at the moment
   of giving birth. The 'stick' refers to the sausage stick
   tied at either end.)

5. While it is boiling, one of you must say, 'Is the sausage-
   holder at home?' The other must reply, 'Yes'. Repeat
   this three times. (Exactly why you have to say this is
   not known, but in Swedish custom many magical
   dialogues have to be repeated three times.)

for carrying out supernatural acts. Without it, how else could we tempt the gods?

In agricultural societies people are controlled by the food they produce. The crops they cultivate and the livestock they rear set the tempo of their lives. The seasonal growth of these foodstuffs dictates what they have to do and when they have to do it. It will not wait for them. Food is coercive. We have to follow its rhythm, and not vice versa. It has power over us.

Food as identity, as our physical selves, as a way of thought, as sex, as power, as friendship, as a medium for magic and witchcraft, as our time-controller – in all these different ways and more, food pervades our culture and gives meaning to our lives. It plays a central role in our societies, and provides us as much with intricate symbols and metaphors as with nutritional substance. By examining its different uses in any one group of people, we can uncover their basic values, aims, and attitudes. As the French gastronome Brillat-Savarin declared, 'Tell me what you eat, and I'll tell you who you are.'

1
THE CALL OF THE WILD

On the morning of 8 January 1800 a filthy, almost naked boy emerged from the woods and entered the village of Saint-Sernin in southern France. He seemed about twelve years old. Kindly and curious villagers offered him a meal of raw and cooked meats, rye and wheat breads, apples, pears, grapes, nuts, and an orange. The boy sniffed the food but refused it all, only accepting acorns and potatoes. He rejected wine and would only drink water. The strange child could not speak, wore only the tatters of an old shirt, and, if chased, could run on all fours. He showed no modesty about his bodily functions, relieving himself whenever, wherever. When the wind blew from the Midi, he would look towards the sky and let out great cries, like a dog. In the previous three years peasants in a nearby valley had occasionally spotted the lad digging up root vegetables, which he ate immediately or carried off to his lair. The untamed child of the forest had been captured twice before but had always managed to escape. This time the villagers made sure he could not run away.

They dubbed him the Wild Boy of Aveyron and imprisoned the lad in a local orphanage. There, he slowly became used to wearing clothes and on fine days was taken for a walk on a leash. The Wild Boy started to become tolerant of more foods and began to eat rye bread, peas, broad beans, cabbage, chestnuts, walnuts, hazelnuts, beechnuts and soup. Within four months he had developed a taste for meat, though he never minded if it was raw or cooked. He was uninterested in wheat and other cereals and refused white bread, sugary foods, any seasoning, and cultivated fruits such as apples, pears, cherries, currants, and plums. He preferred wild fruits and the sorts of food found on the forest floor.

One doctor who observed the boy noted, 'He gets everything into his mouth with one flick of the fingers, and does not chew for long. He is greedy and impatient when he sees some food; he wants to swallow it immediately.' Though he ate like a glutton and even devoured sawdust in handfuls, he took great care, when eating fruit, to stack them neatly in a pile. And if he spilled any soup on his hands, he did not dry them with a cloth but in ashes from the fire. When he had eaten enough, the boy swept the leftovers into his shirt and squirrelled them away in the orphanage garden, as a stockpile.

While some mistakenly thought the Wild Boy an idiot, he did know how to get much of what he wanted. For example, once he had acquired a taste for fried potatoes, he used to carry the tubers to any man in the kitchen wielding a knife, then find a frying-pan and point to the cupboard where the oil was kept. When he was offered sausage for the first time, he sniffed the offering and then ate the lot voraciously. The next day, an officer who came to lunch made a sign for the boy to approach him at the dining table. The officer cut off a small piece from the large sausage on his plate and showed it to the lad. With his left hand the boy took the morsel from the captain's fingers – and with his other he adroitly snatched the rest of the sausage.

Victor, as he was later named, was moved to Paris where a young doctor, Jean Itard, spent years educating him. Though some at first thought Victor's whole life centred on his stomach, the boy did learn to read, write and speak in a very simple manner. He came to accept a wider range of foods and even became quite pernickety, fastidiously making sure that everything on his plate was clean. But even by the time of his death in 1828, Victor's food preferences were far more exclusive than those of most civilized humans. Unlike almost everyone else, Victor had never been taught what foods to eat or how to eat them. When first captured, he had no idea how to cook. Instead, during his years in the forests, he had made the most of what he had found around him. With no one to show him what to do, he had taught himself how to gather food and how to eat it. Though born into the species *Homo sapiens*, Victor on the day of his capture had no human culture: he could not cook and had no cuisine.

An even more dramatic case, if possible, of cultural deprivation is that of the Wolf Children of Midnapore, in West Bengal. These two Indian girls, aged about five, were discovered in 1920 when a band of locals killed a she-wolf, entered her cave and found two children inside, huddled together with a pair of cubs. Placed in a nearby orphanage, they shunned the light of day and spent part of each night howling. On hot days they panted and let their tongues loll out. They walked on their hands and knees for short distances, and ran on their hands and feet. Humans who came too near were snarled at; the closest friend they had was a captured hyena cub.

Reared by wolves, these real-life Mowglis ate like them as well. They did not approach their food. They attacked it. As soon as a bowlful was placed in front of the girls, they would sniff it quickly, then hurl their faces into it, and, making repulsive noises and hideous grimaces, bolt down the lot in seconds: they literally wolfed it down. Sometimes they ate so ferociously they made themselves sick. Though used to a meat-only diet, they prevented constipation by swallowing earth and pebbles after eating. When thirsty they did not hold a bowl to their lips, but had to crouch down and lap up the water noisily.

At times the parish priest who ran the orphanage could scarcely believe what he saw. On the tenth day after their arrival, the older of the pair, Kamala, automatically bent down to eat with the local dogs, competing for scraps of meat and offal. With convulsive shakes of her rib-cage, she gulped the food. Seizing a bone she carried it off in her mouth to a quiet corner, where she held it down with her hands as though they were paws. Gnawing at her food, she rubbed it on the ground to separate the meat from the bone. On one occasion, when Kamala saw vultures – as tall as herself – picking at the remains of a dead cow, she scared them away in order to grab some meat for herself from the carcass.

The younger of the pair died within twelve months. Although the priest tried to civilize the remaining wolf-child, it took five years before Kamala even learnt to walk on her feet. She was slowly weaned on to a mostly vegetable diet and gradually learnt to tolerate salty and sugary foods. But if given meat, she instantly forgot all the table manners she had been taught so laboriously and immediately reverted to her dog-like conduct.

Kamala came to be very fond of the priest's wife; she learnt to hold simple conversations and to call people by name. By the time of her death in 1929 she could also perform simple chores like frightening off crows that were eating grain, collecting eggs from the hen-house, and caring for the smaller children in the institution. In her own limited way, Kamala had managed to find a place for herself in the orphanage, which she might have called home – if she had had the vocabulary.

Like Victor, Kamala had taught herself to adapt to life in the wild; unlike Victor, she was never completely isolated. Deprived of human contact during her crucial early years, she had survived by imitating the behaviour of her foster-parents, the wolves of Midnapore. Unlike the Wild Boy, who had been a herbivore with the diet of a squirrel, the Wolf Child had been a single-minded carnivore with the behaviour of a beast. She had no time for hazelnuts or other forest fruit.

Tragically, Victor and Kamala are not the only examples of wild children. They are simply the most notorious, well-documented cases. Today, tabloid newspapers sell thousands of copies by printing sensationalist stories about the latest cases of grossly neglected children. Effectively abandoned by their parents, these toddlers are left to compete with the family dog, snarling at anyone who chances upon the scene. In November 1970, officials in California were appalled to discover Genie, a thirteen-year-old girl whose sadistic father had fed her baby foods and soft-boiled eggs, pushing them into her mouth as fast as possible. Those later put in charge of Genie tried to give her solid foods. However, since she had never learnt to chew, she would instead stuff her mouth until her cheeks bulged like those of a chipmunk storing nuts. She would wait until the saliva had softened the food and would then swallow it whole.

These wild children – storing acorns, howling like dogs, living off raw meat, unable to use their teeth – seem more animal than human. With their unpalatable mannerisms they appear less than primitive, more unpredictable than any household pet, and further removed from us than even the most exotic of peoples studied by anthropologists. They lack the basic forms of self-control and self-restraint that we were all taught as youngsters. These children do not learn the rules of any tribe but make up their own, or, like Kamala, adopt those of their animal caretakers. Ignorant of how to behave with fellow humans, they are not the sort of person one would invite to a dinner-party. When Jean Itard took Victor to a formal lunch-gathering at a chateau outside Paris, the boy paid no attention to the highly distinguished guests but ate voraciously and then ran into the garden and up a tree. Having no understanding of the intricacies and subtleties of human life, these isolated individuals have no sense of mealtimes, of sharing, or of manipulating others through the use of food. Unlike our food, which we can use as symbols or metaphors, their food has no meaning beyond that of fulfilling basic nutritional requirements. For them food is not something 'good to think with' but simply a means to a biological end: satisfying their hunger.

Maybe Romulus and Remus could found a great city but, outside the realms of myth, those not brought up by humans do not learn to become full functioning humans. By the time of their capture or discovery it is often too late to civilize wild children completely, for no one was around during their early, critical, formative period, when some of our most basic attitudes are moulded and fundamental skills developed. Children who are not taught a language at the right time never learn to speak or be able to communicate properly. In a similar, though not quite so drastic, manner wild children never come to appreciate the full range of a cuisine. Even after years of training by humans they still have peculiar gastronomic habits; they continue to reject a variety of popular foods and their taste never extends beyond an almost inhumanly narrow assortment of foods. Their palate, like their ability to speak, remains crude and unrefined. A wild child's inability to appreciate anything more than a few favourite flavours shows he belongs to a society of one: his own.

These children learnt to survive in their own way, in the wild. Their condition is like a mirror reflecting back upon ourselves, reminding us how we might have turned out. Their uncouth behaviour and restricted diet reveals just how essential is our upbringing – gastronomic and otherwise – by affectionate, responsible caretakers. Without their constant love, example, and company, we would remain stunted for life. Isolated from our parents and other children, we would not only act like the animals we had in effect become. We would eat like them as well.

2

CULTURE vs NATURE

The Original Scene: Primordial Man strolling through the bush, with his Woman, their children, and a small band of companions. They do not cultivate crops, they have no fixed abode, and they spend their time picking fruit or killing the occasional animal. They are not discriminating about what they eat, so long as it is edible. They gorge on nuts, pull up a few plants, or roast some roots. When they have digested that lot, they potter on until they feel hungry again.

It is an idyllic scene, an innocent paradise inhabited by people who do not have to worry about where to find the next mouthful. They seem like Adam and Eve in an appleless Eden: nothing is forbidden – it is all up for grabs. In fact, of course, things are not that simple.

Gatherer-hunters, as nomadic peoples who do not practise agriculture are known, do not just lunge for the nearest food to hand. They like some plants and some kinds of meat, and they reject others. Far from being indiscriminate omnivores, they are among the most choosy peoples in the world. The Mbuti pygmies of the Angolan tropical rainforest, for instance, have their own rules about what to eat and what not to touch. Because leopards devour humans, some Mbuti will not consume them: in their eyes, eating the flesh of an animal that might have been fattened itself on some of their own kind is a bit too close to the bone. Similarly, some will not kill chimpanzees or monkeys because they are too human-like; buffalo is considered tough and unpleasant; and fish is regarded as food only fit for children. But they crave honey and can distinguish the taste of over ten different types. They particularly relish combs full of white maggots, which they heat slightly to soften the stiff honey and make the little white blobs wriggle, before eating the lot with gusto. The Mbuti know what they like and are prepared to work to get it; they do not hunger for everything in sight nor do they gobble everything around them.

12

Although the San (they used to be known as 'Bushmen') of the Kalahari Desert live in a completely different environment from that of the Mbuti, they are just as pernickety. To them the desert is no sun-scorched wasteland but home to over 200 species of plants, almost half of which they regard as edible. Despite this variety, the San choose to eat only fourteen types of plant most of the time. These are called 'strong' or 'big foods', which are thought tasty and/or highly nutritious. Other foods are 'weak' or 'small', and the San do not usually waste their time over them. While their women and children are left to gather fruit and nuts, the men go off to hunt warthogs, antelopes, or giraffes. Though ostrich is perfectly edible, they do not kill the big bird because, to them, its meat tastes bad; similarly, they leave most zebra alone because, they say, its flesh smells. Monkeys and hyenas they never even touch. In short, the San class certain foods as good to eat and others as not worth the bother. Their desert Eden provides them with more than sufficient foodstuffs to create a varied and appe-tizing cuisine. Their taste may not be the same as ours, but that does not mean they are not picky.

Most Westerners think the diet of 'traditional' peoples is per-fectly adapted to their environment. If that were not true, so the reasoning goes, they would all be dead by now. If they were not completely in step with nature, nature would have had done with them. This idea might be appealing, but it is as wrong-headed as the image of Primordial Man as Greedy Gobbler. Contrary to what most Europeans think, the eating habits of many groups around the world are *not* perfectly in tune with their needs. In nutritional terms, they are maladapted to their environment. The gastro-nomic rules of a society do not always ensure that its members receive the sorts of foods necessary to keep them all hale, healthy, and ready to face the next day. For a society to survive, its diet does not have to be exactly right, just adequate. So long as most people in a society get enough food to stay alive and reproduce, they will not disappear as a group. This is not survival of the fittest, but extinction of the least fit.

In the dry parts of north-central India, farmers sow their fields with a mixture of wheat and a legume called *Lathyrus*. If the rains fall, the wheat chokes the legume. If they do not fall, the wheat dies and the locals reap harvests of *Lathyrus*. Making the legume part of your diet, however, is a risky business: eat too much over a period of time and you will be left crippled for life. It is like playing roulette, with your body as the chips.

OUT OF STEP WITH NATURE

In many parts of the world, pregnant women are denied high protein foods – which are usually the most prized parts of a cuisine – because they are thought too 'strong' for people in such a fragile state. Though these women need to eat for two, they are not even getting a balanced diet for one. Mbum Kpau women of Chad, for example, are told that if they eat chicken or goat while pregnant, they risk having a painful childbirth and abnormal children. Mothers in some West Malaysian villages do not give certain nutritionally important foods to their children because they think these substances will 'weaken' their offspring. But, medically speaking, prohibiting these foods does not strengthen youngsters, it only leaves them more open to disease: because children are banned from eating papaya and freshwater scaly fish, many of them lack vitamin A and so develop eye ailments, while those with skin infections, who need to rebuild their tissues, are not allowed eggs and many kinds of meat and fish.

This sort of nutritional mistake and the finicky habits of gatherer-hunters show that while people are influenced by their environment, their lives are not determined by it. The ecological conditions of peoples' habitats do not dictate to them precisely what they must grow, rear, and hunt. They just restrict their choice, laying down the natural boundaries within which people can play out their lives. Operating within these biological confines, the particular crops cultivated and the animals pursued by different societies are a matter of cultural choice.

Similar societies living in the same ecological zone can produce and consume very different foods. The Moussey, Massa, and Toupouri of north Cameroon and Chad all live in the same geographical area, have the same technology, intermarry frequently and share a common genealogical origin. Yet each group grows a different variety of sorghum. Though the strain favoured by the Moussey yielded much less than those of the other two groups, the Moussey stubbornly kept to their favourite until finally persuaded by Westerners of the economic 'benefits' of change. While the Moussey cultivate abundant crops of cow peas, bambara nuts and sesame seeds, the Massa and the Toupouri virtually ignore them. Moreover, women and children from the three groups do not gather the same wild foods, and each has a separate approach to fishing and to raising livestock. They even sneer at one another's food habits: the Moussey mock the Toupouri for eating rotting legs of beef in their rituals, while they in turn are derided by their neighbours for adding the juice of centipedes to their sauces. Though all three groups occupy the same ecological habitat and endure the same climatic conditions, each one stubbornly maintains its own specific diet.

In Kenya, the neighbouring Masai and the Akikuyu are even more divergent in their culinary lifestyles. The Masai drink lots of milk and blood from their cattle, while the Akikuyu cultivate cereals and potatoes. On the whole, the Masai are fit and hale, and the Akikuyu are anaemic, have deformed bones, and suffer nutritional diseases. The Akikuyu could modify their diet and so end much suffering but they choose not to. Culture wins out over ecology, even if it seems something of a Pyrrhic victory at times.

As a general rule, anything humans can do, monkeys are not bad at either. Like gatherer-hunters and unlike most other mammals, primates select their food very carefully. Gorillas are so fussy they only eat certain parts of plants, and they pick and choose from the wide variety available at any given time. Some baboons are so fastidious they develop their own individual preferences: though the bulk of their diet consists of grasses, flowers, and seeds, some learn to snack on eggs, lizards, chicks, and insects. Chimpanzees go for ripe foods or only the most tender of buds. Meticulous about what they consume, they select every item with care and inspect it before eating. Though their diet is more diversified than that of the San, they, like the Kalahari desert-dwellers, rely heavily on just a few staples. In packs of up to forty individuals, chimps will also hunt other monkeys and then share the corpse. Unlike the San they can at times turn cannibal, killing and eating members of their own band.

It may not be surprising that these chimps have developed such a fastidious diet, but it is startling that one type of primate displays the possible beginnings of a cuisine. In the 1950s, primatologists studying a colony of *Macaca fuscata* monkeys on Koshima Island in Japan observed that some of the young females spontaneously learnt to wash sweet potatoes in a stream before eating them. Older monkeys in the colony imitated the females' example and then taught it to their offspring. Some of the monkeys even came to prefer salt-water to fresh, dipping the tuber into the sea between bites.

This crude kind of 'seasoning' may seem devilishly clever but the simple truth is that no gorilla, orang-utan or chimpanzee is capable of cooking. With the one exception of the 'salted-potato' monkeys, there are no primates that know anything about culinary operations. They do not know how to use fire for gastronomic ends; there are no chefs in primate societies. Only humans have complex ways of preparing food, which they teach to their children. Monkeys have instincts; we have traditions. Primates might have brains, but they do not have recipes and they have no concept of 'a proper meal'. Keepers at London Zoo might stage a Chimps' Tea Party, but just what the chimpanzees think they are doing during this performance is another matter completely. To put it a different way, place a plate of kedgeree in front of a baboon and it will be incapable of thinking, 'Ha! If it's fish for lunch, then it must be Friday!'

Samuel Johnson fully understood the point:

I had found out a perfect definition of human nature as distinguished from the animal. An ancient philosopher said, Man was 'a two-legged animal without feathers', upon which his rival sage had a cock plucked bare, and set him down in the school before all his disciples as a 'Philosophick Man'. Dr (Benjamin) Franklin said, Man was 'a tool-making animal', which is very well; for no animal but man makes a thing. But this applies to very few of the species. My definition of Man is, a 'Cooking Animal'. The beasts have memory, judgement, and all the facilities and passions of our mind, in a certain degree; but no beast is a cook.

3

DESERT ISLAND DISHES

Let's play a game. Imagine you become famous. Everybody knows about you, and some of them even like you. You wake up one morning on a beautiful desert island in the South Pacific, with the archetypal palm-trees, long white beach, and crystal-clear water. It looks idyllic, so perfect you could still be dreaming. But you cannot go into the sea because of the deadly stone-fish, the poisonous sea snakes, and the hungry sharks; the rays of the sun reflecting off the water blind your eyes; you cannot tread on the beach because the toasted sand burns your soles; and you cannot sit under a coconut tree in case a nut drops and cracks your head open. You are in what is popularly known as paradise.

A tall man in late middle-age and a suit approaches. He says he is from the BBC and that he can play six songs of your choice. Anything you want, so long as it is not modern, or longer than thirty seconds. He asks a few questions about your childhood and personal life. You tell him your best short anecdotes and he laughs politely. After half an hour, he says he must depart. But before he does, he will leave you two foods of your choice. The sixty-four-thousand-dollar question is: What do you choose?

When asked this question, most of us tend to choose flavours we have grown up with: porridge and peanut butter, roast beef and chocolate, bacon and eggs. These are the foods of our childhood, ones that evoke memories of mealtimes at home with mother looking after everything. We have been with these foods for so long and so intimately we say we love them. And unlike the fickle, romantic sort, this love is steady, dependable, and consistent. It will not do us down, run off with someone else, or send us a Dear John. As George Bernard Shaw put it, 'There is no love sincerer than the love of food.' It is with us until the very end.

We can become so attached to certain foods that we are not prepared to switch under any circumstances. When upper-middle class Englishmen, who were deprived of their mothers while at boarding school, lunch at their West End or City clubs they do not ask for sophisticated French desserts but for their crude old-school fare: jam roly-poly, spotted dick and sticky toffee pudding, with lots and lots of custard. Middle-class Americans can be just as conservative: in almost every foreign city with a sizeable American community, the expatriates organize a commissary so they can keep away from local dishes and stick to their home staples of breakfast cereals and tinned soups. Some Britons are so fixed in their habits and unbending in their tastes that they even take their standard fare with them when they go on holiday. A British travel firm offering self-catering holidays in Spain and France found that the great majority of their customers left the country bearing foods they could not do without. Most packed tea, and more than half carried cornflakes or other cereals. Nearly everyone shunned locally bought bacon and eggs, and over 60 per cent did not buy any food they did not usually eat at home. One resolute family of four, not seduced by the charms of French cuisine, carried tea, coffee, pot noodles, eight packets of cereals, eighteen tins of baked beans, fourteen packets of Angel Delight, and four tins of rice pudding. They were not going to try any of that foreign muck. They were more than content with the food they had always had.

Such beloved foods are the taste of our lives, a steady source of comfort and succour in hard times. To exiles, these foods come to represent the home life they are denied, and they pine for their familiar flavours. In the last century, missionaries in Hawaii rejected the local diet of taro, fresh fruit, and fish; they preferred to wait for slow ships from their native Massachusetts to bring supplies of salt pork and wheat flour, though the meat was by then rancid and the flour lively with weevils.

The arrival of such familiar foods is like the appearance of an old friend. Small wonder then, that American GIs fighting the Japanese yearned for fresh milk and drank as much as possible when they returned home; almost to be expected, that the passengers stranded in the Andes when their plane came down had to ban discussions of what they would eat on their homecoming – the pain of remembering such gastronomic pleasure was too great. And unsurprising, that during the Gulf War US Army food technologists tried to invent a chocolate bar that would not melt in the desert, or that members of 20 Squadron RAF Regiment wrote home pleading, 'It's hot, but we've got used to that, but one thing we can't get accustomed to is a lack of Marmite. Morale is quite high despite the conditions . . . but, oh, for a reminder of home. So come on, Mate, send us some Marmite.'

> ### TRUE GRIT
>
> A Cajun woman from Louisiana who married a New
> Englander did not realize her mistake until she tried the
> food. 'Those winters and snow, *cher*. That was bad enough,
> but what I really missed was my grits and coffee in the
> mornings. When I went in the grocery store up there and
> asked for a box of grits, they didn't understand me. Like I
> was speaking a foreign language or something. They had
> never heard the word before! Grits, I told them, grits, and
> they asked me what grits were. I had to explain it to them.
> I couldn't believe it. I still cannot believe it.'
> She persuaded her husband to move to Lousiana.

People can become so attached to certain foods that they begin
to assume personalities in their own right. When market researchers in Britain asked people 'If Brand X came to life, what sort of
person would it be?' they received immediate and vivid answers;
people did not regard the question as unreasonable or inappropri-
ate. They thought Heinz soup would be an older person, someone
in their sixties, 'very sweet, very understanding, but a little
narrow'. An Oxo stock cube was pictured as 'a great big fat, beefy
man, about forty, strong, solid, stolid. Not a bright sprightly
disposition – but even-tempered.' 'I'd be employed by him,' one
woman said, 'in a secretarial capacity. He reminds me of my
company chairman.' Oxo Man is reliable, trustworthy, and authoritative: 'He'd have a fairly large family saloon – car rides to see
his friends; they wouldn't go too far really.' When your favourite
foodstuffs have so much character, mealtimes are never a lonely
business.

A strong attachment to particular foods is a peculiarly human
habit. Monkeys do not get upset if they cannot find what they
want – they just eat something else. And as a specifically human
characteristic, this learned love for specific items can override
biologically predetermined preferences: culture overcomes nature. Smear sugared water on the lips of a newborn babe and it will
make the closest thing to a smile a twelve-hour-old is capable of;
then give it very dilute lemon juice and it will scrunch its face up
like an old man. This instinctual aversion is probably adaptive, as

many naturally occurring poisons have a bitter taste. But if we *Homo sapiens* are innately attracted to sweet foods and automatically avoid bitter ones, how come over half of the world's population have made a powerful chemical irritant the centre of their gastronomic lives? How can so many millions stomach chillies?

Biting into a tabasco pepper is like aiming a flame-thrower at your parted lips. There might be little reaction at first, but then the burn starts to grow. A few seconds later the chilli mush in your mouth reaches critical mass and your palate prepares for lift-off. The message spreads. The sweat glands open, your eyes stream, your nose runs, your stomach warms up, your heart accelerates, and your lungs breathe faster. All this is normal. But bite off more than your body can take, and you will be left coughing, sneezing, and spitting. Tears stripe your cheeks, and your mouth belches fire like a dragon celebrating its return to life. Eater beware!

As a general stimulant, chilli is similar to amphetamines – only quicker, cheaper, non-addictive, and beneficial to boot. Employees at the tabasco plant in Louisiana rarely complain of coughs, hay fever, or sinusitis. (Recent evidence, however, suggests that too many chillies can bring on stomach cancer.) Over the centuries, people have used hot peppers as a folk medicine to treat sore throats or inflamed gums, to relieve respiratory distress, and to ease gastritis induced by alcoholism. For aching muscles and tendons, a chilli plaster is more effective than one of mustard, with the added advantage that it does not blister the skin. But people do not eat tabasco, jalapeño, or cayenne peppers because of their pharmacological side-effects. They eat them for the taste – different varieties have different flavours – and for the fire they give off. In other words, they go for the burn.

After salt, chilli is the most popular seasoning in the world. Normally used to make otherwise bland staples more appetizing, it is an integral part of people's diet throughout Central and South America, West and East Africa, India, and Southeast Asia, as well as parts of China, Indonesia, and Korea. In rural Mexico, almost all villagers over the age of six eat hot peppers at all three meals. They consume chillies whole, cooked in stews, sliced on foods, or ground up and mixed with tomatoes as a sauce to go with tortillas. Only non-sweet foods escape the addition of a little hot pepper. Mothers gently introduce their one- or two-year-old children to the taste by giving them chillied soups or stews. It is not forced on them: if they fail their baptism of fire, they are offered something else. But by the age of five, most Mexican village children have suppressed the innate rejection and have acquired a liking for hot pepper, adding it to food themselves. By eight they are eating as much of it as their parents. They have learnt to turn pain into pleasure, agony into ecstasy. They have transformed a negative feeling into a positive experience.

Eating chillies makes for exciting times: the thrill of anticipation, the extremity of the flames, and then the slow descent back to normality. This is a benign form of masochism, like going to a horror movie, riding a roller-coaster or stepping into a cold bath after a sauna. The body flashes danger signals, but the brain knows the threat is not too great. *Aficionados*, self-absorbed in their burning passion, know exactly how to pace their whole-chilli eating so that the flames are maintained at a steady maximum. Wrenched out of normal routines by the continuing assault on their mouths, they concentrate on the sensation and ignore almost everything else. They play with fire and just ride the burn, like experienced surfers cresting along a wave. For them, without hot peppers, food would loose its zest and their days would seem too dull. A cheap, legal thrill, chilli is the spice of their life.

Until recently, most English cooks regarded these fiery fruits from foreign parts with xenophobic suspicion. For them mustard was quite enough already. Middle-class Americans associated chillies with the lower orders and snobbishly raised their noses. Even today, the more fastidious among northern Spaniards claim that the addition of chillies murders the distinctive, delicate flavours of different dishes. In contrast, Mexicans take pity on those too timid to be able to appreciate the delights of hot food. As far as they are concerned, it is the gringos' loss, not theirs. Mexicans can even turn chilli-eating into a test of suitability for marriage. When the prospective son-in-law comes to lunch for the first time, his fiancée's mother may give him an especially hot dish. If he can swallow that, check his tears, and still manage to say how delicious it tastes, then he is considered sufficiently polite to wed her daughter.

In the rural areas of Mexico, men can turn their chilli habit into a contest of strength by seeing who can stomach the most hot peppers in a set time. This gastronomic test, however, is not

DEATH ON A PLATE

A serving of the Japanese gastronomic delicacy *fugu* (puffer-fish) can be the meal to end all your meals, as it can kill you.

Strictly trained chefs carefully remove the fishmeat, then soak it for several hours, changing the water periodically. The meat is then cut into almost transparent slices, which are beautifully arranged on a plate in the form of a peacock. The most skilful of chefs ensure that these choice slivers contain only the merest piece of skin, ovaries, liver, or intestines, for all these parts contain tetradotoxin, a poison hundreds of times more deadly than strychnine or cyanide. As you eat, the tiny amount of the toxin makes the lips tingle. You are exhilarated, maybe even euphoric, as you flirt with death while, hopefully, avoiding its embrace.

What if the chef should misjudge his task by even the narrowest margin? First you will feel dizzy and your mouth will tingle, then your fingers and toes. You get cramps in your muscles, your lips go blue, you breathe with difficulty. You feel a desperate itch, as though insects are crawling all over your skin. You vomit, your pupils dilate, and you move off into a zombie-like sleep. Your meal is over and you have left your guests, and without paying the bill. Puffer-fish restaurants keep the number of an emergency doctor by the telephone. But there is little point in calling. The poison is too quick.

The most macabre detail of this whole process, however, is that though you may be out for the count, you are not necessarily dead. Like something out of a horror movie, tetradotoxin poisoning brings on a neurological paralysis that leaves its victim aware of what is going on, but totally unable to react. Most people then die. But some do not. The lucky few eventually wake up and return to life. From time to time cases are reported in the Japanese press of *fugu* eaters who, though conscious, were forced to attend their own funeral, only managing to arise, Lazarus-like, at the last moment.

Despite the demanding and lengthy training that *fugu* chefs have to undergo, puffer-fish still claim over 300 Japanese a year. For these fatalistic thrill-seekers this popular dish is not just the spice of their life, but also of their death.

used as a way to prove one's machismo, for women can play the game as well. In this context, chillies are a non-sexist form of acquired love for those with strong hearts and fiery passions – a steady source of hot sauce for their lives.

The enjoyable sensations of a running nose, crying eyes, and dragon-like mouth belching flames are clearly not for the timorous.

More tabasco, vicar?

4

OF LIFE, RICE AND
REGULARITY

For some peoples, food is not just fuel for the body's motor or a collection of biochemicals needed to maintain existence. Food does not only sustain their life, it physically constitutes their bodies. As far as they are concerned, they are food.

In many parts of Thailand, rice is not regarded purely as a collection of essential nutrients conveniently packed into the form of husks. It is part and parcel of people's very bodies. Every single grain of rice is thought to be alive and to contain part of the soul of the Rice Mother goddess. When the rice flowers bloom, villagers say that she has become pregnant, and that like any mother-to-be she has her particular cravings, which must be satisfied. Her preferences are scented powder and bitter fruits like limes or lemons, which the people dutifully bring to her. At harvest-time, her children – the grains – must be carefully collected and stored. When a buyer from a local mill comes to purchase the grain, the farmer keeps back a small amount, a handful of 'rice-soul', which he uses to 'impregnate' next year's crop. In order to shield the rice from the fact that one day it must die in order to feed others, people mill and cook the grains as far distant from the paddy-fields as possible. Best not to hurt its feelings.

Thai villagers believe that the foetus inside a pregnant woman sits in her stomach eating the food she eats. Because the mother relies on a diet of rice, the growing child's tissue in turn comes to be made of rice. In the same way that women give their food and bodies to feed their children, so the Rice Mother goddess yields her body and soul to nourish the body of humankind. Thus villagers in Thailand, as well as parts of Burma, Malaysia, Bali, and Vietnam, see themselves as physically and psychically made up of rice. The Christian God made man and woman in His own image; Southeast Asians think in the same general way, but their self-image is one of rice. For them, rice is literally 'the bones of the people'.

Unlike Asian rice-growers, the Hua people living in the Highlands of Papua New Guinea did not restrict their beliefs about indispensable foods to just one staple. Hua believed that they stayed alive and did not die a lingering death because each of them carefully monitored their *nu* or 'vital essence', the source of all fertility and growth. In order to remain fit and active, they constantly strove to top up their levels of this precious substance. None was to be wasted. By working in their gardens, people automatically transferred some of this animating stuff to the fruits of their labour: the food they produced was a kind of congealed *nu*. Hua were therefore very careful about whom they gave their food to. They did not want the wrong people gorging on a bit of their vital essence. Consumers too had to be wary. If they accepted a meal from the wrong person, the food would enfeeble them – a perilous condition, given their active lifestyle. Since these people did not believe in gods and did not worry too much about the spirits of the dead, *nu* was seen as the single source and sustainer of life, the means of saving oneself. In short, the Hua did not care about their souls, but about their bodies. This was their religion, and it was based on food.

For most urban Westerners, the notion that we are fundamentally made up of the foods we grow and eat is a bit too alien to be easily palatable. Just so long as we eat the right general sorts of food in the right quantities, we believe our bodies will look after themselves, while the health of our psyches depends more on our upbringing and behaviour than on our diet. However, though Westerners might disagree with the Hua and the rice-growers about the details of their beliefs, the general similarities between the three systems of thought are clear. Asian and Hua beliefs about the effects of diet are not so very different from some of the Western ideas about the central importance of food: skip on calcium and your bones go soft; wholesome food is said to be full of 'goodness' – without it our bodies go bad and eventually we die.

The more imaginative of Western pseudo-nutritionists, moreover, have never questioned the idea that we are deeply and psychologically influenced by what we ingest. Carrying the notion of 'you are what you eat' to an alimentary extreme, they argue that we cannot live life as it should be enjoyed until we are prepared to radically alter our diets, chewing habits, and bowel rhythms. These extremists see the salvation of the human race in gut terms. In England, the prize for such nutritional wackiness goes to Eustace Miles, while Horace Fletcher would be a strong contender for the American award. Together, this eccentric pair make the Hua's and the rice-growers' theories about body chemistry seem positively staid.

At the turn of this century, Eustace Hamilton Miles started to preach his gospel of 'simpler foods' as the key to a better, more fulfilled life. He argued that to achieve greater well-being, people had to forsake irritants in all parts of their daily diet. Instead of relying on stimulating foodstuffs, they should learn to relish plain fare. Heading his list of dangerous and tabooed foods came shellfish and red meat, followed by fish, white meat, hot sauces, peppers, mustard, vinegar, curries, ginger, and alcohol. He even dared to suggest – a radical proposal for the England of his time – that tea should be avoided.

Adjusting one's diet, however, was not enough according to Miles. The foods one was allowed to eat had also to be leisurely chewed. No more bolting it down, just lots of muscular mastication. Miles claimed such assiduous chomping broke up the food, mixed it with saliva, counteracted its overacidity, and left less 'unpleasant waste' in the body. The combined effect of eating the right food and then grinding it down to an unappetizing pulp was meant to be better digestion – in other words, Regular Bowel Movements, which expelled the unwanted and left one physically and mentally fitter. Constipation poisoned the whole body and depressed its energy and spirits. It was to be avoided at all costs.

Miles claimed that those who could keep off stimulants and put a bit of rhythm into their gut would enjoy a host of benefits. One appeared more healthy, had clearer skin, a more upright carriage, greater endurance, and 'a more rapid and harmonious co-operation between eye, ear, brain, hand, etc.'; breathing would demand less effort; the heart would feel easier. Overall, one would be more active, lithe, and alert. Intellectually, the Milesian regime was said to improve one's memory and augment one's versatility of mind. As for its effects on morality, he confessed grandly that he could not imagine 'a truly healthy man whose characteristics would not be truthfulness, honesty, mental activity, kindness, and the wish to teach and to help mankind'.

Growing lads, otherwise tempted to do that of which they would be afterwards ashamed, would also benefit greatly from Miles' diet. In his *A Boy's Control and Self-Expression*, he asserted that constipation clogged the alimentary canal, making it press against 'the tender seminal vessels'. By removing the threat of such dangers, good digestion led to greater tidiness and cleanliness – in every sense of the word. Foul thoughts had to be excreted, not stimulated. Mastication would win the day against the threat of masturbation.

There were economic advantages to boot, as those on the diet would spend less time digesting or sleeping, and people would feel less need for holidays. In fact, men and women would be generally more happy: they would eat less, stop craving stimulants, be more resistant to disease, and be more content with cheap and simple things. In sum, as Miles stated, watching what and how one ate held 'advantages for the Whole Nation, for All Nations, and for Posterity'. His ideas were not to be regarded as an interesting suggestion, but as an obligation. It was 'our duty to God to adopt simpler foods'. If there was hope for Edwardian Britain, clearly it lay in munching the right edibles into a tasteless mash.

Miles himself was the best example of his regime's benefits. Besides being a tennis world champion, he also won British and American national prizes for his skill at squash and racquets in 1900 and 1902. Though a busy lecturer at Cambridge, he still managed to find the time to write over fifty books and to edit two nutritional journals, *The Eustace Miles Quarterly* and *Healthward Ho!*

Miles, though, was no pioneer: he was simply the most industrious and most extreme from a long line of scientifically orientated Englishmen obsessed with the workings of their guts. Gladstone, arguing that God gave us thirty-two teeth for a good reason, religiously chewed everything he ate thirty-two times. Up until the Second World War, anxious parents continued carefully to monitor their charges' bowel habits. Even away from home children were not free from supervision, as the 1930 prospectus of a Sussex prep-school states: 'Every visit a boy makes to the lavatory is recorded in a book, which is regularly inspected by the Nurse who is, in this way, able to check this very important duty.' In 1952 one could still find a brochure for a preparatory school that mentioned the 'matutinal duties supervised by Matron' at 7.55 a.m.

Miles' American counterpart and near contemporary was Horace Fletcher, a rich, retired businessman who propounded an even more muscular theory of good nutrition. Fletcher believed there was a filtering mechanism at the back of the mouth which, thanks to the action of saliva, was responsible for most digestion. To make the most of their food, people had to masticate every mouthful so thoroughly that after a while it was swallowed involuntarily. There was no need, Fletcher claimed, actually to count how many times one was chewing because once one had become used to the routine any food not completely mashed would be involuntarily returned. While he thought thirty times might be sufficient for a morsel of bread, he admitted that a piece of shallot onion had once required 720 chews. He also recommended eating less, eating only when hungry, and switching to a low-protein diet. As a warning against the ill-effects of not following his regime he used to proclaim, 'Nature will castigate those who do not masticate.'

Fletcher gained so much attention because he had the money to fund scientists interested in researching his nutritional theories, and because, as an extremely robust man in his fifties, he was his own best advertisement. While not a sports champion like Miles, he could walk up and down the over 800 steps of the Washington Monument without pause, and in 1903 he ice-skated – for the first time in thirty-five years – for three hours without feeling sore, or so he claimed. Though already in late middle-age, Fletcher would trek across Asia or brave blizzards in the Himalayas and could weight-lift better than any member of the top Yale rowing team.

With a talent for self-promotion that matched the size of his ego, Fletcher would send packets of his remarkably odour-free stools to nutritional scientists in the post. As he put it, his 'tell-tale excreta' revealed the wisdom of his nutritional ways. John Harvey Kellogg – he of the cornflake – was so taken by the man and his ideas that he was inspired to write a 'Chewing Song', for chanting at meals to advance the Cause. Though Fletcherism was at first laughed at as 'the chew-chew cult', it went on to win many, some very distinguished, converts. In London his methods were taught at 'Munching Lunches', where a master of ceremonies would time the treatment of the first morsel taken by each of the guests. Vigorous jaw action, it seemed, would carry the day.

But death comes even to a Great Masticator, and by the time Fletcher's heart stopped in 1919, his movement had already entered a terminal decline in popularity. Though many middle-class Americans had accepted his admonitions about reducing their unnecessarily high protein intake, they finally balked at the idea of giving up dinner-time conversation for the sake of thorough chewing. In the words of one, Fletcherizing 'added a new horror to dining out', as 'these strange creatures seldom repay attention. The best that can be expected from them is the tense and awful silence that always accompanies their excruciating tortures of mastication.' Americans wanted to put a bit more taste back into their food, and some chat back into their mealtimes. Horace Fletcher was forgotten.

THE LAST OF THE MILESIANS

For the last twenty-three years, Stanley Green has been spreading his nutritional message up and down the streets of London's West End. Though often mocked, sometimes attacked, and occasionally spat upon, he continues to hawk his hand-printed booklet about 'Passion Proteins' for a few pence. On a good day he might sell as many as fifty copies. 'People do begin by laughing at me, but many come back later and buy the book. Protein wisdom changes your whole life, makes it easier. I've seen some remarkable changes in people. The first thing a woman does when she takes up protein wisdom is change her hairstyle.'

Today, thanks to works like Audrey Eyton's *The F-Plan Diet* – the fastest-selling book of all time in Britain – most Westerners have heard about the suggested link between low bowel motility and colonic cancer. Though some still think roughage and fibre are different concepts, and that the former is found in green vegetables and the latter in cereals, most know that the message is: 'Consume insufficient roughage, get bunged up, and unless you change your ways, you might be a candidate for getting a tumour in the gut.'

But while some people might be prepared to modify their diets in order to avoid specific diseases, only a determined few creatively extend their ideas about digestion way beyond the present bounds of scientific knowledge. Only a reduced band of New Age nutritionists think that certain categories of food crucially and directly influence the very core of our psyche. They may not believe their bones are made of rice, or that they have to husband their *nu*, but they do maintain that life would change radically if we got our guts into shape. As *Green Farm* magazine put it, 'If your colon isn't happy, the rest of you won't be either.'

These alimentary extremists have elevated 'inner hygiene' to a new, higher, almost spiritual plane. In their moralistic language they speak of 'cleansing' and 'purifying' one's gut. Registered therapists of colonic 'irrigation' or (more pretentiously) 'lavage' will wash away your worries and, as they are quick to emphasize in their ads, 'Only disposable equipment is used.' For leaders of the Bowel Movement, obeying the call to stool has become a daily ritual observance of quasi-mystical importance, enabling one to expunge the pollutants that contaminate our food and thus ourselves. Indeed the old idea of emptying your large intestine daily has been replaced by the more energetic injunction of 'three times a day after meals'. You might be kept on the trot, but always remember, the exercise is good for your soul. Though these colon-centred characters know that fibre bulks out the stool and pushes it on its way, they do not often mention that it can also inhibit the absorption of important nutrients into the blood, while too much of the stuff does not 'scrub' the gut, it scours it, carrying away essential microbes as it accelerates down the intestinal path.

These high-fibre zealots find common cause with the naturopathists, who believe that all diseases are caused by 'the accumulation in the system of waste materials and bodily refuse, which has been steadily piling up in the body of the individual concerned through years of wrong habits of living'. To overcome the effects of this amassed reject matter and to empower one's weakened body, they advocate – among other measures – fasting, scientific dieting, and hydrotherapy. The years of stockpiling the wrong substances must be countered by a planned process of excretory elimination. The bad will out, leaving the good to revive.

I do not wish to be misunderstood. I am not suggesting that the ideas of these gut revolutionaries are fundamentally untrue. Since some of their arguments are moralistic and edging on the mystical, they cannot be criticized within the terms of conventional medicine. If, on balance, their ideas appear to do more good than harm, then perhaps we should not damn these imaginative romantics too readily but instead be quietly grateful for the way they add to the variety of Western culture. By focusing on brown matter they add colour to our lives.

5

TABOO OR NOT TABOO

When I was doing anthropological fieldwork in a South Pacific village called Sulfa Bay, I used to get out of bed shortly after dawn. Once the mother of the family I was staying with had made a fire and boiled the kettle we would have a breakfast of tea and cold cooked yam (very tasty sprinkled with the local sea-salt). Then, like many villagers, I would walk off into the bush, find a secluded spot, drop my trousers and get on with the job. One morning, while still squatting, I heard someone behind me parting the long grass. Staying in position, I carefully swivelled my head to find I was eyeballing a large, fat grey-haired pig only a yard away, patiently waiting for me to finish so it could start on its own breakfast. I pulled up my trousers and left the hungry beast to get on with it.

Poor *Sus scrofula*! This innocent, relatively clean-living creature is the cause of the world's most popular food prohibition. Millions of people regard members of this unjustly maligned species as abominable, defiling, and unclean, and their meat is strictly taboo. Orthodox Jews regard the innocent pig as repugnant, while Muslims single the animal out as the focus of their disgust. The Jews were the first to ban pork, and the Prophet Mohammed borrowed the idea, possibly in an attempt to win a few over to his new religion. Muslims justify their ban by pointing to the creature's filthy habits. But this image of the squalid pig is very much a result of attempts to rear them in dry parts of the Middle East, for pigs only roll about in their own dilute waste when there are no other damp spots to be found. In their natural environment they do not defecate haphazardly, but in particular areas well away from their nests. They are only dirty if brought up in a confined, parched space.

While pork is virtually the only flesh tabooed by Islam, Judaism prohibits a variety of different foods, and the Jewish justification of their porcine ban is a little more involved than that of Islam. Reading between the lines in Genesis, God's original intention becomes reasonably clear: He wanted all animals, humans included, to be vegetarian. After the Flood, the Almighty relented slightly, allowing people to consume the flesh of other animals. Humans were to eat meat, and animals plants. Carnivorous creatures that blurred this distinction were considered unclean. On top of that taboo, the Book of Leviticus also banned animals that do not both part the hoof and 'chew the cud'–in other words, are ruminants with several stomachs that mash the food swallowed. Since pigs have cloven hoofs but are not ruminants and since they do consume carrion, they were considered doubly unclean and so came to be especially despised. 'Pinky and Perky' might have been a great success in Britain, but it is difficult to imagine either Israeli or Saudi television broadcasting a programme about the lives of two very pink, rounded porkers that act like humans.

PARLIAMENTARY PIGGISHNESS

The idea of pork is so hard to swallow that members of the Agudat Yisrael party in the Israeli parliament tried in November 1990 to push a law through banning sale of the meat to anyone but Christians. In reaction to this gastronomic coercion by the ultra-orthodox, less strict Jews decided to stage their own demonstration: a free lunch of ham sandwiches. As one concerned bystander at the crowded meal said, 'I've never touched pork, but once you let these Agudat characters into your sandwiches, they'll want to climb into bed with your wife as well.' As of the time of writing, the pig-headed MPs have yet to get their way.

The Jewish dietary laws do not stop at the curly tail-end of a pig. They are made up of a whole set of kosher dos and don'ts, of which the ban on pork and the separation of meat and milk are merely the most well-known. Though these dietary rules are still central in the lives of many Jews, they were even more important in Jesus's time, when each Jewish sect interpreted God's gastronomic intentions in its own way. What foods you ate and with whom you ate them were a key means of saying what particular group you belonged to. The Essenes would only have a meal among themselves, and neither they nor members of the

Pharisees, the Maccabees, the Sadducees, the Hasidim, the Sicarii, the Herodians, the Hellenists, or the Therapeutae, would even think of sitting down at the same table with a gentile. For Jews, their food rules came to stand for the whole of their law, and violating any of them was seen as equivalent to leaving the faith. God had founded His covenant with His chosen people through the medium of food, and His followers were not going to break this holy agreement by nibbling the wrong edible in the wrong company. When forced to eat swine by the Romans, some chose to die rather than pollute themselves and profane their sacred pact with the Almighty.

Any new prophet who wished to preach the salvation of all humanity and not merely that of one lucky tribe had to breach these dietary rules. If he wanted to attract all and sundry, he had to create a new, less restrictive code of dining. To scandalized Jews, Jesus was just such a gastronomic radical. They regarded him as a subversive glutton for being prepared to eat indiscriminately and with anyone. What was worse, He seemed especially keen to share his mealtimes with people from the most despised groups: Samaritans, tax-collectors, and sinners. In the Last Supper and the events following, the Son of God went so far as to establish the revolutionary innovation of ritual self-sacrifice, one with cannibalistic overtones: to fulfil His wish, His disciples had to transgress the Judaic taboos by drinking His blood and consuming His flesh. As far as Christians were concerned, their Saviour was the fount of all food, and in Holy Communion they joined with their Lord by eating Him. This sort of dietary rule-breaking was too much for His enemies; to maintain society as they knew it, they could not allow such a culinary rebel to continue.

Hindus do not crucify people for their culinary beliefs, nor, more interestingly, do they kill cows. Though millions go hungry in India, cows can wander the streets at will, eat crops without fear of disturbance, and, when old and infirm, may be cared for in special retirement homes. Moreover, Hindu law, by banning the elimination of substandard stock, hinders any effective cattle breeding. In fact, the cow protection lobby is so powerful that, despite the many Muslims in India, several states have passed total bans on killing the animals.

Hindus persist in their economic irrationality because cow worship is central to their religion. Cows are treated like deities because each one has over 320,000,000 gods and goddesses packed into her body; Krishna, the popular god of mercy and childhood, was brought up by a cowherd; the Earth, in times of distress, will take on the form of a cow to seek the aid of the gods; and praying to the cow deity aids one's progress towards achieving Nirvana. This animal is so holy that its products are seen as sacred as well. Polluted Hindus ritually purify themselves by taking a mixture of cow's milk, curd, ghee (clarified butter), dung, and urine. I suppose that if you were prepared to take a brew like that, you would have to think it was holy.

MOTHER'S DAY

'Just to look at a cow,' states the anthropologist Marvin Harris, 'gives many Hindus a sense of pleasure. The priests say that to take care of a cow is in itself a form of worship, and that no household should deny itself the spiritual enjoyment which comes from raising one.' At the same time, the cow is seen as a mother, one whose milk provides nurture, and whose sons supply labour and beef. So some Hindus, when asked about the apparent illogicality of caring for old cattle in special shelters, will answer smartly, 'Would you put your aged mother into an abattoir?'

Jains, members of one of India's oldest religions, have a much, much longer list of culinary prohibitions than those of the Jews, Muslims, and Hindus put together. To them, this life on earth is one of pain and suffering. Death offers no escape as people are reborn, often in a different form. To transcend this never-ending cycle of rebirths and attain enlightenment, they must deeply respect all forms of life. To act like a good Jain, and so gain merit and become a candidate for Nirvana, you have to follow these rules:

1. Filter all water to save the microscopic organisms you would otherwise swallow.

2. Do not drink water after dark – you might swallow a small insect by mistake.

3. Do not cook or eat at night – the heat could kill insects

attracted by the fire and by mistake you might eat a few of them in your food.

4.   Do not kill mosquitoes. Gain merit by letting them settle and have their fill of blood.

5.   Do not eat meat of any kind. Establish asylums for old and diseased animals. Leave out food for rats if need be.

6.   Do not drink alcohol, it stirs the passions. One must be calm and non-violent. Keep off honey: in the heat it might ferment and so intoxicate those who consume it.

7.   Reduce the number of sweets you eat. Jains believe the *nigoda* (tiny creatures that inhabit almost every corner of the universe) are especially prevalent in sweet food.

8.   No tubers or root vegetables, as they are thought to contain many 'life forms'. Anyway, digging for food kills insects and other organisms in the soil.

9.   Do not eat seeded food such as tomatoes, figs, and pawpaw as each seed is alive.

10. Restrict your consumption of green vegetables and fruit. Cut down the amount of rice, chapatis, and dal (cooked lentils) that you eat. Generally, limit how much you eat and drink every day.

11. Share your food with others. Presenting alms to an ascetic will bring you closer to salvation. *Thank* a holy man who crosses your path for giving you an opportunity to perform a meritorious act.

12. Go on lots of fasts, which can last from twenty-four hours up to two years. While fasting, the food you are allowed to eat should be bland and unappetizing.

13. You can choose to renounce a certain food for a period, or, if you are particularly determined, for life.

14. If you suffer from a terminal illness or have reached an infirm old age, you may consider death by fasting. Your Jain teacher will only let you embark on this noble and sacred act if you have already attained the level of discipline and spiritual development needed. Follow his directions, as you gradually cut out all solids in your diet and start to rely on liquids, which become progressively less and less sustaining. He may tell you

to drink milk, then move you on to fruit juice, and finally restrict you to plain boiled water. Your last moments should be especially holy, as your kin and friends chant for you. The ideal is to die chanting quietly along with them.

These rules differ slightly among different Jain communities but the main thrust of them is clear: avoid accidental violence to almost any living thing. Not all Jains follow them strictly, however. Besides the thousands of monks and nuns, many of India's four million adherents to the creed are well-to-do merchants and jewellers. In cities they tend to live in the same part of town and, most important, assist one another in business. As far as they are concerned, their financial success shows they are upright Jains: they make money *because* they are honest characters who do not gamble, do not spend their money on drink, and do not make crooked deals. Though they may have splendid houses and fine clothes, they also stage lavish feasts at which they give away cutlery, sarees, blouses, and petticoats to all the women attending. By sharing their wealth and thus, in a sense, renouncing worldly goods they gain prestige and merit. In other words, financially it pays to be a good Jain, but religiously you pay to be a good Jain.

Agnostic Westerners may scoff at these different religious rules as superstitious and nutritionally nonsensical, but on investigation their own ideas about pollution can seem pretty odd too. They may not abominate pigs, revere cows, or try to keep off seeded food, but many of their own gastronomic prohibitions are just as peculiar. Hindus, for instance, have no monopoly on economic irrationality for while the English do not consider asses sacred they are still prepared to foot the bill for homes for distressed donkeys. Besides prohibiting the consumption of insects and most types of meat, Americans will not eat carrion-eaters or decayed flesh unless it is game. Some even find crayfish repulsive because they live in the muddy bottom of rivers. As one finicky local in southern Louisiana confessed, 'I can't believe my eyes when I drive along the interstate and see all those people digging up vermin from the scum of the drainage ditches, and taking them home to eat.'

Until very recently, most Britons and Anglo-Americans regarded the eating of garlic as a filthy foreign habit. According to one British journalist, young Englishwomen who took their holidays on the Mediterranean used to regard the local lads not as potential lovers but as 'greasy perverts' because they all stank of the stuff. Distaste for garlic still exists in parts of Britain. When in 1989 an American visiting a Scots isle used it in the food she served at a local women's group, some of their husbands refused to sleep with them that night. In the United States, consumers of garlic were deemed offenders against public decency and morals. While newspaper editors wrote scathing articles about garlic-reeking immigrants, children who smelt of it at school were punished, and adults guilty of the same sin were asked to leave buses, cafés, and other public places. It was OK for smokers to smell like a dirty ashtray, but garlic-eating migrants had to confine their habit to quiet weekends spent apart from Anglo-Americans. Since garlic was seen as a medicine rather than a foodstuff, those who would not curb their intake were viewed as antisocial and unsavoury characters. Such immigrants clearly did not wish to become 'real' Americans.

Garlic might now be somewhat more acceptable, but insects remain taboo. Chances are, if you offer an American or European a tasty insect as a midday snack, they will react in horror and regard you quizzically. If they are finally prepared to gobble the titbit up, they look upon themselves as intrepid explorers of exotic foodways, as either martyrs or heroes of science. This Western taboo on eating insects has been, and is, so thoroughly observed that even strong-stomached sailors in Victorian times would knock out the nutritious worms from their sea-biscuits before eating them. Yet this particular prohibition turns out to be a peculiarly Caucasian phenomenon, for people throughout the rest of the world rely on and relish a vast variety of delicious creepy-crawlies. Among the thousands of different dishes prepared regularly are locust dumplings (Arabic north Africa); red-ant chutney (India); water beetles in shrimp sauce (Laos); and moth caterpillars (South Africa), which, when fried, have a delicate taste similar to sugared cream or sweet almond paste. Every summer Australian Aboriginals used to gather in the Bogong Mountains to feast on the moths there. Pounded up and made into a cake, they were said to be 'extremely nice and sweet, with the flavour of walnuts'. Nowadays, their successors enjoy witchetty grubs, honey ants, and shipworms.

Including insects in your daily diet both adds variety and makes good nutritional sense, for these small animals are usually rich in protein, fat, and calories. In contrast to beef, which is only 20 per cent protein, fly larvae are 63 per cent protein, and locusts 50–75 per cent. Moreover insects, unlike larger wild animals, are easy to catch and breed extremely rapidly. In fact, it is only in areas where people can be assured of a balanced diet in adequate quantities from cultivated crops that the nutritional potential of insects can be ignored or neglected.

While free-thinking nutritionists have been aware of the advantages of eating insects for a long time, the contradictions of Western gastronomic prejudices have on the whole proved too much for them. One early campaigner was the Victorian naturalist Vincent Holt who argued that insects are clean, palatable plant-eaters and not, as his peers branded them, 'filthy, loathsome things'. Wise farmers could battle their minuscule enemies by eating them; if they had not the time, then the poor could collect the pests as a way of improving their diet. Cockchafer beetles, for instance, ravaged the foliage of fruit and forest trees, yet as grubs were 'of a most serviceable size and plumpness'. (Salt and pepper the grubs, roll them in flour and fine breadcrumbs, wrap in aluminium foil, and bake in the hot ashes of a wood fire.) Holt thought woodlouse sauce equal, if not distinctly superior, to shrimp, while grasshopper fried in butter with parsley, salt, and pepper was 'delicious'. One of his sample menus runs:

Snail Soup
Fried Soles with Woodlouse Sauce
Curried Cockchafers
Fricassee of Chicken with Chrysalids
Boiled Neck of Mutton with Wireworm Sauce
Ducklings with Green Peas
Cauliflowers with Caterpillars
Moths on Toast

Despite the impeccable logic of his arguments, the English would not accept any insect product other than honey or cochineal. They still will not. Holt's words are as valid now as they were then: 'I can never understand the intense disgust with which the appearance at the dinner-table of a well-boiled caterpillar, served with cabbage, is always greeted.'

Most Westerners feel sure that insects will taste bad, even if they have never tried them. Yet many rural European children, not yet completely socialized by their parents, suck the sweet crops of bumble-bees, crunch the meaty legs and rumps of beetles, and delight in the sweet honeydew excretions of aphids. The further irony is that urban Westerners are in fact eating insects almost all the time. In the mass-production of certain foods today it is often impossible to remove all traces of insect carcasses. Legislation tends to be less concerned with *which* insects we ingest than with the dosage. It seems the last laugh is reserved for Holt's successors.

Many Americans, ever fearful of 'germs', seem obsessed with sterilization and domestic sanitation. In 1967 the great French gourmets Henri Gault and Christian Millau claimed that this pervasive fear of microbes retarded any development of American gastronomy: 'We French swallow an impressive number of microbes and we even boast of having got along well with them for a score of centuries.' The more fastidious among Americans will not touch the left-overs on someone else's plate and would not consider eating something that has fallen on the floor, even a squeaky-clean floor. Some people are so particular they will not eat from a stew that has been stirred with a *brand-new* fly-swatter, straight out of its plastic wrapper.

To most people, ordinary foods become disgusting simply through contact with something repulsive. No matter how many times one washes it, Westerners will still balk at drinking tea from an ex-spitoon. The object has become permanently polluted by human waste and it can never be used for containing food. In the 1940s, the American psychologist Adam Angyal found that if people inadvertently touched some disgusting object, they experienced a lingering, unpleasant after-sensation, even after washing their hands. The disgust could not be removed with a wipe; one just had to wait for it to go slowly away. This emotion is not innate, for people from some other societies will eat droppings while in any culture children less than three years old will put almost anything into their mouths – as most exasperated, anxious mothers know. By the age of six or seven, however, most Western children have gained some idea of 'contamination': show a child a picture of a glass of milk with a blob of dog turd added and she will say she would not drink it.

Ironically, many Westerners are regarded as defiling and filthy by the very people *they* consider unclean and insanitary. The Gypsies see all non-Gypsies as potentially polluting and they are constantly on their guard when visiting their homes, schools, hospitals, or welfare offices. In public toilets some Roms will even use paper towels to turn on taps or open doors. If they move into a house previously occupied by non-Gypsies they will paint and bleach, and then try to cover up lingering traces of the earlier tenants by hanging tapestries and drapes and by putting down thick carpets. They avoid food not prepared by one of their kind. If forced to buy something while on the road, they prefer wrapped food to a meal on a plate. When they have to eat in restaurants, they use their hands instead of the utensils, and they drink out of plastic cups – washed, but used, mugs would defile them. Other customers might be shocked but the Gypsies know that the truly dirty are not they, but their observers.

If you want to eat like a Gypsy, there are certain rules you cannot ignore:

1. Purity is essential. Food must be kept away from anything that might pollute it, like pregnant or menstruating women, or non-Gypsies.

2. Wash your hands thoroughly. Wash all utensils that touch the food in a special basin, one that is only used for kitchen items, with its own bar of soap.

3. To prevent women defiling the meal, it is better if men handle the food.

4. If sexually active, cleanse yourself weekly by abstaining from all animal products (meat, eggs, lard, butter) except fish, on Fridays.

5. Food for a Gypsy ritual must be especially pure. Buy fruit in unpacked cases (so they have not been touched by the retailer). Buy drink in cases and beer in kegs. Do not go to butchers. Purchase a live animal and get experienced Gypsy elders to butcher and carve it up.

6. At feasts use only new cups, plates, napkins, and tablecloths. Buy plastic ones, it's cheaper. At the end of the meal, throw them away, plus any food that has been touched, no matter how much of it there is.

7. As a general rule, cook hot, spicy, greasy food for your family.
    (It will fatten you, constipate you thoroughly, and push you
    closer to haemorrhoids.) Make it in one pot. Throw in green
    and red peppers, tomatoes, potatoes, some meat, garlic, and
    lots of chillies. Make soups of butter beans, hot peppers, ham,
    and jellied pigs' feet and ears. For meat, barbecue huge hams
    or lamb steaks smeared with hot sauce. For rituals, roast a lamb
    or a pig on a spit. Fry or bake your own bread.

8. If you are a woman and you wish to be judged a good cook, you
    must learn how to make *sarmi* (cabbage leaves stuffed with
    pork, onions, peppers, rice, and tomatoes).

Whether for Muslims, Jews, Americans, Hindus, or Gypsies,
culinary dos and don'ts designate the cultural boundaries between insiders and outsiders, setting each group off from the rest.
They mark the dividing line between the edible and the inedible,
the sacred and the profane, and – above all – the clean and the
dirty. At the same time, they express important religious concepts,
so that the faithful, when they sit down to eat, are reminded of,
or act out, moral teachings. Christians say 'Do unto your neighbour as they would do unto you', and so *should* welcome any
unexpected guest to their table. In Judaism meat is seen to come
from a dead animal while milk is thought a life-giving substance,
so the orthodox keep their meat and milk dishes on separate
plates: life and death must not be mixed up. The absence of beef
from the Hindu diet is similarly laden with morality. As Gandhi
said, 'Cow protection to me is one of the most wonderful phenom-
ena in human evolution. It takes the human being beyond his
species. The cow to me means the entire subhuman world. Man
through the cow is enjoined to realize his identity with all that
lives.' In all these cases we have food for thought, religious
thought.

The dietary rules of various societies are so different that when
put together they crisscross like crazy paving: one group bans the
pig, another makes bacon a key part of its diet; some put dung in
their drink, others cannot consider the idea; Americans think the
Gypsies disgusting, and the Gypsies regard Americans as defiling.
This inability to define 'filth' universally reveals just how relative the Western notion of 'dirt' is. Possessed by an obsessive fear
of invasive germs and anxious about keeping to 'good, clean
habits', we turn our noses up at potentially useful sources of food.

We are all too ready to sneer at the customs and cuisines of others, yet our own fantasies about filth make us ignore many kinds of meat and protein-rich food. Our ideas about pollution are just about as culture-bound, and as irrational, as anybody else's. We are not special.

6

NO FOOD

People forced to go hungry are constantly thirsty. Their mouths run dry, they lose weight rapidly, and they constantly crave food. If they are starved for a prolonged period, they begin to feel weak all over. Their libido disappears, leaving them impotent. Unable to work or to do almost anything, they become apathetic and depressed. They always feel cold. Their flaky skin wrinkles all over and dirty brown blotches appear. Then they age years in weeks and retire to their beds, without the will to do anything but await the end.

When food first runs short, people do not tend to sit around bewailing their condition but actively search out alternative sources of nourishment. Instead of feasting on their normal fare, they make do with unpalatable items that are often bland, tiresome to prepare, and somewhat indigestible. These are 'famine foods'. When the rains do not fall in central Tanzania, for instance, the Sandawe farmers have to gather wild plants. They chew raw roots for their juices, and they boil leaves, roots, and pounded seeds. They may taste bitter, but they keep the Sandawe alive, while their ignorant neighbours, who do not know how to exploit their environment, go hungry. In fact, during mild famines in certain areas, children have a more balanced diet than normal because they supplement their meagre meals with a wide variety of nuts, berries, and roots, which they would usually scorn. In places where crop shortages are a constant threat, some people occasionally eat famine foods in times of plenty so that when the harvest is poor, the new meals are not too great a gastronomic shock. In early modern Europe, some people used to force themselves to consume bark bread from time to time so their stomachs would always be able to digest it.

Today, Westerners are no longer used to drastic food shortages and they have to learn afresh each time one occurs. In 1940 the British were cut off from Europe, and their transatlantic supply lines were threatened by German submarines. 'The English were left alone', as one French wag put it, 'with their cuisine.' Food was rationed, and a revitalized Ministry of Food urged people to grow their own, dig for victory, and scavenge the countryside for elderberries, sloes, crab apples, rowan berries, hips, and haws. Members of Britain's 'Kitchen Army' (housewives) learnt how to substitute potatoes for meat and how to prepare dishes that

---

SURVIVAL KIT
(Sixteenth-Century Seamen's Fare)

ENGLISH VERSION:	SPANISH VERSION

Every day:
  1 lb biscuit,
  1 gallon beer
	Every day:
	  1$\frac{1}{2}$ lb biscuit or
	  2 lb biscuit,
	  1$\frac{1}{3}$ pints wine or
	  1 pint Candy wine
	  (Cretan Malmsey,
	  preferably)

Sundays, Tuesdays, *Thursdays:* 2 lb salt beef	

Mondays:
  1 lb bacon,
  1 pint peas
	Sundays, Thursdays:
	  6 oz bacon,
	  2 oz rice

Wednesdays, Fridays,
Saturdays:
  $\frac{1}{4}$ stockfish or
  $\frac{1}{8}$ salt ling,
  4 oz cheese,
  2 oz butter
	Mondays:
	  6 oz cheese,
	  3 oz beans or
	  chickpeas

	Wednesdays, Fridays,
	Saturdays:
	  6 oz salt fish (tunny
	  or cod, squid or 5
	  sardines),
	  1$\frac{1}{2}$ oz olive oil,
	  1$\frac{1}{4}$ pints vinegar,
	  3 oz beans or chickpeas

	Wednesdays only: 6 oz cheese

used runner bean leaves, tansy, sorrel, lovage, rose petals, borage, and chestnuts. To make dull ingredients more appetizing, chefs invented new recipes with patriotic names like 'Dunkirk Delight', 'Blackout Cake', 'Commando Casserole', 'Inspiration Pie', 'Turnip Tommies', and 'Potato Jane'. The most famous of all Second World War economy recipes, Woolton Pie, was thought up by the chef of the Savoy Hotel and named after the then Minister of Food. A vegetable stew covered with pastry, it was described at a public meeting as 'looking on the outside exactly like a steak and kidney pie, and on the inside just like a steak and kidney pie – without the steak and kidney.'

FRONT-LINE CUISINE

In the First World War the British Army biscuit was so hard that according to one gunner, 'you had to put them on a firm surface and smash them with a stone or something. . . . Sometimes we soaked the smashed fragments in water for several days. Then we would heat and drain, pour condensed milk over a dishful of the stuff, and get it down.' An alternative recipe was to smash the biscuit into a pulp, pour this into a sandbag, add water and a few sultanas, and then boil. Once cool, this 'pudding' could be carried down to the trenches where each man could saw off a piece, sandbag and all. As one private who tried it confessed, 'I revolt at the memory.'

Wartime meant that previously innocent animals were suddenly seen in a new light: the house sparrow was branded an 'enemy of the nation' for its raids on allotments while the *Daily Express* ran an article entitled 'Herr Rabbit – Fifth Columnist', which called for the mass killing of the agricultural pests. People were discouraged from giving a dog a bone to chew; instead they should boil it to make soup. Since lard was rationed and olive oil could only be obtained at a chemist's on a doctor's prescription, some taught themselves to fry with paraffin. When the few Chinese restaurants that existed in London finally ran out of rice, they served 'soyaghetti' – spaghetti cut to look like rice. The US government helped out by sending, among other foods, tins of economically packed meat, known as 'Specially Prepared American Meat'. In short, SPAM.

During the Nazi occupation, the Dutch suffered chronic food shortages. The only bread they had, made from ground rye mixed with a flour extracted from peas and barley, was heavy and sour. Since meat, cheese, butter, and margarine were scarce, they filled sandwiches with raw vegetables or a paste of brown beans, chopped onions, tomatoes, and salt. As the fighting moved into Holland in late 1944, food became so short that people ate sugar beets, which formed a mushy pulp when boiled, or, since they were Dutch, flower bulbs. Syrup was made from beets, and the remaining mash was blended with tulips and wheat to produce a black and slightly sweet bread. According to one participant in 'The Hungry Winter', people 'greatly enjoyed delicious' soups of nettles, herbs, and cat – the pelt was made into mittens.

HOW TO COOK A TULIP

At first bite, tulip bulbs seem like potatoes, but this is followed by a very bitter after-taste. To improve the flavour, remove the core and the dark, outer skin. Cook in a vegetable stew, or cut into very thin slices and fry – they will taste like chips.

As a famine deepens, the usual rules and taboos are laid aside and the social order begins to fracture. By this stage people will eat anything, and will not let anybody get in their way. When Leningrad was besieged by the Germans in autumn 1941, almost three million people trapped in the city were forced to try new sources of sustenance. Cats and dogs disappeared off the streets; the trees emptied of crows and sparrows; old briefcases were boiled up to make 'meat jelly'. Potatoes, frozen by the severe cold, were fried in linseed oil. People ate lipstick and used the grease for frying what little bread they had – often made of cellulose, sawdust, and floor sweepings. They stripped off wallpaper and devoured the paste, which was said to be made from potato flour. Some ate the wallpaper as well. Later, in a drastic attempt to put something in their stomachs, they moved on to chewing plaster. The besieged became so desperate that when bombs landed near food queues, the survivors would wait for the planes to fly off, then gingerly step over the bodies and reform the line. Driven by hunger, even the rats became bolder. Formerly law-abiding citizens formed murderous gangs that snatched ration cards, preyed on lone pedestrians, and launched attacks on bread shops. As rumours of cannibalism became more and more widespread, parents kept their children at home. Men and women with fat faces and rosy cheeks came to be regarded with great suspicion, and fear. 'In the worst part of the siege,' one survivor remembered, 'Leningrad was in the power of the cannibals. God alone knows what terrible scenes went on behind the walls of the apartments.'

Some people cannot adapt, even in emergencies. Blinkered by their culture's cuisine and taboos, they regard anything strange as inedible, and they do not let even the threat of their imminent demise change their minds. Prepared to die for their dishes, they choose to starve rather than consume something exotic. Captain Scott and his men perished in the Antarctic because Edwardian gentlemen did not feed on their dogs, and so the explorers left their huskies where they dropped. In the Korean War some American POWs died of malnutrition because they could not eat the meals doled out by their Chinese and Korean captors. Pilots shot down in the Pacific in the previous war ignored their survival training and went hungry rather than consume island grubs, grasshoppers, lizards, and toads.

The most tragic example of gastronomic conservatism overriding biological needs, however, is the Great Famine of Ireland. By the late 1840s the country was badly overpopulated, land was short, and when the potato crop failed for two successive years millions died. Many could have saved themselves if they had started to cultivate and eat maize. But they did not know how to cook this unfamiliar edible, and they were not prepared to make it an important part of their diet. American corn did not fit into the Irish idea of food.

Resistance to dietary change among the famished is not usually so widespread or so disastrous. Today, aid agencies providing relief in famines try to overcome this sort of problem by ensuring that the food they bring has a familiar taste and colour, and that it can be prepared like traditional foods. Even the down and out, after all, have standards.

7

MOVABLE FEASTS

As schoolchildren, my sisters and I used to return home before four everyday. Our mother would already have the kitchen table prepared with sandwiches, jam, biscuits, cake or pastries, butter-drenched crumpets, and the odd maiden aunt or two. Our father would then come in from his afternoon calls. Rubbing his hands vigorously together and with a grin that aimed for each ear, he would proclaim, 'Saved another life today!' On days when he was particularly pleased, he would amaze us all and amuse himself by ending the meal with a little fruit - throwing a grape in the air and scoring a hole-in-one every time.

Afternoon tea was a light, happy occasion. It was a gentle break in the day, between calls and the evening surgery for my father, between school and homework for us children, between cooking and yet more cooking for our mother. Not a closed gathering but an open event, anyone who knocked on the door between half-three and five was invited to join the table. Tea-time was a social occasion, a simple, relaxed meal for easy conversation and good company. Family rows were saved for other times.

But these are memories, and so is afternoon tea. This brief meal has since disappeared from our working days. By the late 1970s, offering an afternoon guest anything more than a cup of tea and a biscuit or slice of cake had come to seem pretentious and old-fashioned – the sort of event a Young Fogey would stage. These days, urban shoppers pausing from their toils in a 'tea-shop' hardly ever choose more than something to drink and a pastry. Even a male student trying to pick up the girl sitting opposite him in the library does not invite her to a full, cream-rich repast. The chances are that all she gets is a cup of coffee and a query about what she is doing tonight. The Ritz and other surrealist dream-palaces may still offer full-blown 'set teas' (tea, sandwiches, scones, pastries, cream-cakes – and no jeans), but their customers are mainly ageing ladies or tourists nostalgic for a past they never had. And these pricey teas, as a privileged form of 'living heritage', are so popular you have to book, two weeks in advance.

Like the twelve-course dinner, afternoon tea has disappeared into history because times have changed and there is no longer any space in the day for it. Mealtimes map the structure of our waking lives. They are the points around which our days turn because, except for snacks, we do not eat when we feel like it. We eat at certain times, and we eat certain foods at different times of the day. Who has turkey for breakfast, or scones and cream for lunch?

Other than the recent demise of afternoon tea, our present mealtimes of morning breakfast, midday lunch, and evening supper feel as permanent as the Grand Canyon and as natural as flowers budding in spring. Breakfast is to wake us up and prepare us for the hours ahead, lunch is a refreshing pause in the middle of the working day, and supper is a relaxing opportunity to restore spent energies. There is, however, nothing biologically necessary about this tripartite schedule. Our gastronomic timetable is a dynamic, not a static, product of our history and continues to evolve. It only seems unchanging because the changes occur so slowly.

Anyone who goes on holiday abroad learns immediately just how arbitrary their own mealtimes are. The Basques do not eat breakfast, while tourists who dine in Madrid at 8 p.m. wonder why they are the only people in the restaurants. (Local diners do not start arriving until ten.) Visitors also complain that lunch does not begin until half-past two. What they do not realize is that many urban Spaniards break from work at one, meet their friends in a bar and eat a small snack before then going home for their main meal of the day. Others work without a break: they start at eight, finish at three, and then have their lunch. The people of Zumbagua in the Ecuadorian Andes have a very light meal before dawn, a larger meal at midmorning, the same again in the late afternoon, then another very light meal, this time after dark, to end the day. This arrangement suits the local women, who need to pasture their flocks from midmorning to midafternoon without interruption. It would not suit hungry backpackers who turned up at midday, only to find nothing was to be cooked for several hours. Some African communities do not bother with set meals at all; they just nibble and pick at food throughout the day.

Henry VIII had his main meal of the day at 11 a.m. A hundred and fifty years later, Cromwell and his cronies were dining at

2 p.m. At this level of society, changes in the gastronomic timetable seem to have been set in motion by powerful trendsetters. By the end of the eighteenth century, the time of dinner had been pushed back even further: gentlefolk did not sit down to table until 4 p.m. They did not have breakfast when they got up but did two hours of work before starting to eat at 10 a.m., so they were not starving themselves from cock-crow to mid-afternoon. In fact, the day was not divided by the sun, but by the chief meal: until dinner-time, people greeted one another with 'Good Morning'. Tea came four hours later, and supper, usually a substantial one, ended the day at ten or eleven in the evening.

By 1815, people were breakfasting earlier and dining later. To fill the hungry gap, Londoners started to take a midday snack, called 'luncheon', at coffee-houses or pastry-shops. According to Dr Johnson, this twelve-o'clock nibble consisted of 'as much food as one's hand can hold'. Over the following decades breakfast, formerly a highly social occasion, lost ground to lunch, which became a more substantial meal favoured by urban ladies of leisure. For men who could not get home at midday, lunch remained less a set meal than a form of refreshment taken near the office.

The next radical addition to English mealtimes was the invention of afternoon tea. At first a children's meal held in the Victorian nursery, it was soon picked up by young women eager for novelty. Afternoon tea fitted into the social patterns of those days so well that by the turn of the century it had become an integral part of the affluent way of life. In large houses a formal event with cake-stands and hot dishes, tea-time provided ladies with an intimate setting for chatting and sharing secrets. Grand hostesses, with the means and the space to stage elaborate tea parties, would make it known that they were 'At Home' every third Wednesday. Guests arrived in their best dresses, and hired musicians provided the accompaniment to this gossip-shop. Men were not banned, they were just away at work. If *they* wished to natter, they could do so in their clubs.

So by the time Queen Victoria had gasped her last, the well-to-do had completely revised their binary division of the day – morning and evening, before and after dinner – into a fourfold classification: morning, afternoon, between tea and dinner, after dinner. With the recent disappearance of tea-time, we have reduced this schedule to a threefold one.

But even the present tripartite division of the day is under threat. Most Americans now snack rather than fast during the mid-morning and mid-afternoon, and the meals they do eat have become much more snack-like. Similarly, very few Britons now bother to cook anything for breakfast, and more and more are choosing to go to work on an empty stomach. Lunch has also declined in importance. Though in the 1950s the majority of men still went home for their midday meal, these days most just have a light meal or a quick bite in a canteen, cafeteria, or fast-food outlet. In Britain today, almost the only people who prepare their own lunch, and it is not a main meal at that, are housebound mothers and the retired.

The English might be happy following the American example, but other Europeans are holding on to their gastronomic traditions much more firmly. For the Germans and the Swiss, lunch remains the largest meal of the day, eaten either at home, in a small restaurant, or in a canteen. At the end of the day, Germans have only a light meal of cheeses and cold meats. In France, Spain, and Italy many people, though not as many as before, still go home at midday while others patronize restaurants offering three-course meals. Unlike the Americans and the British, many Continentals continue to uphold lunch as a meal worth bothering about. They are not going to overturn their culinary customs and love of food for the sake of a snatched sandwich or a Big Mac.

In strictly-run institutions, like asylums, prisons, and boarding-schools, food organizes both the day and the week: you know where you are if you know what you are having for dinner, no matter what day it is. There is no room for unpredictability and none for choice. Even in some homes, ones where people feel a great need for regularity and order, the week's meals are planned with an almost military thoroughness. In the film *Shirley Valentine*, set in a working-class Liverpool household, one afternoon the dog eats the steak Shirley had bought for the evening meal. As a dutiful wife, she does not desert the house in a panic, leaving the man in her life a note saying, 'Your dinner is in the dog'. Instead, she cooks up a fry. When her hide-bound hubby comes back and sits down to supper, his only emotion is disgust and his only comment, as he pushes the dish at her, 'Egg and chips? But it's not Tuesday! We have steak on Thursdays!'

Meals give form to our days, they organize our weeks. They also structure our year. We mark the passage from January to December with a series of holidays, each with its own particular foods. In Britain, Shrove Tuesday is pancake day; Easter means chocolate eggs; Christmas is turkey, mince pies, Christmas pudding, and brandy butter. In Italy, bakers celebrate an ordained series of religious festivals by making special breads, and in Spain 90 per cent of all the *turron* (almond nougat) consumed over the year is eaten during the Christmas period. In Holland, respectable bourgeois commemorate the season of good cheer by giving one another lumps of chocolate in the form of human excreta. Eating them at the end of Christmas dinner is said to leave people in indigestive fits of laughter.

Most of these foods are not special in themselves: chocolate turds can be found in a joke-shop any working day of the week; bakers can knead dough any way they want; turkey is available any month of the year. We make such foods special by tying them to specific feasts held during the year. We are not making something out of nothing; we are making something extraordinary out of the ordinary. These foods have been turned by us into markers of the passage of time. They have been made into a gastronomic calendar. The people of Vanuatu go one step beyond this, marking not just the change of seasons but the year itself in terms of food. For them, yam is such an important crop that they call it the king of foods. In fact, it is so central to their vision of life that instead of having a distinct word for 'year' they use 'yam'. ('When did your father die?' 'Three yams ago.')

Foods, and the meals we make of them, are our clocks, our faithful calendars. They are, in a real sense, the time of our life. For those who grow their own food, its cultivation, preparation, and consumption sets the rhythm, the pace of their days and weeks while, for the rest of us, the sequential availability of different items underscores the progression from winter to summer and back again. In Britain, the first asparagus in the shops means that May has come. When the skies rain shot-filled game, then the Glorious Twelfth is with us again. In the Solomon Islands, the first yams signify May; in southeastern Papua New Guinea the appearance of edible seaweed shows June has come, while octopus can only be found in August; and when, in Vanuatu, the moonlit sea shimmers with the phosphorescence of the delicious sea-worm shoals, the locals know it is late September and time for a seafood feast.

While people in less developed parts of the world still separate the year into boring or exciting periods depending on what foods are available, such seasonal division is now much harder for us. Thanks to the persistent efforts of the food industry, we can today buy almost any item – at a price – at any time of the year. Rapid transportation, deep-freezing, new forms of cultivation, and the creation of novel variants that ripen especially early or late have all dulled our gastronomic sense of seasonality. Provided you have the money, there is no longer any need to ever go without any of your favourite foods.

Despite all these changes, however, some residual sense of the annual progression remains. Or am I the only person who can still taste the approach of Christmas when offered a tangerine, nuts, and a glass of mulled wine by friends?

What's a Meal?

Every meal has a structure, and every culture has its own way of defining what a meal is. Ignore these rules at your peril, unless you want to get a name as a daring, cranky host and are not worried at the prospect of losing your friends.

The Mambila of Cameroon think *fufu* (manioc porridge) an essential ingredient of any meal. If *fufu* is not included on your plate, then you are only eating a snack, not a meal. For the Amazonians living along the Bajo Urubamba river, 'a meal' (*la comida*) must have game – fish or the flesh of a forest animal – and cooked plantains or manioc. No other possible combination can be called a real meal, not even that most popular of Amazonian dishes, beans and rice. The people along the riverbank eat many other foods, such as fruit, peanuts, maize, fungi, and insect larvae, but these are regarded as snacks, and when eaten at a meal are considered only adjuncts. In contrast, among the people of Zumbagua of the Ecuadorian Andes, mealtime means a *sopa*, a thick or clear soup made of vegetables and some meat boiled with flour or corn. Two bowls of this heavy, starchy stew is often enough for each person, though more is always offered.

To Malaysians, it does not matter how much food one is offered: if it does not include rice, it is not a meal. Similarly, in many parts of India people do not consider a plate of food without rice 'a meal', but 'tiffin'. The Japanese have only one word, *gohan*, for 'cooked rice' and for 'a meal'. As far as they are concerned, a meal does not become a proper meal – no matter how many dishes have already been presented – until the rice is served. All other dishes are *okazu*, 'supplementary articles of diet'. Following this logic, the Japanese may perceive a British meal not as 'meat and two veg' but as a staple (potato) with *okazu*, or meat and one veg. Spanish villagers serve vegetables and meat as separate courses; the French start their meals with a salad, while some Spaniards have it after the main course and before the sweet. Both view the habit of putting a bit of salad next to the meat and vegetables on the same plate as a lack of culinary refinement. How can anyone taste anything if everything is mixed up like that?

In many parts of Britain, people have a very fixed idea as to what constitutes 'a cooked dinner', also known as 'a proper dinner'. For many families this is still the most important culinary event in the week and is never served more than once a day or four times a week. There is always a cooked dinner on Sundays, and never one on Saturdays. Unlike lunch or supper, which are lighter meals, often eaten individually, a cooked dinner is a heavy meal taken by the family together. It is not just 'meat and two veg', because only particular meats and vegetables are eaten: beef, lamb, pork, or chicken are OK; gammon steaks, a bacon joint, sausages, offal, or preserved meats are not. Besides the omnipresent potato, only green vegetables that grow above the ground are allowed: peas, beans, Brussels sprouts, cabbage, and maybe broccoli (people hesitate about cauliflower because its core is white). Other vegetables, like carrots, parsnips, or turnips are only included in the meal as additions. As well, all the ingredients must be recognizable: if you shred or mince any of the food, the result cannot be called a real cooked dinner. Gravy is essential - and it had better be the right consistency and colour. As wives say, 'it makes the meal'; the husband 'must have his gravy'.

The potatoes must be boiled, except on Sundays when they are roasted. If they are chipped and deep-fried, then you are not making a 'proper dinner' but a 'chip meal', that is, fish or sausage and egg, chips, baked beans and/or a tomato, and no gravy – in other words, the very foods excluded from a cooked dinner. Anyone who tries to give a traditionally-minded family chips

MILLET MEAL AS MEAL

To the Bemba [southern Bantu people of Zimbabwe] each
meal, to be satisfactory, must be composed of two constituents: a thick porridge (*ubwali*) made of millet and the relish
(*umunani*) of vegetables, meat or fish, which is eaten with
it. . . . *Ubwali* is commonly translated by 'porridge' but this
is misleading. The hot water and meal are mixed to the
proportion of three to two to make *ubwali* and this produces a solid mass of the consistency of Plasticine and quite
unlike what we know as porridge. *Ubwali* is eaten in hunks
torn off in the hand, rolled into balls, dipped into relish,
and boiled whole. . . . To the Bemba, millet porridge is not
only necessary, but the only constituent of his diet which
ranks as food. . . . But the native, while he declares he
cannot live without *ubwali*, is equally emphatic that he
cannot eat porridge without a relish, *umunani*. . . . The
functions of the relish are two: first to make *ubwali* easier
to swallow, and second to give it taste. A lump of porridge
is glutinous and also gritty – the latter not only owing to the
flour of which it is made, but to the extraneous matter
mixed in on the grindstone. It needs a coating of something
slippery to make it slide down the throat. . . . The Bemba
himself explains that the sauce is not food. It prevents the
food 'coming back'. Meat and vegetable stews are cooked
with salt whenever possible, and there is no doubt that an
additional function of relish in native eyes is to give the
porridge taste and lessen the monotony of the diet. Ground-
nut sauce is also praised as bringing out the taste of a
number of different relishes such as mushrooms, caterpillars, etc.

In general, only one relish is eaten at a meal. The Bemba
do not like to mix their foods, and despise the European
habit of eating a meal composed of two or three kinds of
dishes. They call this habit *ukusobelekanya* and one said, 'It
is like a bird first to pick at this and then at that, or like a
child who nibbles here and there through the day.'

A. Richards, 1939

instead of boiled potatoes as part of a cooked dinner will be accused of cutting corners, maybe even of cheating. And in this sort of community, a woman who cannot cook the meal right is not considered a good housewife.

The Course of History

The present structure of Western meals as a short series of usually simple, separate courses is a relatively recent invention. Our forefathers organized their repasts in a very different manner.

During the Middle Ages the diet of peasants in northern Europe was too meagre for meals to be divided into courses. Most of the time they had to subsist on dark bread, cabbage, beans, and salt pork, followed by curds. In order to appreciate the distinctive style of medieval cuisine, it is best to look at the dinners of prosperous town merchants. For each course the table was covered with an array of dishes. As in a modern buffet, the diners helped themselves to whatever took their fancy, picking at some dishes and gorging on others. Abundance, rather than a skilful harmony of flavours, was the gastronomic order of the day, as hosts wished to create a sense of plenty, not of balance. At the turn of the fourteenth century, a typical Parisian merchant might have presented his guests with the following:

First Course
Miniature pastries filled with cod liver or beef marrow
A cameline 'brewet' (pieces of meat in a thin cinnamon sauce)

Beef marrow fritters
Eels in a thick, spicy purée
Freshwater fish in a cold green sauce flavoured with spices and
    sage

Large joints of meat, roasted or boiled
Saltwater fish
Fritters
Roast bream and darioles
Sturgeon
Jellies

Second Course
'The best roast that may be had'

Freshwater fish

Broth with bacon

A meat 'tile' (pieces of sautéed chicken or veal, with a spiced
sauce of pounded crayfish tails, almonds, and toasted bread,
and a garnish of whole crayfish tails)

Capon pasties and crisps

Bream and eel pasties

Blank mang (*blamanger*: a spicy white dish made from
capons)

Third Course

Frumenty (hulled wheat boiled in milk, with cinnamon and
sugar)

Venison

Lampreys with hot sauce

Last Dishes

A variety of sweet and spicy confections (such as pears, comfits,
medlars, peeled nuts, larded milk, vegetable and herb tart,
pastries, figs, raisins)

Spiced wines and wafers

Whole dry spices 'to help the digestion'

This motley collection of dishes might sound like a grand feast,
but it was really just a crudely put together repast when compared
with the much more elaborate Chinese meals of the same time.
Even a royal banquet in medieval Europe would not have had as
many dishes as a family feast in Hangchow. A celebratory dinner
there might have included a dozen soups; forty dishes of boiled,
stewed, stir-fried, steamed, roasted, or barbecued meat, poultry,
and seafood; the same number of fruit and sweetmeat dishes;
twenty vegetables, a dozen different types of rice dishes; and as
many as thirty kinds of dried and pickled fish. Compared to the
developed refinement of Chinese dinners, European meals were
unimaginative and disorganized events. The Occidentals still had
a long way to go before they could begin to rival the sophistication
of Oriental cuisine.

By the time of the French Revolution, the number of courses
had been reduced from four to three, and the content of each had
been made slightly less random. At Parisian feasts, many diverse
dishes were still served together, but they were grouped according

to their nature. The food historian Reay Tannahill has pieced together a representative menu for a feast of the time:

First Course
The appetizers consisted of a tureen of soup (each one different) set at each corner of the table.
Entrées - light 'made dishes', an introduction to the heavier meats that would come later - were arranged along the sides.
Once the diners had drunk the soup, the tureens were removed and four dishes of fish put in their place. At the same time, servants were constantly offering the guests *entrées volantes* ('flying entrées'): dishes of hot kidneys or livers and of salted or preserved meats meant to stimulate the gastric juices.
The *pièces de résistance* were the heaviest foods of the meal: game, poultry, and large joints of meat, usually garnished with vegetables and accompanied by salads.

Second Course
This was still in the medieval style. A haphazard assortment, known as *entremets*, of cold meats, savouries, aspics, vegetable dishes, and sweet dishes.

Third Course
Pastries and ices

The British adapted this new style of serving dishes to suit their particular tastes. Contemptuous of any French food that seemed fanciful, they kept the roast and boiled meats of the *pièces de résistance* in the first course, while the remaining *pièces* (roast poultry and game) were included with the *entremets* in the second. That way, unadventurous diners could ignore all the fancy dishes and stick to 'plain and wholesome' food in both courses.

The main difficulty with *service à la française* was that much of the food went cold before anyone had a chance to sample it. By the time diners had carved off and tried some of the meats within immediate reach, the other dishes were already lukewarm. In the mid-nineteenth century, hosts tried to overcome this problem by switching to *service à la russe*. Here, the food was cut up in the kitchen, and the servants then offered guests helpings: first meat, then potatoes, followed by vegetables, and finally the sauce. While this new style of service reduced the number of dishes (the servants could not be running back and forth *all* the time), it increased the number of courses, as diners now had less choice and had to accept what they were offered.

The full version of this new style of dinner consisted of up to twelve courses: *hors-d'oeuvre* (or oysters or caviare); one thick and one clear soup; a large boiled fish and a small fried one; an *entrée*; the joint, or *pièce de résistance*; the sorbet; the roast and salad; a dish of vegetables; a hot sweet; ice-cream and wafers; dessert (fresh and dry fruits); coffee and liqueurs. In France, some meals became so elaborate that diners were given sherbet between fowl courses to clear the palate. According to the social historian John Burnett, a turn-of-the-century hostess might choose to delete or combine some of the courses. A typical menu would have read:

Soups

Consommé Desclignac • Bisque of Oysters

Fish

Whitebait (Natural & Devilled) • Fillets of Salmon à la Belle-Ile

Entrées

Escalopes of Sweetbread à la Marne
Cutlets of Pigeon à la Duc de Cambridge

Relevés

Saddle of Mutton • Poularde à la Crème
Roast Quails with Watercress

Entremets

Peas à la Française • Baba with Fruits
Vanilla Mousse • Croûtes à la Française

By the first decades of this century, hosts started to make their meals lighter and less elaborate. Partly this was due to a fashionable reaction against earlier excesses and partly to the increasing evidence from the new science of nutrition about the dangers of consuming too much meat and too few vegetables and fruit. In 1817 when the Prince Regent gave a dinner, there were over a hundred dishes; a hundred years later, the guests at the

THROUGH ORIENTAL EYES

Although the present European style of organizing meals may seem more informal than its Victorian version, it would not suit the Jorai of central Vietnam. At mealtimes the Jorai do not talk or drink but quickly help themselves to as much or as little as they wish from each of the dishes, which are all served at the same time.

To them a French dinner would mean sitting on a rigid chair, before a rigid table, between two rigid persons. A dish is served, but you never know what will be served after; you have no choice, you cannot combine tastes. The menu is imposed; worse, the host or hostess compels you to take your share of each dish, and to take again; sometimes it is served dictatorially on to your plate, and you must eat it all, even if you dislike it. Wine is poured into your glass; if you do not drink during the meal you will appear odd, and this will cause comment. At table people talk loudly and talk throughout. The meal takes such a long time that people smoke cigarettes after each dish. If you are bored you cannot leave, and belching is forbidden.

Parisians might think their meals the height of sophistication. To the Jorai they would be the height of constraint: too lengthy, too noisy, and with no concern for individual taste. Best to stay at home.

coronation feast of George V were served only eleven dishes, followed by prepared peaches, petits fours, and fruit. When Elizabeth II was crowned in 1953 the celebratory banquet was even shorter: it consisted of only four courses and was all over within thirty-five minutes.

A Short History of Mealtimes
(Mainly for 'Gentlefolk')

1780

Breakfast
10 a.m. A substantial and highly conversational meal, to which

visitors are invited, and which can last hours. Cold roast beef, cheese, ale, fish, eggs, often chops and steaks. Tea, toast, bread, butter, and – for those who can afford it – coffee, chocolate, and cakes.

Dinner
Any time between 3 and 5 p.m. The main meal of the day. In grand houses, often lasts four or five hours. Formal dress.

Tea
7 p.m. in 'modest households', 8.30 p.m. in the homes of the rich. More a meal for women than for men. Tea, sandwiches, and cakes.

Supper
Between 10 and 11 p.m. Fairly substantial. A buffet rather than a set meal. Cold meats, sweets, fruit, and wine on ordinary occasions; a choice of hot dishes when company is present.

1815

Breakfast
For the leisurely, 10 a.m.; for the less leisurely 9 a.m.; for busy lawyers, copyists, shop assistants and so forth 8 a.m. or earlier. Tea and coffee, replacing ale.

Luncheon
Midday. A snack, or an informal light meal. Those with the means and the free time held *pic-nics* – a fashionable gathering with each person contributing a share of the food, often eaten in the open in the countryside.

Dinner
Unchanged since 1780.

Supper
Also unchanged since 1780.

1835 (Transitional Period)

Breakfast
Now more commonly held before 9 a.m. Less formal and punctual

than before. Losing some of its social flavour and prestige to luncheon. Though still including a variety of grilled dishes, hot toast, fancy breads, butter, and jams are becoming more prominent.

Luncheon
A set meal, for women rather than men.

Dinner
For bachelors, clubbable men, and widowers, 6 p.m. or earlier; where women had a say, 8 p.m.

Supper
Its hour and size are dependent on the timing and substantiality of dinner.

1860s

Breakfast
In town 8–8.15 a.m., in the country 9–10 a.m. For the middle and upper-middle classes in town, a brief family meal, including cold meats and hot dishes. No guests unless especially invited. In the country, a more leisurely meal.

Luncheon
Between 1 and 2 p.m. Less of a social occasion than before. More and more men are now eating this set meal, with their family.

Dinner
For the urban middle-classes, when *en famille*, a solid simple meal at about 6 p.m.; when staging a formal dinner-party, 8 p.m. In the country, held at 5 or 5.30 p.m., and usually followed, hours later, by a light meal called either 'supper' or 'tea'.

These, mainly middle-class, meals should be compared to the contemporary diet of a farm labourer:

Breakfast
Husband – milk and bread; family – tea, bread, and butter.

Dinner
Husband – bacon, daily; others – bacon three days weekly, potatoes or bread, tea.

Tea
Tea, bread, and butter.

1900

Early Morning
8 a.m. For the fortunate, a tray with tea and bread and butter brought to them, while still in bed, by a maid.

Breakfast
London businessmen and their families, 8–8.30 a.m. Chops and cold meats are no longer served; instead, kedgeree or a fried slip with buttered eggs and bacon.

Luncheon
Luncheon parties are coming into vogue, mainly for wives and unoccupied gentlemen.

Afternoon Tea
In big houses, this is a formal and elaborate occasion, starting at 5 p.m. or later.

Dinner
At 7.30 p.m.; for dinner-parties, at 8 p.m. or later. A large, often lengthy meal of several courses.

At this time, Americans are known for their huge appetites. For breakfast, upper-class American hotels offer their guests beefsteak, broiled chicken, broiled salmon, and other fish, liver and bacon, kidneys, lamb chops, tripe, clams, omelettes, cold cuts, many kinds of potatoes, beans, breads, and so on.

1930s

Breakfast
About 8 a.m., earlier for the poor, later for the rich. For the rich, toast, butter, marmalade, porridge, other cereals, eggs, bacon,

fruit. The poorer classes do without fruit, cereals, and marmalade, eat less bacon and eggs, and often substitute margarine for butter. The well-to-do drink coffee and tea, others only tea.

Midday ('lunch' for the upper classes, 'dinner' for the rest)
1 p.m., somewhat earlier for the lower classes, later for the upper. Most men eat this meal with their families. Dinner is usually meat, potatoes, and sometimes green vegetables, pudding, and tea. Lunch is often a four-course meal of soup or fish as first course, and fruit and cheese after the sweet. Poultry, mutton, fish, salads, green vegetables, and fruit are much more common for those with money. Sausages, stews, and meat pies are more popular among the less affluent.

Afternoon Tea
About 4 p.m. An upper- and upper-middle class event. Usually a light snack of tea, cakes, biscuits, bread, and butter.

High Tea
Usually between 5 and 6 p.m. A substantial meal for the lower classes, eaten when the husband and children return home. Tea, bread, butter, meat or fish, potatoes, and vegetables. (Afternoon tea is more popular in London and southern Britain; high tea is more common in the north.)

Dinner
7–8 p.m. For upper-income groups only. The main meal of the day. Often soup and fish rather than meat and vegetables, followed by coffee.

Supper
9–10 p.m. For lower-income groups only. A snack. Usually bread and cheese, with cocoa or tea.

Compare these with the following traditional mealtimes in the far north of Scotland:

7.15 a.m.
Tea and oatcakes (bread made with oats, barley, and fat from melted dripping).

10.30 a.m.
Porridge and milk.

1.00 p.m.
Tea and 'something cold to eat': oatcakes, scones made from wheat flour or barley meal, 'plain bread' (a sliced loaf), homemade rhubarb jam, butter, and cheese.

4.30 p.m.
Dinner: a vegetable or meat soup, or potato and boiled/fried fish, or cabbage and pork; pancakes with rhubarb ham, biscuits, oatcakes, and scones.

8.00 p.m.
Supper: tea, white bread, oatcakes, scones, pancakes.

Finally, the daily mealtimes of three non-Western cultures:

Zumbagua
(Ecuadorian Andes)

Café (Before Dawn)
Machica (finely-ground, toasted barleymeal) mixed with *panela* (concentrated sugar-cane juice) boiled in water, or bread and water flavoured with instant coffee and white sugar.

Almuirzu (Midmorning)
S*opa*, sometimes followed by sweet gruel.

Almuirzu (Late Afternoon)
As above.

Café (After Dark)
Machica again.

The Tharu
(Plainspeople in Nepal)

Early Morning
8–10 a.m. Rice and vegetables, sometimes with soupy lentils. Tharu usually do some work before this meal.

Midday
1–3 p.m. No meal unless there is enough left over from the morning. Usually only a drink of thinnish rice soup. (Boil water, with a little rice, a few beans, and the water from the second or third washing of the rice. What you get is starch water with rice at the bottom which, the Tharu say, drunk cold, is very refreshing.)

Evening
6–8 p.m. Rice and vegetables again, maybe with soupy lentils. After the wheat harvest, Tharu eat *chapatis* instead of rice at the evening meal.

Snacks
Roast maize.

The Mambila
(Lowland Cameroon)

Predawn
For those going to work in the fields, beer; for those staying at home, nothing.

Main Meal
About 10 a.m. *Fufu* (maize porridge thickened with manioc flour) plus a sauce made from fish/meat/green leaves and okra, which makes the sauce gelatinous.

Early Evening
6–7 p.m. Same as the main meal; sometimes omitted.

Snacks
White manioc, plantains, fresh maize.

8

SQUEEZE MY LEMON

For D. H. Lawrence, the vulgar way to eat a fig,

*Is just to put your mouth to the crack and take out the
    flesh in one bite.*

Every fruit has its secret.

The fig is a very secretive fruit.
*As you see it standing growing, you feel at once it is
    symbolic:*
And it seems male.
*But when you come to know it better, you agree with the
    Romans, it is female.*

*The Italians vulgarly say, it stands for the female part;
    the fig-fruit:*
The fissure, the yoni,
The wonderful moist conductivity towards the centre.

Involved,
Inturned,
The flowering all inward and womb-fibrilled;
And but one orifice. . . .

To Lawrence the seed-filled fig is 'like a ripe womb', one that
flowers 'inward, womb-ward'. Unlike flowers, which stand aloft
and reach towards heaven, these fruit are like women who hide
their secret beneath fig-leaves, 'Where everything happens
invisible, flowering and fertilization'. As you might imagine, he
then goes on to make a great play about the crimson interior
showing through the purple slit of the fruit 'like a wound'. When
finally ripe the fig bursts forth, like a fearless female making a
show of her vaginal secret.

Nowadays, Lawrence's vision of human sexuality is regarded as
quite peculiar and very much his own fabulation. These days few

follow him in regarding the Phallus as the Holy Ghost, or adhere to his belief that individuals are reborn through struggle against the female force of Law. Despite the eccentricity of his viewpoint, however, he is only one among a long line of artists who have exploited the erotic potential of foodstuffs. For edibles, like bits of our bodies, can be firm, hot, juicy, soft, moist, and well-shaped sources of pleasure. While Lawrence lingered lasciviously on the metaphorical vaginality of ripe figs, Adrian Mitchell was inspired by the spiced heat of Indian cooking, Edward Weston was drawn to capsicums that seem all biceps and bum, and in the late 1970s the photographer David Thorpe became famous for his series of *Rude Food* books which skilfully combined sections of the female torso with tasty morsels of real food.

RIDDLE

Their tongues are knives, the forks are hands and feet.
They feed each other through their skins and eat
Religiously the spiced, symbolic meat.
The long oven cooks them in its heat -
Two curried lovers on a plain clothes sheet.

Adrian Mitchell

Sometimes the physical similarity between food and sex is so patent you do not need to be a talented artist to make the connection. Over-polite women refuse to eat bananas by peeling back the skin and then lunging, lips open, for the fleshy head of the fruit. Instead, they keep the object firmly on the horizontal, on their plate, and daintily cut it up with a knife and fork. Some people blush or giggle at the sight of a *phalloides* mushroom while mischievous professors of botany like to enliven their lectures on chillies by displaying that notorious variety of *Capsicum annum* nicknamed the 'penis pepper'. When a Spanish provincial government tried to promote its regional produce by commissioning a television commercial showing a horizontal, oversized asparagus with a bulbous head slowly entering from stage right, local women complained and the ad was withdrawn.

Wags bent on adding a low note of eroticism into the midst of their meals have felt the need for something more provocative than naturally occurring priapic forms. At banquets in sixteenth-century England and France, hosts titillated their guests between courses by decorating the table with carnal 'subtleties' – sugar and pastry models of the male and female genitalia; perhaps the modern-day equivalent would be to add a dark, edible member to the tray of after-dinner chocolates. In the early 1980s, Baltimore confectioners did a roaring trade in 'adult' gingerbread cookies and 'erotic chocolates'. 'I have people coming in,' marvelled one sweetshop owner, 'and saying, "I want to see the gynaecologist special." Some women actually give their doctors these candies after an examination.' In contemporary Sicily, sexually shaped food is not confined to adult eyes but can be viewed by anyone in the shopfronts of Palermo bakeries. One can spot phallic breads, baked images of what look suspiciously like a man and a woman coupling, and small, hemispheric almond treats called 'breasts of the virgin', created by local nuns and still highly prized by them.

Eating and loving are perceived as such similar activities that we tend to talk of one in terms of the other. We say we have lusty appetites, we hunger for love, feast our eyes, eat out our hearts, and suffer devouring passions. Vulgar Frenchmen do not seduce their womenfolk, they fry them (*faire frire*) or put in the pot (*passer à la casserole*), while English-speaking lovers of either gender can whisper to one another between the sheets, 'Do you want me to eat you?' A couple may together seek carnal knowledge (from the Latin *carnis*, 'fleshy, meaty'); others can indulge their appetites in carnival (from *levare*, 'to put away'), the Festival of Meat held just before the Lenten period of abstinence. Some Louisiana Cajuns, nicknamed 'coon-asses', use their car bumpers to advertise their omnivorous attitude to sexuality: 'Coon-asses make better lovers because they'll eat anything.'

This equation of food and fornication crops up again and again in societies all over the globe. In culture after culture we find that people use the same word for 'to eat' and 'to copulate'. The Ancient Greek term *parothides* can mean either 'hors-d'oeuvre' or 'foreplay'. Among the Yoruba, 'to eat' and 'to marry' are covered by the same verb, one which has the general sense of 'to win, to acquire'; the French make a similar connection, for the term *'consommer'* can apply to both meals and marriage. The Yanomami of the Amazon use one verb to mean 'to eat like a pig' and 'to copulate excessively', while their adjective for 'full, satiated' can also signify 'to be pregnant'. In the Aboriginal language of the Koko Yao of Cape York Peninsula, northern Australia, the term *kuta kuta* denotes both incest and cannibalism: you are not meant to make love to the wrong person or make a meal with the wrong food. The Ilahita Arapesh of Papua New Guinea make the link between food and sex in a rather different way, for they have the saying, 'Cooked meat goes in the mouth and *down* the body; raw meat goes in the vulva and *up* the body.'

THE PLEASURES OF THE TABLE

Most peoples are prepared to leave the link between food and foreplay as a metaphor. But the hippies turned it into reality by making oral sex a feast. Both men and women – when not too drugged to do anything physical – used to decorate their partner's 'plates' with edible items like cottage cheese, chocolate sauce, yoghurt, and strawberry mousse. Some also bought tubes of strawberry, mint, or vanilla flavours, while one notorious rock star 'gave' his girlfriend a Mars Bar.

But these additive-rich sex aids went out of fashion with the hippies themselves. Nowadays, the middle classes desire healthy food and healthy sex. Who today wants to smear their partner's parts with E493?

For many peoples the connection between eating and copulating is not merely linguistic. Their attitudes towards these twin pleasures and the ways they should be indulged are the same as well. The Victorians considered food, like sex, an unfortunate carnal necessity to be endured. Neither activity was to be enjoyed, but simply performed. In a similar fashion, the Jorai of central Vietnam eat their food quickly and without interruption. No one talks or drinks during the meal. Jorai married couples are said to unite in the same silent, dry, perfunctory manner. In both cases the aim is to get the job over and done with. The Wamira of the New Guinea coastline are much more anxious about food and sex, for they see gustatory and sexual appetites as frightening forms of ravenous, rapacious desire. Both must be controlled if their individualistic, competitive society is not to splinter apart from within.

The Mehinaku villagers of central Brazil do not have such worries. They say sex is the pepper that gives life and verve and that copulation is a kind of eating. Men are said to eat women, and women men. His genitals give 'food' to hers, and vice versa. A young Mehinaku man may point to his girlfriend and say, 'Her vagina is my penis's food', while a man who asks where his wife is might be told, 'Your penis's food has gone to get water'. Even the quality of sex is judged in gastronomic terms. Good sex, like good food, is *awirintyapai*, 'delicious, succulent'. Dull sex, like dull food, is *mana*, 'tasteless', a term usually applied to unspiced edibles such as cold manioc porridge and water. Villagers told Thomas Gregor, the anthropologist who studied them, that copulating with your spouse is *mana*, while having sex with lovers is almost always *awirintyapai*.

Mehinaku say they should be as generous with their sexuality as they are with their food for a person whose hunger – sexual or gastronomic – has been frustrated may fall sick or lose their soul to a spirit. In a small-scale society like theirs, the general well-being of the whole community depends on every member of the village. So for the sake of others and the commonwealth of the community, 'a reasonable request for food or sex is seldom turned down without good cause'.

Card-carrying Freudians claim that food and sex are so often linked because our first pleasurable sensation comes from feeding at the breast. According to them, we put eating and desire together from Day One, and we spend the rest of our lives confusing the two. But there is no need for us to rely on a theory that is based on the particular psychological make-up of the Viennese middle class at the turn of the century, especially when so many societies have their own explanations. As Gregor points out, many peoples' conception of biology intertwines natural mechanisms and social relationships. In almost every community, men and women co-operate in the production of food and for the production of human beings. Copulation results in new humans, who will produce food, which will enable them in turn to produce further humans, and so on. The only real difference, in this sense, between societies is that some, like that of the modern West, do not develop their ideas about the symbolic links between food and sex, while others, like the Mehinaku, expand them into full-blown philosophies of life.

Though Europeans have not made the connection between eating meals and one another into a central part of their vision of how the world functions, they still recognize the association between feeding-then-fornicating. Married couples try to keep their love afloat and their bed-times lively by going out for special meals or by having one at home after the children are asleep. This sort of 'quiet dinner for two' is deliberately intended to lead on to coupling: what starts as a *tête-à-tête* is meant to end as body-to-body. The well-known danger, however, is that a good meal can induce sleepiness.

Since eating together can be as intimate as having sex, and sometimes almost as exciting, quiet dinners *à deux* come to loom large in secret adulterous affairs. On these extramarital excursions, clandestinity and expectation are the pepper to the illicit lovers' feast. As one hitherto faithful wife confessed:

> When I started the affair with Tony, who was married to a girl in my husband's office, food assumed a great significance in our lives. It was almost more of a thrill than the sex!
>
> We'd phone each other at the beginning of the week, pick a restaurant about twenty miles away, then drive separately to the rendezvous, parking in different streets, about a quarter of a mile from what we called base food camp. I'd get there first, and order avocado with prawns – always the same starter. I used to dip my fingers in the garlic dressing, and pour it slowly over the prawns, thinking about him, and imagining what we'd do. Then I'd rub the dressing over the avocado and wait for the phone call. He phoned the restaurant after he'd parked the car to make sure no one had spotted us. If I said it was all clear, he'd arrive just as the waiter brought the second avocado. Sometimes he would feed me small pieces from his spoon. It was all so intense and special. Eating had become something private between us.

Similarly, when a heterosexual woman embarks on her first lesbian relationship, secret meals together can become one of the most emotionally charged events in their affair. Food here takes on a significance almost unknown in more straitlaced romances. In the words of one woman reflecting on her initial experience of lady love:

I think the mystery comes because in a first homosexual relationship you have to go to ground; eating becomes a positive thing you
do together, rather than a passing way of doing other things. That
relationship only lasted six months but it changed the pattern of my
ordinary eating. It gave me, with those meals, an intensity of
feeling I have never experienced again.

These private feasts sound romantically memorable but –
lesbian liaisons apart – the underlying sexism remains stubbornly
present. As feminist critics point out, men speak of hunting the
(edible) object of their desire and of cornering their prey. Moreover, food metaphors for the male torso imply masculine muscle
and strength, while those for the female form suggest pleasure –
men's possessive pleasure of female bodies. A man can be 'beefy'
and has a 'hot dog', 'sausage', or 'piece of meat' between his legs,
together with a 'couple of nuts'. Masturbation becomes 'beating
the meat' and copulation 'hiding the salami', 'sinking the pork
sword', or 'a beef injection'. In contrast to these meaty male
metaphors, a woman is said to have a 'bun', a 'breadbasket', a
'snapping turtle', or, to use the Ancient Greek phrase, a 'bowl of
sauce'. On her chest she has a pair of 'fried eggs', 'apples',
'oranges', 'grapefruits', or 'melons'. Looking at her overall, she
might be called a 'tomato', a 'mushroom', a 'bit of mutton', a
'chick', a 'peach', a 'cookie', a 'honey pot', a 'piece of cake', or,
more simply, 'sweet enough to eat'. In contrast, tell a man he is
'sweet' and he will think you are questioning his masculinity; call
him 'sugar plum' and you deserve the black eye you will get.

Women are even expected to enjoy eating sugary confections;
one without a taste for sweets is thought insufficiently feminine,
too hard to 'sweeten up', a real 'sourpuss'. Like the all-too-perfect
food in glossy advertisements, women are also expected to present
themselves as beautifully prepared and highly palatable objects.
They are supposed to let themselves be appreciated and then to
serve themselves up for consumption: 'What a dish! I wouldn't
mind a bit of her!'

Feminists can take heart, however, as women are linguistically
just as capable of 'eating' men as men are of women. And in
certain cultures that is just what they are said to do – gobble men
up. This male nightmare tends to occur in two sorts of societies:
highly eroticized ones where men feel pressured to perform sex

well, and ones where the ideological separation between the sexes is so great that the womenfolk appear to local men as distinct, and dangerous, creatures.

BAKING BABY

Having a 'bun in the oven' is not a new phrase but an old European metaphor. Since French people in the sixteenth to nineteenth centuries used to say that women 'cooked' the foetus until it was properly done, the skin of a new-born babe was called its 'crust', and a premature baby was thought 'uncooked'. Louis Bourgeois, a seventeenth-century physician, took the oven metaphor seriously: for relief of haemorrhage after birth he recommended taking 'clean earth, such as is used for the floor of an oven, mixing it with strong vinegar, spreading it on a cloth and putting it on the loins: this moderates the warmth and stops the flow'. Since the womb was seen as an oven, those who consumed human and animal afterbirths as aphrodisiacs called the placenta a 'cake, loaf, tart, or biscuit'. One researcher working at the turn of the century found that midwives in the Diois region used to put a hot loaf on the abdomen of the woman in labour and would make her drink an infusion of wood ashes. This image of the foetus as rising dough has not completely disappeared, as even today people in the Vivarais and Forez regions say of an immature person, 'He has not been well cooked', or, 'There wasn't enough fuel on his fire.'

The Mehinaku fit the first bill well. Among these Amazonians, as we have seen, a person of either sex regards the genitalia of their partner as their own sex organ's 'food'. Villagers carry this oral imagery further by describing the anatomical details of women's genitalia in facial terms. Female sex organs have 'foreheads', 'noses' (the clitoris), 'mouths' (the whole vagina), and 'lips' (the labia). Thus when a Mehinaku man enters a woman he is symbolically allowing a female sexual mouth to eat his penis. Hardly surprising, then, that the menfolk recount fearsome stories about toothed vaginas able to bite off members, or that they suffer such anxieties about castration.

The second type of society is especially prevalent in many parts of Melanesia. Wola men, of the New Guinea Highlands, for instance, believe women to have a power associated with their reproductive abilities capable of polluting and killing men by eating away at their vital organs. During their periods, they are particularly dangerous. A man who has sex without taking special forms of protection beforehand is 'eaten': his hair is said to thin, become wispy, and then fall out; his skin dries up, wrinkles, and turns ash-grey; he loses weight, his muscles waste away, and his bones stick out. His vitality sapped, he rots away in a sweaty stink. He has indeed been consumed, and there is little of him left for anyone else.

For a Mehinaku man, 'Good fish get dull, but sex is always fun.' And many Westerners might be tempted to agree. The flavours of food are fine but they are outstripped by the sensationality of sex. Candlelit dinners, after all, are only so romantic because they are a prelude to further, even more satisfying, pleasures.

Gustation, however, has its ultimate revenge over the tyranny of lust, for the sensitivity of the palate outlasts erotic desire. As the French politician Talleyrand said in his old age, 'Show me another pleasure which comes every day and lasts an hour.' The libido may die away, but the taste buds, or the majority of them anyway, remain. Chances are, the taste you will take to the grave will not be that for sex, but for the next meal.

9

LOVIN' SPOONFULS

A short list of aphrodisiacs might include anchovies, ant juice, artichokes, barbel, bamboo shoots, basil, wild cabbage, calves' brains, camel bone, caper berries, stuffed capon, caraway, caviar, milk of chameleon, crab-apple jelly, crocodile tail, preserved dates, deer sperm, dill, doves' brains, eel soup, egg-yolk in a small glass of cognac, fennel, flea-wort sap, dried frog, gall of a jackal, game birds, garlic, ginger omelettes, goat's testicle boiled in milk and sugar, goose tongues, grapes, halibut, hare soup, haricot beans, herring, horse penis, horseradish, mackerel, lamprey, leeks, powdered lizard with sweet wine, marjoram, milk pudding, mugwort, musk, ninjin, nutmeg, oysters, paprika, pâté of bone-marrow, Parmesan cheese, pepper, plaice, quince jelly, ray, radishes, rhinoceros horn, rocket, rosemary, saffron, sage, salmon, candied sea holly, shallots, sheep's kidneys, spinach, swan's genitals, tarragon, terrapin soup, thyme, turmeric, viper broth, woodcock, and pineapple fritters.

The Ancients also recommended beets, boiled cress, chickpeas, crocodile droppings, dried liver, hippopotamus snout, hyena eyes, mallow-root in goat's milk, mare's sweat, narcissus root, nettle seeds, pine nuts, pomegranates, sows' vulvae, and necks of snails taken with a little wine. Cleopatra, in true queenly style, preferred pearls dissolved in vinegar, while Elizabethan Britons thought so much of prunes that brothel-keepers fed them free to their clients.

This incomplete inventory of Western aphrodisiacs appears bewilderingly diverse and apparently indiscriminate, as though anxious lovers were ready, in their search for sexual satisfaction, to believe in the efficacy of almost any food or philtre. Their gastronomic choices, however, are not as random as they at first appear. A number of simple principles underlies the selection of most supposed love-aids.

Sometimes the reason why a food is believed aphrodisiac is obvious, as with animals' sex organs or the meat of mammals, such as goats and rabbits, famed for their fecundity. Nor is there much difficulty in understanding why the sea-slug is highly prized by the Chinese: when touched, this cucumber-shaped food swells and enlarges like an excited penis. Some foods are thought aphrodisiac because of their resemblance to the human form: the anthropomorphic mandrake root, lauded by Pliny the Elder and celebrated by Machiavelli, has been infamous for centuries. Medieval tricksters used to uproot the plant, insert seeds into the section of the root corresponding to the genital region of a human, and then return it to the soil. When the mandrake was finally removed a few weeks later, the root – with the aid of a little carving and the sprouting of the seeds – not only looked like a man, but like one with pubic hair. The claimed stimulatory effects of mandrakes are not restricted to humans, for according to a Victorian erotologist female elephants that eat their leaves are seized with such a desire for copulation that they charge wildly in any and every direction in desperate search for males to mate with.

Like mandrake, ginseng was thought aphrodisiac because its root can appear so humanoid. Nowadays there is also scientific work suggesting the existence of some pharmacologically active ingredient in the plant which increases stamina and endurance. What is so unusual about ginseng is that, unlike caffeine, cocaine, and amphetamine, its stimulatory mechanism operates unconsciously and does not seem to have many harmful side-effects other than a possible increase in blood-pressure. The bad news – for those seeking a reliable sex-aid – is that there is no firm evidence about its aphrodisiac effects. Some animals, however, do react directly when treated with extract of ginseng. Hens lay more eggs, the ovaries of frogs grow faster, and female rats become more responsive to the advances of males, while male rats dosed with the stuff and then let loose among the opposite sex ejaculate faster and more often. But, as with elephants and mandrake leaves, scientific experiments with ginseng and animals do not necessarily tell us anything about the plant's effects on human sexuality.

The supposed potency of sea-slugs, mandrakes, ginseng, bananas, figs, and other suggestively shaped foods relies to a great extent on the idea that like acts for like. The efficacy of other aphrodisiacs is based on the related, but distinct, principle that an intimate part acts for the whole. Germans in the Middle Ages believed in the power of an apple steeped in the sweat of the loved one. In the seventeenth century, an Englishwoman got her man by making 'cockle-bread': after kneading a small piece of dough, she impressed it against her vulva and then baked it. If the male object of her passion ate the little loaf, he would be unable to resist her. If that failed, she could always insert a fish into her vagina and then serve it up to him.

Some suppliers claim aphrodisical powers for their products as a way to boost consumption. In Britain in the Second World War, the rumour was put out that white bread – the most common and unexciting of English staples – was a potent aid to love-making. Today, guarana, the seed of an Amazonian berry, is marketed as 'the go-anywhere, get-going, pick-me-up drink that you can feel giving you a lift. Use it . . . to give yourself that extra boost for long and demanding days – and nights!'

Some foods are touted as aphrodisiacs because of their rarity or novelty. Previously unknown plants newly released on to the market are at first perceived as exotic, strange, and redolent of obscure powers. Until these mysterious foodstuffs become familiar and common, people give their imagination play and hold their scepticism in check. When tomatoes were first brought over from the New World, Europeans thought these 'love apples' were the forbidden fruit of Eden, while chocolate was considered so arousing that monks were forbidden from drinking the libidinous brew. Though it is hard for us to imagine a stodgy staple as a sexual stimulant, sixteenth-century Britons also prized that other native American plant, the sweet potato, as a potent love-aid. In Shakespeare's *Merry Wives of Windsor*, Falstaff boasts to his love of his ability to resist lustful temptation by listing the aphrodisiacs of his day: an imported tuber, an erotic tune, and two varieties of candied sea-holly. 'Let the sky rain potatoes; let it thunder to the tune of "Green Sleeves"; hail kissing-comfits, and snow eringoes; let there be a tempest of provocation, I will shelter me here.'

Other plants have been called aphrodisiacs because their physiological effects – however mild, or violent – are similar to those experienced by people in the process of making love. Chillies, curries, and other combinations of spices excite the sex organs, get the heart pumping, and may even cause sweating. In the past, Puritans and prison governors have banned these foods for precisely that reason. At the turn of the century, young Cajun men took the very opposite view: they wanted to excite others, female others, and would sprinkle cayenne on dance floors, in the hope that the powder, shaken up by the shuffling feet, would arouse their partners enough to overcome their Catholic inhibitions.

Wholesome recipes like almond soup, herrings, and egg ome-lette may seem unlikely aphrodisiacs, but they were meant to induce a general feeling of well-being and a mild state of euphoria which could, in the right circumstances, lead to an amorous encounter. In this sense, as the anthropologists Peter Farb and George Armelagos have pointed out, almost any food is a potential love-aid, as the very act of eating raises blood pressure, increases the pulse, and boosts body temperature. So long as you have not eaten too much, your body is now energized, ready for further action.

Some sexual stimulants are much more specific and localized in their effects; one recipe calls for a mixture of thorn-apple powder, black pepper, honey, and other ingredients to be applied directly to the penis shortly before sex. The atropine and hyoscine in the powder excite the member, the pepper makes it burn, itch, and engorge, and the honey acts as a lubricant, easing entry. But quite honestly, if this sort of peppered, gooey potion is meant to be the food of love, perhaps it would be better to stick to plainer fare.

The consequences of consuming cantharides, the notorious 'Spanish Fly', are even more dramatic *and dangerous*. Made from the pulverized remains of a dried blister beetle found in southern Europe, it burns the mouth and throat intensely, causes severe abdominal cramps and vomiting, and then empties your bowels in a diarrhoeic rush. The shock to your system and the assault on your kidneys are so great that the chance of death within twenty-four hours is high. And all this for the sake of a brief, violently induced erection of the penis or clitoris. For the sake of public health, wise governments prohibit its sale.

Those seeking much less harmful stimulants might consider trying pheromones. Animals naturally produce these volatile chemicals, whose biological function is to attract members of the opposite sex. They are also found in parsley, celery, celeriac roots, carrot tips, young parsnips, cheese, asafoetida, Bombay Duck, anchovy sauce, and Asian fish sauces. Truffles, 'the black diamond of the kitchen', contain substantial quantities of anderostenone, a chemical variant of the male sex hormone testosterone. The odour of this pheromone, according to the Australian wine-grower Max Lake, suggests 'musk and sandalwood with the merest nuance of urine'; the meat of wild boars and uncastrated domestic pigs is so full of the pungent scent that to some it seems tainted and repellent.

The research done on the influence of pheromones on human behaviour, however, has not yet provided any conclusive results. Subjects sitting in a room scented with an unnoticeable amount of anderostenone rated photographs of women as more attractive and sexy, and shots of men as warmer and more friendly than when performing the same task in an unscented room. In a separate experiment, psychologists sprayed anderostenone on to certain chairs in a dentist's waiting room. The receptionist observed that a significantly higher proportion of women, and a significantly lower proportion of men, chose the scented seats. But the women's response was only significant when the concentration of anderostenone was high or low, and the scientists are unable to explain why women showed no chair preference when the chemical was sprayed at a moderate level of concentration. All in all, this is the trouble with much of the research into pheromones: some experiments suggest that they do influence people's moods and attitudes, while others suggest that they do not.

The unexciting, and perhaps reassuring, conclusion to this brief tour of the world's sex-aids is that mood itself is the ultimate aphrodisiac. The spiced ingredients of a meal may get our bodies going; the phallic or vulval shape of the food served up may reveal our intentions; a wholesome, but not heavy, dish may put us in the right mood; and a pheromone-filled truffle may just possibly influence our attitude, but none of these has any chance of success without the right ambience. No culinary concoction of chemicals is going to turn your guest's head unless you provide him, or her, with the right setting. The food is supplementary to the romantic task at hand, and *that* job is up to you.

10

ASKING FOR IT

My mother, heavy with me, cried for apples. She did not mind if they were Cox's, Granny Smiths, or even Bramleys, just so long as they were crisp, sharp, and there in front of her. While she does not openly boast of her cravings, she was clearly pleased that she did have them, as though they helped to confirm her role as a mother. Personally, I suspect they were also a way of involving my father, by making him drive through suburban London before dawn in search of an all-night greengrocer.

Some mothers have cravings. Some do not. My female friends, by nature somewhat more rebellious than my mother, are pleased they do not. They do not want to be part of what they see as the myth-making that surrounds maternity. In this particular case, my acquaintances are out on a limb. Pregnancy cravings are not specific to Western culture and are, it seems, relatively easy to explain in physiological terms. Throughout the world, women who are eating for two long for certain foods, and, what is more interesting, they tend to desire the same kinds of food. Of course, in areas where people are living on a dietary knife-edge, pregnant women are not thought to have special cravings. Instead, they have hunger pangs. But then, so does everyone else in their community.

The items pregnant women crave most are sour fruit, followed by other kinds of sharp-tasting, salty, spicy, hard, or chewy foods. In Britain, that means women cry for, among other things, apples, oranges, ice-cream, chocolate, boiled sweets, raw potatoes, chewing gum, and nuts. Rural Thais give their Rice Mother goddess, when pregnant, scented powder and bitter fruits. On the Indonesian island of Kedang, they pine for tamarinds and mangoes. In the Deep South they go for clay.

Women with cravings do not just have passionate desires for certain kinds of food. Like my mother, they may also want the food at an odd time of day or in an unusually large quantity. On top of that, they may eat much more frequently during the day than normal, or come to crave unconventional combinations, like custard with pickle.

Despite constant attempts to link a mother's needs to her peculiar desires, cravings, which tend to start in the first few months of pregnancy, are unrelated to the *nutritional* needs of the budding mums. The pregnant woman who bends over in the herb-garden to eat parsley off the stem is not longing for the iron in the plant, but for its strong flavour. It is lack of taste, not of minerals, which brings her to her knees. Though a mother in one study said she longed for 'food advertised on TV', it appears most pregnant women crave the substances they do because their senses of taste and smell have become dulled. Foods that are usually bitter now seem sweet; morello cherries, for instance, are eaten fresh, without cooking or sugar. Experimental evidence shows that taste thresholds are indeed raised during pregnancy and that, after giving birth, they return to normal levels very rapidly, in some cases within a few hours. Is this turmoil in the taste buds the price of having loved?

Many pregnant women with cravings have at the same time aversions to other foods. Tea, coffee, and cocoa stand at the top of this list, with vegetables, meat, fish, and eggs coming next, followed by fatty, fried, or greasy foods. One pregnant woman, when asked why tea revolted her, said, 'It tastes funny.' Another, suddenly turned off coffee, confessed, 'It left the most awful taste in my mouth afterwards.' What appears to be common to all these substances is that they tend either to have a distinctive or powerful smell – such as fried chicken or onions – or to be delicately flavoured, or somewhat insipid. In the United States, some pregnant women stop drinking coffee because it provokes nausea, while others cannot stomach oregano-spiced sauces. On Kedang, pregnant women will not eat plain foods such as unsalted maize, and will not touch anything with a strong odour or which is slightly rotten, such as fish. There is a lack of scientific evidence about the physiological cause of such aversions, but they are possibly due to a change in the sense of smell, rather than of taste. Many pregnant women come to find tobacco smoke repellent, and a large number give up the habit (and not just for medical reasons).

In a host of different cultures it is laid down that pregnant women should be given what they want. Rural Guatemalans say a woman may miscarry if her cravings, which are thought to be the direct desires of the foetus, are not satisfied. In eighteenth-century France, it was thought a pregnant female's cravings should never be frustrated. An unsatisfied woman might produce a babe with a cherry-, raisin-, or melon-like birthmark. When chocolate started to become popular, women began to give birth to infants with supposedly chocolate-coloured marks. In one modern study carried out in Michigan, one-third of an inter-viewed group of White, Afro-American, and Latin-American women specifically gave cravings, especially unsatisfied ones, as the cause of infantile blemishes. The danger was particularly high if a mother touched herself while desiring the food. A woman who, without thinking, patted her cheek while longing for straw-berries might produce a child with a 'strawberry mark' on its cheek. One woman said that a pregnant mum who did not get the chicken she craved could give birth to a baby 'looking like a chicken'. The concern to prevent any of these infantile defects occurring is so great in one Afro-American urban neighbourhood in Arizona that locals tolerate pregnant women going from house to house asking for the food they crave. The residents do not want any stains on their community.

Some pregnant women do not long for apples, sweets, or ice-cream. They hunger for clay, starch, dirt, rocks, ashes, coal, charcoal, ice cubes, baking powder, matches, or even match boxes. As far as we can tell, in the West this form of compulsive eating – known as 'pica' – is confined mainly to members of low-income American groups. The women who consume these seem-ingly bizarre substances say they do so because their cravings signal a dietary lack, or because it is customary. Clay and earth in particular are thought to be good sources of valuable minerals. The scientific evidence, however, is contradictory: some types of clay are rich in calcium and magnesium, while others are not; moreover, ingested clay may impair the absorption of iron and so contribute to the development of anaemia. The most convincing explanation to date is that pregnant women consume clay be-cause it is a type of traditional behaviour socially approved by the women's peers. This maternal custom has long been practised throughout central Africa: certain Ewe villages in Ghana, for example, make good money by selling their prized clay baked in the form of eggs.

CLAMPING DOWN ON CUISINE

Africans are not the only peoples to have made a custom of clay-eating; in many parts of Indonesia and Papua New Guinea it is regarded as a delicacy. Admiralty Islanders say their particular variety has a taste similar to chocolate. But whatever its flavour, early plantation owners, especially in the French Antilles, regarded clay-eating with deep suspicion. They thought slaves only ate clay in order to fall ill and so get off work. In a vain attempt to curb their slaves' appetites, the plantation owners clamped mouth-locks on them. Of course, this naive and humiliating measure did not end the practice; it just made it more clandestine.

Africans sold into slavery took the practice of clay-eating with them to the Caribbean and American plantations. In the United States, the habit spread to other impoverished groups who came into contact with the Afro-Americans. When clay was not readily available, women most likely came to regard laundry starch, baking soda, and wheat flour as acceptable substitutes. Today, clay is sold by the shoebox in farmers' markets in Georgia, and friends bring it as a gift to new mothers in hospital. Getting one's supply is so important that Afro-Americans who have moved to northern cities are sent small pellets from relatives in the South. It is important, though, not to eat too much of a good thing. Believers in the efficacy of these 'foods' say that if a mother eats too much clay or starch her infant could be covered with the excess at birth, which might be difficult to wash off. As one lamented, 'My sister's baby was born with starch all over its face.'

For those Western women who normally worry about watching their figure, pregnancy is the one time when, with a sense of joy and none of guilt, they can shed all self-control and indulge their appetite to the full. Who cares if you get fat? Women, after all, are meant to grow large during pregnancy. So why not make the most of your time? As a general rule, mothers who have cravings and aversions during pregnancy tend to have been compulsive eaters as children, to have been smokers before their pregnancy, or to have had a history of appetite change during times of emotional stress. Statistically, the chances are that women who drink are more likely to have cravings than those who are teetotal. In other words, it appears that if you have a strong oral fixation it is much more probable that, when pregnant, you will crave certain foods and push others away. The anally uptight do not tend to suffer the same pangs or hates.

As with most things that women do, men – somewhere or other, at some time or another – try to get in on the act. Some men cook, some men look after their children, and some Melanesian males simulate menstruation. Even childbirth is not sacred. In many areas of the world, especially Amazonia, men practise the 'couvade': they ritually imitate, and perhaps experience, aspects of pregnancy, giving birth, and the postnatal seclusion of the mother. Like their pregnant partners, they may give up their normal routine activities, observe the same prenatal restrictions, and keep to the same food taboos. In the most dramatic examples, they retire to their hammocks and simulate labour pangs. This seemingly cranky conduct is often explained by members of those cultures as being a paternal attempt to aid the spiritual development of the otherwise vulnerable newborn babe. Without the mother there is no child, without the father's contribution the child may not survive.

No modern Western society has a cultural equivalent to this sort of behaviour. However, since the 1960s doctors in England and Sweden have recognized a particular set of symptoms that is shown by almost 20 per cent of their pregnant patients' male partners. Men afflicted by this 'couvade syndrome' tend to be quite strongly attached to their mother, to have lost their virginity relatively late in life, and to be older (on average over thirty) and to have older parents than non-sufferers. Also, their female partners often become anxious about the impending birth within the first months of their pregnancy. These wretched men can suffer morning sickness, gastro-intestinal problems, and toothache; they may gain weight, become irritable, complain of lack of sleep, or even start to lactate. But so far, no evidence has come to light that these miserable males crave or long for specific foods. Perhaps something is sacred, after all.

11

REVOLUTION AT TABLE

Kids know what they like: no adults. Without grown-ups to pester them, they are not told when to eat and what to eat, they do not have to stop fidgeting at table, and they do not need to watch their manners. Adults do not understand what their offspring want, which is simply to enjoy themselves and not be confined by a set of rules that appear meaningless, unnecessary, and petty. Children do not, for example, 'toy' with their food – they eat some of it and creatively employ the rest for other uses, maybe turning their faces into canvases and painting their cheeks with the stuff. If they want to make their peas into projectiles and mould their mashed potato into skyscrapers, why shouldn't they be allowed to?

As Germaine Greer has argued, guilty adults have turned the dining-room into a chamber of horrors for innocent children. A fully dressed table, with its stiff white cloth, stands like an altar over the head of a toddler. The child's only access to it is by climbing a chair, usually designed to topple as the cub moun-taineer ascends. Once on the summit, it is difficult to maintain one's balance for long. Those who do manage to sit it out without falling over the edge come to learn that chairs are aids to indiges-tion, as they force one to sit in a physically awkward position. And all this effort just goes into the preliminaries. Now in place, the child has to learn how to eat the food in front of her.

The adult instruments of juvenile torture start on either side of the plate. To children, knives and forks are not props for a gastronomic performance but sculpted sticks of cold steel with a hard, cold taste. Unlike the warm wood of chopsticks or the familiar feel of one's own fingers, Western cutlery is more akin to surgical implements than eating utensils. It denies us full pleasure of our food and lends a clinical edge to the event. Family meals are meant to be occasions of joy, not medical operations.

Better to use fingers. Though 'hand-to-mouth' is a pejorative phrase in English, suggesting beggars rifling through dustbins for scraps, we should not despise the appendages at the ends of our arms. Excellent at picking things up, fingers are also very easy to

clean: to follow the example of some Indians, simply put them in
your mouth and suck hard as you slowly withdraw them. Then
just a quick wipe with a towel and the job is done. No need to spray
them with detergent or drop them into a dishwasher: no nasty
chemicals and no waste of energy. Fingerlickin' is not just fun, it
is ecologically OK to boot.

Many adults are aware of the violence they must do in order to
programme their children successfully. But they regard a sense of
decorum as a passport to polite society. Not training their offspring in how to hold their knife and fork would mean their
automatic exclusion from 'the right kind of table'. And if the taste
of metal, whether silver spoon or electro-plated fork, is the
gastronomic price that has to be paid, then many parents are
prepared to make their children pay it.

Anyway, grown-ups can argue, table manners are like all other
rules: once imbued, they do not have to be followed slavishly.
They can be played with. Etiquette is not a fixed set of laws etched
in stone, it is a changeable collection of regulations that adepts
may manipulate as the occasion demands. The point about rules
is knowing them sufficiently well to know when you can break
them. At this level, table ritual becomes an adroit performance,
where the more proficient players are able to appreciate the skills
of one another. For such masters of manners etiquette is not a
prose form to be obeyed but a poetics to be enacted.

These subtleties are lost on kids. What they are concerned about
is independence, and they quickly come to understand the games
their parents want them to play and how to exploit their elders'
desires for their own ends.

Children like simple, sweet foods that are easy to eat: baked
beans, spaghetti, puddings, and biscuits rather than unboned fish
and raw vegetables. Meat is hard to chew, and knives and forks are
such cumbersome, awkward objects that they need adults to cut
the stuff up for them. Breakfast and tea-time are not so bad. At
least the foods are easy to eat and often sweet. Sandwiches and
toast are finger foods, and a bowl of cereal can be eaten with a
spoon. It is the main meal of the day that can be the real cause of
strife.

To traditionally-minded parents, a 'proper meal' is central to the
upbringing of their children because it provides them with healthy,
nourishing food, and because they believe families should eat

proper meals together. It is what families are meant to do. Kids are not so sure about that. They know they can influence what sweet is served but that they have relatively little choice about the main dish. That is something they have got to eat, and eat properly under the scrutiny of their father.

In Yorkshire and other parts of Britain, children are told, 'Waste not, want not'. Parents persuade daughters to eat burnt toast by saying it will make their hair curl, and they cajole their sons to finish their cabbage by claiming it will put hairs on their chest. If he or she dares to leave a morsel, the child is reminded of the starving millions in India/Bangladesh/Africa, as though eating the remaining titbit will somehow affect the global system of food distribution. In Newfoundland, parents personify their threats with the terrifying figure of the dreaded 'Crust Man'. A living embodiment of leftover crusts, this big, ugly humanoid is said to wander the streets at night checking that children have dutifully gobbled up everything they were served. Any disobedient kids are bundled into his bag and carried away. In South Africa, Chaga children who refused to eat their soup in the evening were scared into finishing it by the threatening sound of the *koko* (bogey-man) just outside their house. The noise, of course, was not made by a bogey-man (a fearsome Chaga warrior or a White Man) but by the child's dutiful elder brother.

If children want to tip the balance of power back towards themselves the most effective weapon in their armoury is steadfastly refusing to eat what is placed in front of them, no matter what they are threatened with. Tired mothers do not want to see their time and effort wasted. So, to please their children, and thus ultimately themselves, they often end up preparing food they know will be liked. Out-manoeuvred by their children, they should perhaps take some pride in their children's manipulative skills.

When kids are not exploiting their mothers at mealtimes, they are busy creating their own gastronomic world, one which inverts the nutritional and moral values of their parents. Children are told meat and vegetables are 'good' for them and that too many sweet things are 'bad'. And just in case they have not got the message, they are not given any pudding if they will not eat the main course. The sweet dish is turned into a bribe, a pleasurable reward for eating the meat and veg. Simultaneously obeying your

SCHOOL DINNERS

Until very recently, British children had absolutely no choice about what they were served at school. In an effort to assert their own values in this otherwise powerless situation, they mocked the food and renamed it.

While waiting for the meal to arrive, the whole class might launch into a rendition of 'Today's Menu':

> Scab and matter custard,
> Green snot pies,
> Dead dog's giblets,
> Dead cat's eyes,
> And a cup of sick to wash it down.

Meals were dubbed SOS ('Same Old Slush') or YMCA ('Yesterday's Muck Cooked Again'). Stew was called 'spew' or 'dog's dinner', corned beef 'armoured cow', cottage pie 'resurrection pie', and when ham was the dish of the day, the children hummed 'Yum, yum, pig's bum'. Roast potatoes became 'Rocks of Gibraltar', pea soup 'London fog', fried bread 'frizzled monkey', and macaroni 'drainpipes' or 'filleted worms'. Even less complementary terms were used for the last course: milk pudding was 'slosh', chocolate rice 'mud', tapioca 'fish eyes in glue', sultanas in sago 'tadpoles in a pond', pink blancmange 'baby-in-the-bath', currant cake 'flies' cemetery', red-jam roly-poly 'dead baby', and Spotted Dick with warm treacle 'Leper's Arm with Old Man's Dung'.

parents and consuming the unappetising becomes a virtuous act. Both nutrition and ethics are combined in each mouthful: 'Be a good boy and eat it all up, it is good for you.' When this mealtime morality becomes all too much, children rebel by secretly gorging themselves on food that is nice, and bad: sweets.

As the anthropologist Allison James has shown, in the northeast of England grown-ups call things they regard as being inedible, useless, or rubbishy 'kets'. Junk food is ket, and so is cheap paint that will soon peel. In a clever inversion of adult values, local children have appropriated the word for their own ends. For them, kets are the very sweets their parents refuse to buy them and never eat themselves. These sorts of confectionery are the exact opposite on almost every single count of what parents think of as food. Cheap, not wrapped, and made for little hands, these kets have non-food names like 'Smelly Feet', 'Building Bricks', 'Slime Slurp', 'Super Jet', 'Traffic Lights', 'Jelly Wellies', and 'Car Parks'. Others are named after animals, especially those never eaten in real life ('Crocodile Candy', 'Munchy Maggots', 'Jelly Snakes', 'White Mice', 'Gummi Bears'); some smack of cannibalism ('Jelly Babies', 'Hobos', 'Mr Marble'); and one directly pokes fun at adult fears – 'Rotten Teeth'.

Adult confectionery, when it is not being romantic or suggestive, tends to have precise and detailed names: 'Orange Crisp Chocolates', 'Peppermint Lumps', or 'Liquorice Bon-Bons'. You know what you are going to eat. In contrast, the names of kets can be completely misleading: 'Jelly Eels' are not savoury but sickly sweet; 'Rhubarb and Custard' is not smooth and digestible but hard and chewy. The very colour of these juvenile confections does violence to adult notions of what food should look like. Instead of the natural greens of spinach and cabbage, the dull white of potatoes, or the speckled beige of muesli, kets are fluorescent orange, luminous blue, vivid yellow, shocking pink, or bright blood red. Sweets for grown-ups do not use these highly saturated colours but soft pastel shades which are meant to seduce the eater, not shake him or her up.

Kets are not intended for such gustatory niceties. They have distinctive, strong flavours that are meant to assault the taste buds and lay them low: Fizz 'n' Chips makes the mouth tingle; sherbet makes it smart; a gob-stopper physically blocks the addition of anything else. Potato chips, though not usually regarded as exclusively kets, fit the same general pattern. Unlike ordinary, polite foods, crisps cannot be nibbled quietly. Their loud crack and crunch is the whole point of eating them. Their brittle texture is all, and their taste is almost irrelevant, for no one likes a stale crisp, whether it is cheese and onion, salt and vinegar, or smoky bacon flavour. Most sounds reach our hearing organs by passing through the air. But when you crunch into a crisp, your jawbone begins to resonate at over 150 cycles-per-second. These singing vibrations are directly transmitted to the bones of the inner ear, where they are converted into that familiar explosive racket. Crisps are not for eating, they are for listening to.

Kets, these garish, crude taste-bombs, represent youth's rejection of the older generation's values and ideas about nutrition. They are a subversive form of consumption, enabling youngsters to create their own gastronomic lifestyle and their own feeding patterns. By swapping kets between themselves, they set up their own system of exchange, their own petty economic network, one free of interference by grown-ups.

In this juvenile world, fixed mealtimes can even come to be seen as an unwanted interruption of their ket-eating habits. Trust adults to get in the way of kids' desires!

12

KIDS' STUFF

Up in the Highlands of Papua New Guinea, many people still living in the traditional style think that girls naturally grow into women without any aid or assistance from others, but that boys have to be made into men, that they have to undergo a prolonged process of ritual initiation. Boys must pass through a series of trials and must regulate their diet in order to firm their flesh, harden their bones, and dry out their bodies, so removing any residual trace of breast-milk. One Awa man remembered the words the elders told him and his peers at the start of their initiation:

> *You are just small boys and still sleep near your mothers. Now we will take you to sleep with us in the men's house. Now that this is done, you cannot go back to stay with your mothers. If you stay with your mothers, you will not grow quickly. If you stay there you will be like the little ones that still suckle. You will not become grown. You must come into the men's house, you must hear what your fathers have to say, you must grow rapidly. . . . If you disobey your fathers and you go down to where your mother is cooking food and you eat, you will not grow, you will remain thin, and you will stay that way forever. So remain in the men's house and eat with us.*

> *The nutritional message could not be clearer: eat the wrong foods and you will not mature. And in the tough environment of the New Guinea Highlands, no one is interested in a physically weak male.*

Like the Awa, the Tukanoan Indians of northern Amazonia are concerned that their children eat the right foods at the right time. Unlike the Awa, they do not worry so much about the sex of the cook as about the nature of the food itself. To them all food is simultaneously life-sustaining and potentially lethal. Though they say that food makes the body and the soul grow, anything edible is also thought to be dangerous because of the powers associated with it, or because of the way it is produced: if a Tukanoan child drinks boiled manioc-starch soup on the wrong occasion, the stick used to stir it will magically stir up his soul; someone who eats fatty foods might be attacked by a jaguar or snake because these animals can magically see the delicious grease inside the consumer. To save themselves from these calamities, Tukanoans get their shamans – intermediaries between the spiritual and everyday worlds – to treat all their food ritually. An Indian will ask one of these specialists to blow a spell on a sample of a certain category of food, such as 'large fish'. Once he has done his stuff and dispelled all the dangers, his client can then eat any type of large fish without worry.

The Tukanoan approach to nutrition means that shamans have to treat all the different sorts of food that children are gradually introduced to. Since a newborn babe survives on its mother's milk and on soft, sweet-tasting pink gooseberries, the father has to employ a shaman to cast spells over both items. When weaning starts, he is called in again to treat the soft vegetable foods the infant is to be given. Whenever a child moves from one food stage to the next – from tubers to fruits and leaves, to small fish, and finally to large mammals – the shaman has to clear its gastronomic way with his spells. This, however, is not the end of the laborious process, for an adolescent undergoing initiation into manhood is thought to lay himself open to danger, and so the shaman has to go through the whole set of magical procedures one more time. Given this set of beliefs, Tukanoan shamans are kept busy but, thanks to them, the locals are kept alive: the food they cultivate and catch does not become the cause of their death.

Like the Tukanoans, many groups of people around the globe think boys and girls pitiable, vulnerable characters in need of protection from dangerous edibles. As weak, undeveloped individuals they have to be shielded from perilous forms of food. For their own sake they have to be taught what and when they should and should not eat. The Andaman Islanders of the Indian Ocean, for instance, traditionally thought that each type of food had its own kind of power, and that the aggrieved spirits of the dead could kill the living by directing that power against them. A meal would make a victim sick, not healthy. Adults could protect their infants against this danger but children, in order to become sturdy, independent grown-ups, had to be endowed ritually with this food-based force. This lengthy ceremonial process, lasting several years, ensured that Andamanese boys and girls would mature into able-bodied adults, skilful at hunting and other tasks, and strong enough to resist disease. By eating foods in a carefully controlled ritual context, the youths took on the power of the foods. This sort of nutrition was not voluntary or optional, but necessary for personal survival. Anyone who did not pass through this ritual process was sure to die young.

Awan, Tukanoan, and Andamanese ideas about what children should and should not eat may seem exotic, weird, and very distant from anything in our own experience, but there was, of course, one highly idiosyncratic tribe in Western history whose nutritional ideas we must not forget. Like the Tukanoans and Andamanese, members of this group saw children as peculiarly vulnerable to the dangers inherent in many foods. They may not have believed in the therapeutic power of shamans or in the nutritional value of a long, complex ritual, but there are still sufficient similarities to justify the comparison. For this particular Western tribe put their infants on to an extremely restricted diet and kept them on it until late adolescence – all for the sake of their supposedly ever-so-delicate bowels. In the scientific literature this group is known as the Victorians, later called the Edwardians, and the native term for their gastronomic regime is 'Nursery Food'.

This miserable selection of foods barely justifies ranking as a proper diet. Babes were given semolina, a gruel made from arrowroot, crushed biscuits, bread, or flour. Children had to survive on milk, oatmeal, bread, potatoes, mutton, rice, and suet pudding, and almost nothing else. The bread was preferably eight days' stale, and the potatoes old rather than new. With the exception of beef, all other sorts of meat were forbidden; asparagus, broccoli, cauliflower, and French beans were only to be eaten very occasionally, and then only in minute quantities; cakes and sweets were strictly taboo.

Even when away from home there was no escaping the nursery diet. Until the 1840s, the scholars at Eton had boiled mutton and mashed potatoes as their main meal every single day of their school lives. Supper was the leftovers, and if nothing was left over, there was nothing for supper. The reform of the ancient college included the revolutionary introduction of bread, butter, and milk for breakfast and for tea; beef was to replace mutton twice a week; Sunday was to be celebrated with plum pudding.

Food for children was to be plain, dull, and heavy. Victorians justified starving the taste buds of their offspring in this way because they thought youngsters' digestive systems feeble and imperfect. Children quite literally lacked guts: compared to those of adults, their stomachs and intestines were less robust and incomplete – their bodies were as immature as their personalities. Juvenile bodies, it was believed, could not withstand the rough fare of their elders. Mutton, old potatoes, and stale bread only passed muster because they were simple, wholesome, and supposedly easy to digest. Fresh fruit, most vegetables, and any sweet a child might actually *like* were considered unsuitable, unhealthy, and potentially damaging to the delicate constitution of a young Victorian.

Parents' reasons for imposing this rigorous regime were not just alimentary. In the late nineteenth century, authority was everything and children were to be the obedient puppets of their masters. Dictating what a boy ate was a practical, daily way to break his will and teach him the importance of subservience. Some parents, obsessed with the need for discipline, believed that if their charges did not like what they were given, then the food *had* to be good for them. The children of Victorian nurseries were not allowed to develop dislikes, and any sign of gastronomic rebelliousness was overcome by the unrelenting monotony of the same simply cooked, weakly flavoured dishes served up day after day. Food was not to be enjoyed, but tolerated.

If variety is the spice of appetite, it is possible that this trained insensitivity contributed to the appallingly low standard of British cuisine at the time. Many Victorian novels reveal people's lack of enthusiasm, bordering on guilt, towards eating. Instead of relishing their meals, they were meant to get them over and done with. And they learnt these self-denying habits in the nursery.

Luckily, this drab diet was confined to the upper classes. Children from other social ranks ate what they wanted or – more precisely – what they could. Affluent Victorians might have rationalized this socially-based difference in diet by regarding members of the 'lower' orders as a different kind of animal, but they could not say the same about the children of their American peers. Those who made the journey to the United States were shocked by what middle-class children were eating. According to one outraged visitor, they breakfasted on 'fish, flesh and game, fruits, salads and hominy; Johnny-cakes, corn cakes, buckwheat cakes, all hot with molasses; toast swimming in butter'. In the Children and Nurses' dining-room of grand hotels, the young residents would be offered an array of rolls, breads, hot cereals, as well as beefsteak, mutton chops, ham, fresh fish, liver and bacon, codfish cakes, boiled or scrambled eggs, kidneys, corned beef hash, tripe, clams, and various types of potatoes. And that was just for breakfast. In the afternoon, American children were not fed tea in the nursery but sat at table with their parents where they shared such 'unwholesome' food as oysters, jellies, ices, fruit, and preserves. To astonished Brits, the adult diet of these American children had to be one reason why they were so assured, precocious, and altogether unchildlike – and thus another good reason why their own offspring should be kept on plain fare.

This rigid, dull diet has now gone the way of the nursery itself. Both the diet and the room have become part of British history. Nursery food was yet another victim of the Second World War, when all social classes – parents and children alike – were forced to survive on the same rations. People stopped worrying about their children's digestive tracts and started to give them much of what they wanted. The children did not complain nor, apparently, did their bowels.

Nursery food has gone for good and English children today have become some of the most faddish eaters in the world. Compared to the omnivorous appetites of their French counterparts, young Brits are extremely finicky, and their list of food dislikes is long. Tomatoes are the most unpopular, but the juvenile inventory of undesired foods also includes salad, carrots, cabbage, sprouts, beetroot (among other vegetables), strawberries, fish, pork, lamb, stew, and nuts. It may well be the case, as some scientists say, that children prefer soft and moist foods because their mouths produce insufficient saliva to lubricate it as they chew. But this still fails to explain why French children have so few food aversions, and the English so many.

Most probably, they are so irritatingly particular in what they eat because their parents allow them to be. Reacting against their own parents' horror stories of nursery food, many of today's adults want their children to *express* their likes and dislikes. They wish to be loved as caring parents, not as domestic Hitlers dictatorially imposing their own ideas about diet. Instead of smothering the individuality of their sons and daughters with unappetising, unchanging dishes, they nourish their children's personalities by catering to their food preferences. Kids, after all, have rights too.

13

HOW TO MAKE FRIENDS

In hard times, Irish mothers used to stretch the family meal (and their imaginative powers) by serving 'fish-and-point'. This apocryphal recipe consists of a large serving dish with a herring painted on it and a pyramid of salt in its centre. Each diner forks one of the potatoes on his plate, dips it in the salt, and points it at a section of the fish, crying, 'That's my bit!' On eating the potato he then exclaims, 'Hmm! How good the fish tastes. Perfectly cooked! It's so true – you can't beat a fresh herring!' To entertain themselves and to take their minds off the monotony of potatoes three times a day, family members would compete with one another for the most original way of expressing their fishy appreciation.

Most European families, like Irish ones, regard mealtimes as a way to draw everyone together. A mother's provision of cooked food is an excuse for all members of her family to sit down *en famille* and enjoy themselves in one another's company. They are meant to appreciate the food and, above all in middle-class homes, the chance to chatter with their nearest and dearest. If, in the pointed Irish case, the food could not provide much pleasure, then the family members could take pleasure in a collective fantasy. Since they could not physically share the non-existent herring, they could share a joke about it instead.

At its most dramatic, the dinner-table acts as both a stage and the stalls. It is a domestic theatre where members of the family in turn play the roles of performers and audience. No one is in the pits and, in the more accommodating of households, they are not all fighting to occupy the critic's seat. My father usually granted himself the star-role in the continuing production staged by his wife. Occasionally he would deign to give us children bit-parts in what was essentially a one-man show. He acted the in-house comedian with our mother as the straight guy feeding him lines. We giggled dutifully while the meal went cold and the sauce over the meat congealed into a mucous film.

When not serving as a drama-school for unpaid hams, mealtimes can become a clearing-house for the family's news, information, and experiences. Since they are one of the few regular occasions when parents, brothers, and sisters are all present at the same time, family meals are regarded by most as a privileged opportunity to catch up on the gossip and contribute some of their own. The dinner-table is also used as an arena for parents and children to discuss matters of interest and common concern. Individuals express their different points of view, maybe modify them as the debate progresses, and – on the more successful of occasions – combine to produce something approaching a group attitude or judgement: the family forum has made up its mind.

Communal meals are so fundamental to Europeans' sense of what a family is that they will go to great lengths to ensure they can all eat together. If the husband has to work shifts or regularly comes back late, his wife may delay dinner and prevent the children from going to bed so they can all eat at the same time. In South Wales and other parts of Britain, mothers will put aside a plateful for each of those who will come later, as though it were important that every member of the family is at least served at dinner. Besides feeding their husband and children, women will also cook for all their single male kin, even distantly related ones. Some grown bachelors still have lunch at their mother's every working day, and when she dies, other female relatives cater for him.

As these examples suggest, the general idea in Europe is that the eating of food together is what helps to keep a family together. For what kind of family would it be if the mother, father, and children never sat down to the same table together? Households surviving on such low incomes that they physically cannot all sit together in the cramped kitchen say they feel the lack of an adequate table keenly. Pushing the father into the sitting-room and having older children eat off their knees is no way, they complain, to bring up a family.

Since Sunday is seen as a special day for the family, Sunday lunch becomes the key meal of the week. All the family members are meant to turn up, and for once the television and the radio are turned off. This meal is so central to people's idea of what a family is that women managing the home budget on low incomes will scrimp and save during the week to ensure their husbands and children can be given a 'proper Sunday dinner', with a roast joint as the centrepiece. Research done in the north of England suggests that those families which never bother with roasts or providing anything special for the Sunday meal are not seen by others as 'proper' families or as having a 'proper' family life. The logic underlying this attitude is, if you do not make meals according to the same basic pattern as us, then we cannot regard you as people like us; if you do not eat like a family, we will not consider you as a family.

While these family eating patterns are still culturally dominant in much of Western Europe and parts of North America, they no longer occupy quite the central position they formerly held. In Britain today, working mothers cook fewer meals for their families because their husbands and teenage children are often out in the evenings. Even Sunday lunch is no longer religiously observed week in, week out, but sometimes skipped if the family decide to go out for the day. In the United States, thanks to the creation of one-person microwave meals, children can indulge their individual preferences and 'cook' their own food by pressing a button. Seventy-five per cent of American families no longer have breakfast together, and they only meet up for dinner three times a week, or less. Instead they snack more, throughout the day. Despite all these changes, however, and even though many families today do not have most of their meals together, many still cling to the idea of eating together as important to their sense of family as a miniature community. So, for members of the middle-class at least, the meals they do manage to have together are turned into almost celebratory feasts.

STARRY-EYED AND HUNGRY

Until NASA realized that eating together was a good way to keep astronauts happy, the space-travellers ate their food by lifting their visors and sucking tubes of puréed meats, vegetables, and fruits. Nowadays, they sit down to meals of frankfurters, turkey Tetrazzini, bread, bananas, almond crunch bar, and apple juice – at a triangular table so all three crewmen sit in equal position with respect to one another. To give them a real feel of a home away from home, they are even allowed to do the washing up.

CHRISTMAS

Since Christmas is the most important family meal of the year, women with little money make an extraordinary effort to provide their homes with special foods for the festive feast. In the words of one woman, speaking in 1982:

We pay so much for a hamper every year – we get that off the milkman. We got a meat pack last year, didn't we? We paid so much a week, and we got £25 worth, and we got these vouchers and we went to [the butchers] in town. We got everything. It was lovely to have meat, you know. We even got steak, so you can tell it was a treat, a real treat. The kids loved it, 'Cor, look what me mam's got in the freezer' – things they'd never seen before.

There is, of course, nothing 'natural' about the Anglo-Saxon custom of planning meals along familial lines. Their meals are only staged that way because the family remains the primary social unit in much of British society. Other cultures have different customs, and to members of those groups their way of doing things is just as 'natural'. In many traditional African societies the women prepare the meals but men and women dine separately. The Nuer of southern Sudan, for instance, regard eating, like excreting, as a corporal operation which draws attention to one's body. Since ingesting food rouses the consciousness of one's physicality and thus brings on feelings of shame, Nuer avoid eating in front of members of the opposite sex unless they are close kin, and a husband will not eat together with his wife for the first years of their marriage. In northern Vanuatu, some men join ranked male societies where members of each rank cook their own food at their own hearth. They only eat with each other and leave their families to look after themselves. In India, upper-caste Hindus who marry women beneath their station cannot eat meals with them if they do not wish to pollute themselves. The couple can share sex but not food, and the man has to dine with his mother, sister, or other wives. Either way, however other peoples organize their mealtimes, it is worth remembering that the Anglo-Saxon custom of eating *en famille* has not always been observed by Britons themselves.

In many well-to-do Victorian and Edwardian homes parents ate in the dining-room and children in the nursery.

Feeding time does not have to be staged as though it were a family event. In fact, for some peoples, the daily task of eating does not even have to be a social activity. The Amazonian Bakairi, for example, prefer to eat on their own: at mealtimes each goes off into his hut, or quietly scoffs the lot behind a tree. When a visiting explorer began to eat a piece of fish he had been given by one of them, all the men sitting round turned their faces away, ashamed at the sight. One of the more friendly locals told their ignorant guest to take the fish into his hut and finish eating it there.

A LEAVENING INFLUENCE

In 1945, when the Germans pulled out of Auschwitz under the threat of the Russian advance, the starved inmates had their first-ever chance to search the camp. The Italian writer Primo Levi and two friends found potatoes and a stove, which they took back to their freezing hut. Once they had managed to get the stove going, the other occupants of the hut spontaneously gave the three of them slices of bread in thanks. Until that moment the unwritten law of the camp had been 'eat your own bread, and if you can, that of your neighbour'. To Levi this bread offering was 'the first human gesture that occurred among us'. By sharing food, they had re-asserted their humanity.

Exactly who you eat with may vary from country to country, but one global generalization we can make is that giving and exchanging food is fundamental to any sort of human relationship in any society, whether in Britain, India, or Vanuatu. Among the Bantu of Zimbabwe, two people make a temporary contract by swapping food: they call this 'a clanship of porridge'. We make, and keep, friends by sharing food with them. Even the Bakairi and the Nuer, who eat on their own, give and take food from one another, while the English term 'companion' comes from a Roman word meaning 'one who breaks bread with another' (*com* = with, *panis* = bread). The Christian notion of consubstantiality is based on the idea that people who share food together, whether in meals like the Last Supper or Holy Communion, may also share a common moral substance. Judas' betrayal was thus all the worse because he had so recently supped with the Lord.

A gift of food can express many things: concern, sympathy, gratitude, affection, love. Thus not giving food to others is equivalent to debarring oneself from much of ordinary day-to-day life. Children who do not pass their sweets around are not asked to play with others, a housewife who will not reveal her recipes to her neighbours is not trusted by them, and businessmen who do not take colleagues out to lunch make fewer deals. The only people who will not share any food at all are misers and hermits, and what friends do they have?

Anyone who gives, however, normally expects – eventually – to receive something in return. A gift of food carries with it a set of obligations. University tutors know this all too well: if a student brings them an apple at the beginning of the tutorial, they can safely assume it is a sweetener for teacher because the essay is not up to scratch. When a European explorer thanked a group of Arctic Inuit (Eskimos) for the piece of meat they gave him, an old man quickly corrected him:

> You must not thank for your meat; it is your right to get parts. In this country, nobody wishes to be dependent on others. Therefore, there is nobody who gives or gets gifts, for thereby you become dependent. With gifts you make slaves just as with whips you make dogs.

In societies where all food should automatically be shared, locals often have to be devious in order to eat in peace without being constantly pestered by hungry others. While extolling an ideology of great openness, they quietly become masters of secrecy. It is for these reasons that the Siriono, living in the Bolivian rainforest, tend to eat at night. If a family prepares a meal during the day, it is usually surrounded by a crowd of people begging for morsels. So, to avoid difficulties and to be able to eat without interruption, Siriono often wait until their neighbours are asleep before tucking in. But even this tactic does not make for relaxed mealtimes. As the anthropologist who lived with them remembered:

> When I was on the march with the Siriono . . . a few of my loyal Indian companions, who developed a certain interest in my

welfare, used frequently to wake me in the middle of the night to share food, which they hated to display during the daytime because of the possibility of their having to divide it with someone else. . . .

Eating takes place without benefit of etiquette or ceremony. Food is bolted as rapidly as possible, and when a person is eating he never looks up from his food until he has finished. . . . The principal goal of eating seems thus to be the swallowing of the greatest quantity of food in the shortest possible time.

In order not to appear mean, the Siriono are forced to feed at midnight. They keep their friends by keeping quiet about their meals.

Food ties the living together. It can also connect the living to the dead. At funerals and memorial services in rural Greece, the bereaved give *koliva* to everyone who turns up. Locals claim that this spicy fruit-and-nut, wheat-based dish is eaten by participants 'so that the dead may eat'. Though some are ambivalent about these beliefs, most say that the food somehow finds its way to the other world: eat up and speed the dead's advance to the land of eternal rest. If the deceased person had, for example, a passion for caramels, her recently widowed husband might give some to others saying, 'Here, eat a caramel, so that my wife will eat it.'

In contrast, at Anglo-Saxon funerals, bereaved families may share food with their relatives and friends, but they make no special claims about feeding the dead. Instead, simply by eating together, they collectively celebrate life in the face of recent death. The communal meal is meant to breed a sense of community. One problem, though, is that after a few drinks some people almost inevitably start to remember what an old bastard the deceased really was.

It is often said there are as many deer in the park of Magdalen College, Oxford as there are dons in its senior common room, and that when one of these learned men finally passes on to that great library in the sky, his fellows feast on one of the parked beasts. Whether this is a now-extinct custom, or a myth kept up by outsiders who like the idea of the Great and Gowned doing eccentric things in an ancient foundation, the cultural logic of the event is still clear: by consuming one of 'their very own', these clever men and women simultaneously commemorate their colleague's demise and their collegiate survival over death. Without the fellow, high table may not be the same again, but the Great Leveller will not stop formal dinner in hall, nor Magdalen itself.

However, as animal rights' activists have pointed out, when one of the herd dies, their keeper does not get his gun and go stalking dons in the cloister. Is this what is meant by academic freedom?

14

HOW TO MAKE ENEMIES

A narrow-minded friend of Cicero's decides to stop attending dinner-parties. The Roman orator, wiser in the ways and pleasures of the world, tries to change his mind:

> Really Paetus, I advise you to spend time in honest, pleasant, and friendly company. . . . I am not thinking of the physical pleasure [of dining], but of community of life and habit, and of mental recreation, of which familiar conversation is the most effective agent; and conversation is at its most agreeable at dinner-parties. In this respect we Romans are wiser than the Greeks. They use words meaning literally, 'co-drinkings' (symposia) or 'co-dinings' (syndeipna), but we say 'co-livings' (convivia), because at dinner-parties, more than anywhere else, life is lived in company.

Cicero was right: a successful banquet is the very height of civilization.

Renaissance writers largely agreed with the Roman orator but, unlike him, they did not run down the importance of the food. According to them, a well-run feast satisfies a gamut of human needs, from some of the most earthy to some of the most refined. It is an opportunity for total pleasure, uniting the physical and the intellectual, the body and the spirit. Good food, in good company, makes for good times.

But hedonism, while given play, is not given free rein. Diners appease and delight their appetites, without giving in to gluttony. A playful civility overcomes unbridled animality; sensuality is reconciled with constraint. Though conversation is part of the menu and guests obey no rule other than that of controlled improvisation, seriousness must alternate with entertainment, and erudition with comedy. The best of Renaissance feasts celebrate human nature. They do not debase it into low farce.

This recipe for success sounds very inviting, but moralists from the time of the Ancient Greeks have recognized that the pleasures of eating can release subversive, as well as creative, powers. The theory might be that eating together breeds conviviality and a

TABULATING PERFECTION

How, in this year of grace 1825, must a meal be contrived in order to combine the conditions which procure the pleasures of the table in the highest degree?

Let the number of guests be not more than twelve, so that the talk may be constantly general;

Let them be chosen with different occupations but similar tastes, and with such points of contact that the odious formalities of introduction can be dispensed with;

Let the dining-room be well lighted, the cloth impeccably white, and the atmosphere maintained at a temperature of from sixty to seventy degrees;

Let the men be witty without being too pretentious, and the women charming without being too coquettish;

Let the dishes be few in number, but exquisitely choice, and the wines of the first quality, each in its class;

Let the service of the former proceed from the most substantial to the lightest, and of the latter, from the mildest to the most perfumed;

Let the progress of the meal be slow, for dinner is the last business of the day; and let the guests conduct themselves like travellers due to reach their destination together;

Let the coffee be piping hot, and the liqueurs chosen by a connoisseur;

Let the drawing-room be large enough to allow a game at cards to be arranged for those who cannot do without, yet still leave space for postprandial conversations;

Let the tea not be too strong, the toast artistically buttered, and the punch mixed with proper care;

Let retirement begin not earlier than eleven o'clock, but by midnight let everyone be in bed.

Brillat-Savarin, 1825

warm feeling of fellowship, but in practice, as we all know only too well, meals can provoke division as much as unity, anger as much as joy, violence as much as peace. The table talk can turn too lively and even shift to the level of delirium as manners are forgotten and the over-excited guests surrender themselves to wild impulse. Verbal jousting is replaced by the physical sort. The diners drop their forks and close their fists. They take to the floor, turn the tables, and end the meal with a punch-up. Not to be recommended, I would have thought, on a full stomach.

Most of us can recognize this sort of aggressive scenario, even ·if our own meals seem almost miserable in comparison with the splendour of Roman or Renaissance banquets. Gangster feasts in films, for instance, do not usually end with handshakes all round, but with the hoodlums forking one another in the neck. Suburban family meals can often be just as violent, if not quite so bloody. Parents and children begin the meal with good-natured intentions, but gastronomic pleasure is quickly put on a side-plate as an old grudge resurfaces or a rebellious teenager flexes her muscles. The scab is picked off an old family sore and the row commences: Father bangs the table; Mother is in tears; the seditious child flees the scene; the food stays in the pot.

Christmas dinner, as the most important meal of the domestic year, is also the site of the greatest battles. If there is tension in the family circle, then this is the time for it to break out, for the temptation to spoil the meal is almost too great to resist. By the time the pudding appears (suitably aflame) and the old arguments have done the rounds, it is almost a race to be the first to quit the table in a temper and slam the door as you go. What would Christmas be without at least one good row?

Eating together can bring you all together. It can also break you apart, especially if you have to share meals with the same people every day. One facetious don tried to justify his college's annual series of banquets by claiming that he and his colleagues spend so much time looking at the same faces on high table that they have especial need of good food. Benedictine monks adopt a different strategy: they keep a rule of silence during mealtimes while one of their number reads to them. This rule is only relaxed over the Christmas period. One monk confessed to me that he and his brethren are greatly relieved when this period ends and the taboo on talking is reimposed. 'If one is teaching all day and rather under strain, to make conversation with one's brethren (and remember we are with the same people probably much longer than others are with their families) is an extra burden.' These monks contain the potentially divisive power of table talk by keeping mum and listening to the written words of another.

We can use food to forge friendship. We can also employ it to make enemies. One reason the Civil Rights Movement got going in the United States was that Afro-Americans were not allowed to eat at the same counter as Whites. In societies with carefully graded rules of hospitality, it is all too easy to offend others by not treating them with the respect they deserve. According to Alice B. Toklas, 'If you wished to honour a guest [in Parisian society between the wars] you offered him an omelette *soufflé* with an elaborate sauce, if you were indifferent . . . an omelette with mushrooms or *fines herbes*, but if you wished to be insulting you made fried eggs.' In Ancient Roman society, the easiest way to humiliate an unwanted guest was to relegate him to the lowest place in the dining-room. In the parish of Zumbagua, up in the Ecuadorian Andes, superiors give *wanlla* ('treats, snacks') to inferiors: men give them to women, parents to children, the wealthy to the humble poor. Giving *wanlla* to one of your peers, such as a brother or sister, offers them pleasure and wins you a little prestige at their expense. But giving *wanlla* to people who look down on you is considered presumptuous and insulting. Well-intentioned visitors are best advised to find out where they stand before offering others fried fish, boiled eggs, sweets, or biscuits.

The giving of food is very much a double-edged device, as the Kalauna of Papua New Guinea know all too well. They say that before the Australian colonial authorities imposed peace in their area they used to fight with spears. Nowadays they fight with food, competing with one another as to who can give the biggest gift. If a Kalauna man is provoked to anger by, say, an insult or catching his wife copulating with someone else, he will publicly shame his enemy by giving him such a large amount of food that it cannot be repaid immediately: the recipient is left quivering in a violent, impotent rage. Unlike the mild English version, shame is one of the strongest emotions in New Guinean psychology.

Kalauna guard against famine, whether caused by hurricanes, tidal waves, or drought, by working hard in their gardens and so producing more food than they need. If the big wind does not blow, if the sea stays calm, and if the rains come as normal, they can use their surplus crops for putting people down. To ensure a greater surfeit than that of potential opponents, they also practise a special sort of magic to suppress hunger. As they say, a successful Kalauna man is one of strength, with a full garden and a small belly. How much he will have stored in his house they will not know, for he and his wife will have carried their best yams home in the dark of night. To avoid inciting envy and thus possible attack by sorcery, it is best to keep others guessing as to exactly how many you have tucked away.

When a prominent man wishes to put down an opponent in another village by besting him in a competitive food exchange, he has his supporters visit the enemy camp before dawn. They challenge the adversary by offering him a small yam. If he accepts it, and thus the challenge, his leading supporter comes forward and starts to insult the visitors. 'You think we cannot pay back your yams? You think we have no pigs? You think we do not know how to garden? You think we are birds or dogs and cannot plant food? You think we remain idle all our lives? Well, we'll show you! You'll see who can plant better! We do not spend all our time copulating with our wives like you!' The fight has started. Now it is time for both sides to gather their weapons.

The challenger and his party immediately raid their stores and dig up their gardens. They lay out their yams, taros, bananas, and pigs for their adversary's men to collect next day. Once the latter have removed all this food and taken it home, they start plundering their own reserves. The challenger's supporters then turn up on the morning of the following day to collect the return gift. This is the crucial moment: if the challenged has not enough food to equal what he and his supporters received, he will be openly shamed; if he can give even more than the challenger expected, then the challenger's party must take the food, return home, and scour their stores and gardens for food to pay back the excess. The challenger and his helpers must be able to return this surfeit in kind within a day or else stand shamed. But if they are able to give even more than that then, instead of being put down, he puts his opponent down. He will have won the contest.

The dinner-partying classes of Britain may not be as openly aggressive in their food exchanges as the Kalauna, but they can be just as competitive and cunning. Hosting a formal or important dinner-party is not an undertaking lightly entered into. The stakes are high and no one wishes to drop a few notches on the social scale. The hostess – for, in Britain, it is still mainly women who stage these performances – must first check her social debts. Who does she owe dinners to? (This is important: remember what

CLASS WAUGH

I remember the dinner well – soup of *oseille*, a sole quite simply cooked in a white wine sauce, a *caneton à la presse*, a lemon *soufflé*. At the last minute, fearing that the whole thing was too simple for Rex, I added *caviar aux blinis*. . . .

[Rex arrives.] He looked around the sombre little place with suspicion as though expecting to see apaches or a drinking party of students. All he saw was four senators with napkins tucked under their beards eating in absolute silence. I could imagine him telling his commercial friends later: ' . . . interesting fellow I know; an art student living in Paris. Took me to a funny little restaurant-sort of place you'd pass without looking at – where there was some of the best food I ever ate. There were half a dozen senators there, too, which shows you it was the right place. Wasn't at all cheap either.' . . .

He plainly wished to talk of his own affairs; they could wait, I thought, for the hour of tolerance and repletion, for the cognac; they could wait until the attention was blunted and one could listen with half the mind only; now in the keen moment when the *maître d'hôtel* was turning the blinis over in the pan, and, in the background, two humbler men were preparing the press, we would talk of myself. . . .

'Ah.' The cream and hot butter mingled and overflowed separating each glaucous bead of caviar from its fellows, capping it in white and gold.

'I like a bit of onion with mine,' said Rex. 'Chap-who-knew told me it brought out the flavour.'

'Try it without first,' I said. . . .

The sole was so simple and unobtrusive that Rex failed to notice it. We ate to the music of the press – the crunch of the bones, the drip of blood and marrow, the tap of the spoon basting the thin slices of breast. There was a pause here of a quarter of an hour, while I drank the first glass of the Clos de Bere and Rex smoked his first cigarette. He leaned back, blew a cloud of smoke across the table and remarked, 'You know, the food here isn't half bad; someone ought to take this place up and make something of it.'

Brideshead Revisited, 1945

the wicked witch who was not invited to the feast did in *Sleeping Beauty*.) Then she has to juggle the potential guests, countering the bores with the lively, the serious with the flippant, and the mute with the garrulous. Next comes the food: a well-tried favourite, or something new but difficult? To get the menu right she has to balance the crisp and the smooth, the sweet and the sour, the bright and the drab, the bland and the spicy. No social or gastronomic detail is too small. Above all, this laboriously planned and prepared meal must be presented as though its production had been effortless. Any hint of pressure, and the guests will become tense.

The strain is too much for some. Cooking meals for others to judge is too nerve-racking an ordeal and they give up formal entertaining completely. If hubby has got to give the boss a meal, best to take him out to a restaurant. Perhaps these cowardly non-cooks have the right attitude for there are so many possible pitfalls in giving a dinner-party it is impossible to avoid them all. Culinary knowledge fills whole libraries and none of us is a walking encyclopaedia. There will always be someone who knows more than you about Burgundy vintages, the best way to buy truffles, or how long to marinate the Tahitian salad. Try to cook something fashionable and someone will gently but firmly point out that gastronomic trends have moved on. Others will perceive your gesture towards elegance as piss-elegance, your hint at formality as stuffiness, and your courageous combination of dishes as a clear sign of an unrefined palate. 'What is this woman trying to tell us?' the guests mutter to themselves.

Of course, if you do somehow manage to get the dinner right in all its aspects, if you are – against all the odds – skilful enough to stage a banquet of almost Renaissance finesse, your guests may be so impressed they will be scared to invite you back. Instead of being shamed by them, you make them anxious of being shamed by you. You will have won the implicit contest so well, you will have no real competitors – nor any return invitations. It is lonely at the top. But take solace, for the Kalauna would approve of your winning strategy.

15

A CLASS ACT

Do not play with your food. Do not bolt it either. Eat it with the same care and consideration that was put into cooking it. Your knife is for cutting, not for writing – do not hold it like a pencil. Do not wave it in the air and never stick it in your mouth. Keep a straight back. Lift the food to your head, do not lower your head to the food. Licking is for lovers, not for the plate. All joints on the table will be carved, so keep your elbows by your side. Control all bodily urges: do not sniffle, snort, weep, yawn, shout, read, belch, or fart (silently or otherwise). Unless you have something to say, keep your mouth shut: other diners wish to see the food on the plate, not some semi-masticated mash inside your oral orifice. This is your first lesson in British table manners. You have a lifetime to learn and practise the rest.

As we all know, these rules are not important: they are essential. The dons of All Souls College, Oxford, recently refused to give a visiting fellowship to a most distinguished foreign academic because no one could bear to sit near to him on the narrow dining tables. It was not simply that he gripped his knife and fork like murderous weapons between mouthfuls, or that most of his talk was about himself. What the dons could not tolerate was his habit of talking frenetically while eating, so spraying those opposite with half-chewed particles and decorating his beard with gobs. Eccentricity they could abide, but such bad manners was too much.

Since the number of table dos and don'ts increases as one 'ascends' the classes, you can rapidly gauge the social position of almost every Westerner by watching how they use their knife and fork. And the more subtle the rules are, the more finely they grade the hierarchy of social distinctions. Table manners are so much part and parcel of the British way of life that no one can ignore them. Even those who appear to have no manners are really people who have deliberately decided to react against any form of class pretension. Letting others worry about the 'correct' way to eat, they slurp their soup to the tune of water going down the plug'ole, thickly paint their plateful with a murky seasoning (gravy, ketchup, or other bottled sauce), and stub their butts into the yellow remains of a fried egg. Vigorously clattering their spoon as they stir in the sugar, they make their message echo loud and clear: 'Damn the lot of you. Manners do not make man. They make ponces.'

The West European fixation with table manners, however, is not some age-old anxiety but a relatively recent concern. Among the medieval nobility it was the done thing to eat using one's fingers and a dagger-like knife. Everyone ate from the same dish. People would only frown on a fellow diner if he grabbed a little too greedily, replaced a bone in the dish after gnawing at it, or dipped a piece of already-bitten bread into the communal sauce. And if one *had* to scratch at itches caused by fleas or lice, it was best to do so, not with one's naked finger, but with a bit of cloth over the finger.

By the end of the Renaissance, courtly society had begun to develop a more elaborate code of table conduct. In contrast to the common mob, gentlefolk were now meant to cultivate a 'delicacy of feeling' and to repress spontaneous behaviour. Spitting, gobbling, licking the dish, and blowing one's nose on the tablecloth were all discouraged. Instead of drinking soup from a common dish or from ladles used by several people, diners were each given a separate spoon and bowl. Napkins and forks slowly started to become more common. (Forks were still unknown in the French regions of Cantal and Maconnais in the mid-nineteenth century, while even as late as 1897 the British Navy was still forbidding their use since they were considered unmanly.)

Delicate diners were meant to use their knives as little as possible. Modern Americans have solved this problem by cutting up all their food at the beginning of the meal. The Chinese, however, had stopped bringing their knives to the table several centuries earlier. Since all their food is cut into bite-sized pieces in the kitchen, the only table utensils they need are blunt chopsticks. To these refined Orientals, we Westerners are the barbarians, uncouth characters who eat with 'swords'.

In the late eighteenth century, the rise (thanks to industrialization) of a new class of very wealthy people began to threaten the previously secure position of the landed aristocracy at the top of the social tree. One way the peerage chose to re-assert their social superiority was by multiplying the rules of decorum; they would only accept the *nouveaux riches* on their own, highly mannered terms. The industrialists, eager to enter the upper echelon of society, proved more than ready to ape the conventions of the blue-bloods. Highly formal dinner-parties became a key social ritual. Meals became ever grander and more ostentatious. Fledgling hostesses, relying on the newly produced books of etiquette, learnt to organize their dinner-parties with an almost regimental thoroughness.

WINDS OF CHANGE

Dinner-parties are about frontal talk, not back-chat, and the first guest to break ranks by breaking wind is also the first person out the door – pushed by his host. Though coming from behind may be a sound military strategy, it is not an advisable tactic at dinner-parties. The only person in recorded European history who could actually *please* fellow diners by letting fly a fart was *Le Pétomane*. But this Parisian performer of the last century only got away with it because he could play all of the 'Marseillaise' on his anal sphincter.

For less musical characters, such as you and me, this rule against rear-guard action is never relaxed. Even though a sadistic cook might serve up baked beans, you must still remain uptight. Help, however, is near at hand, for a Cambridge scientist has recently developed an 'environment-friendly' version. H. J. Heinz has stated, 'We are always interested in any wind-resistant bean.'

The only report I have heard of a group where farting is not openly frowned upon comes from the northwest Amazon: 'One of the things that instantly strikes visitors to the Pira-parana area is that the adult men delight in farting loudly, often modulating the noise with their fingers or cupped hands.'

The order of the day was not so much conspicuous consumption as conspicuous waste, as far more was served than could possibly be eaten. French cuisine became *de rigueur* as a sign of sophistication, and Parisian chefs devised laborious recipes that celebrated complexity for its own sake. The rising middle-classes, not wishing to be left out of this gastronomic game, did their best to emulate their financial and social superiors. They even invented their own form of refinement: the fish-knife. Thus the modern, elaborate versions of table manners and dining style, by-products of the proceeds from industrialization and colonialization, quickly came to take up the central position they still, to a great extent, occupy in West European society today.

These sorts of rules are not merely boundary-markers, ones scoring the social divide between the different classes. They also form a substantial part of class-philosophy. According to the distinguished sociologist Pierre Bourdieu, the French bourgeoisie follow these rules as ways to display their control over their own biological natures and to advertise their command over their own instincts. You might be achingly hungry, but you still must not eat like an animal; you do not start to eat until everyone is served; you are not greedy; and you never appear over-eager. Restraint and self-discipline are the keynotes of this bourgeois code.

To well-heeled Frenchmen and women, breakfast, lunch, and dinner are not regarded as mere occasions to fulfil bodily needs but as opportunities to assert a class-based love of order, propriety, and style. Mealtimes have their own rhythms, their own aesthetics. The table is set; diners have their particular places; the dishes come in a preordained sequence and are arranged to please the eye; nutrition takes second place to shape and colour; quality is emphasized over quantity (which is why portions are so small in Parisian middle-class restaurants). Refinement is everything. Formality wins out over substance.

French manual workers interpret this obsession with etiquette as bourgeois posturing. As far as they are concerned, only the insincere and pretentious would wish to maintain such a snobbish sham. In contrast, labourers present themselves as uncomplicated characters, and they do not let their families become obsessed with table ritual. At their meals all the food is served at much the same time; any hint of ceremony is viewed with suspicion; the style is free and easy; people sit where they wish; quantity comes before quality. Substance is the central concern. Formality is pushed to the sidelines.

Gastronomic taste follows roughly the same pattern. The labouring classes go for cheap and nutritious foods, the ones that will give them the energy needed for their jobs. As one ascends the particular stretch of the French social scale that goes from manual workers to foremen to industrial and commercial employers, the diet becomes increasingly rich, both in cost and calories (for example, game, *foie gras*). Doctors, lawyers, and senior executives sneer at this sort of popular taste, which they brand as heavy, fat, and coarse. To them, the cuisine of the *nouveaux riches* is gross, vulgar, and ostentatious. Professionals and company directors avoid this sort of working-class fare writ large. Instead they opt for the light, the refined, and the delicate. In restaurants, they wince at anything *flambé* and order *bouillabaisse* rather than *pot-au-feu*. Valuing slimness over strength, they choose health-giving and non-fattening foods. They want to be lean, not heavy with muscle or incipient flab: Giscard d'Estaing, not Rambo.

Teachers and downwardly mobile members of the upper middle class (*les nouveaux pauvres*) fit, somewhat uneasily, somewhere between these two groups. They might have the knowledge, but they do not have the money. So, as in all aspects of style, they tend towards the ascetic. Seeking originality at the lowest price, they opt for exoticism or culinary populism. If they invite you to dinner, you know it is not going to be truffles but Chinese, Vietnamese, or peasant dishes.

British class differences in eating styles are similar to those in French society. Standing in a supermarket queue it is astonishingly easy to decipher the social status of other shoppers by glancing at the contents of their baskets and carts. If they are piled high with tinned and convenience foods, large bottles of vegetable oil, steam puddings, manufactured desserts, bags of sugar, biscuits, cakes, potatoes, white bread, and soft drinks, then you are standing behind D's or E's. (How nice to know that food wholesalers do not regard us as numbers or names, but as letters.) A's burden their carts with brown breads, pulses, unprocessed cheese, rice, olive oil, and fresh vegetables, fish, juice, and fruit. They have the sort of salaries to be able to worry about the 'goodness' of the food they buy, unlike those on low incomes who cannot afford such anxieties.

But cost is not the only consideration determining proletarian diet. Surveys suggest that – in the North of England at least – the lower classes are generally more hidebound than others in their culinary habits. They are not so keen on fresh fruit and salad vegetables because they do not fit into their idea of 'a proper meal', that is, meat and two cooked veg, followed by a sweet pudding. Lentils they're not even interested in.

Though the British generally pay less attention than the French to the refinement of what they cook (no wonder they feel gauche in Parisian restaurants), English women of all social classes bother to teach their children table manners. Mothers want their off-spring to say please and thank you, to use their utensils correctly, and not to bring books or toys to the table. Even if the food isn't up to much, at least the kids can eat it in a socially approved manner.

The impression given by American writers on class is that many of their compatriots are deeply uncertain of their exact position on the social ladder. Food books aimed at the upper-middle-class market seem more concerned with presentation than with cuisine. 'Elegance' comes first, and the food a distant second. Rather than worrying about what to serve, hosts and hostesses busy themselves working out the correct place for the candelabra, flowers, linen, silver condiment holders, wine basket, and other kinds of table clutter. They will eat at 8 or 8.30 p.m., the lower middle classes at 7 or 7.30 p.m., and workers as soon as they come in from work, at 6 or 6.30 p.m.

FRYING TONIGHT

I have a thing about chips. I can't rationalize it. I always feel that chips are associated with the lower classes. I hate the smell of chips, the cooking smell associated with it. . . . I've always thought – do I dare say it? It smells like a council house when you come in and it stinks of chips. That's awful, isn't it? Some of our best friends live in council houses – never mind. I just associate it with cheap and nasty, to be honest with you. . . . I associate chips with slap-happy cooking. You know, like I say, cheap and nasty.

Middle-class husband

When Sir Raymond Carr, the distinguished historian of Spain, was recently asked why he had been so keen to leave the working class environment of his childhood, he confessed, 'Couldn't stand the food.'

Sweet food offerings laid before a revered figure the day before his idol is installed in a Jain temple in India. (*Marcus Banks*)

RIGHT 'I haven't liked it since I was a little kid and my mother made me eat it. I'm President of the United States and I'm not going to eat it (broccoli) any more.' (George Bush)

OPPOSITE The last of the Milesians. Stanley Green on his beat in Oxford Street, London.

ABOVE Early lessons in inflation? As a food technologist, Margaret Thatcher's speciality was seeing how much air could be pumped into ice-cream before it collapsed.

RIGHT Lovin' spoonfuls? At bullfights the Spanish dictator General Primo de Rivera used to eat the warm, raw testicles of the first bull to fortify him later for sex.

LEFT Futurist frolics. Marinetti's recipe for love 'manandwomanatmidnight': *Pour some red Zabaglione onto a round plate so as to form a large pool. In the middle of this place a nice big onion ring transfixed by a stalk of candied angelica. Then lay out two candied chestnuts, as shown in the illustration, and serve one plate per couple.*

RIGHT 'We'll fight them on the beaches, we'll fight them on the shores and we'll hit them over the head with rolling pins as we haven't any weapons.' (Attributed to Churchill)

BELOW Those Nigerians who eat dog think the animal resembles a Peugeot and name its parts accordingly.

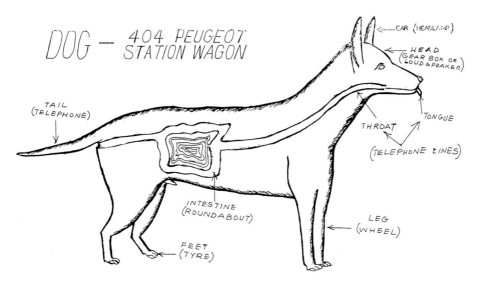

DOG — 404 PEUGEOT STATION WAGON

EAR (HEADLAMP)

HEAD (GEAR BOX OR LOUD SPEAKER)

TAIL (TELEPHONE)

TONGUE

THROAT

(TELEPHONE LINES)

INTESTINE (ROUNDABOUT)

LEG (WHEEL)

FEET (TYRE)

RIGHT The European imagination at play: such graphic 'evidence' of cannibalism was used by nineteenth-century do-gooders to convert Africans to Christ and Mammon.

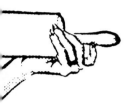

LEFT Kamala, one of the wolf children of Midnapore in India, photographed in the 1920s. She walked on all fours, gobbled her food like a dog, and preferred to socialize with animals.

ABOVE Tharu rice-growers in Nepal prepare their mid-morning meal. (*Christian McDonaugh*)

BELOW Sugar-daddy sweetening his baby: he is flesh and blood, she is chocolate, the roses are sugar.

ABOVE For the Mambila of Cameroon, *fufu* (maize porridge) is their staple food. They eat it twice a day, every day. (*David Zeitlyn*)

BELOW Yam! At their exchange rituals, the Tannese of Vanuatu in the South Pacific swap yams, pigs, puddings, giant kava roots, and blows from pieces of cloth.

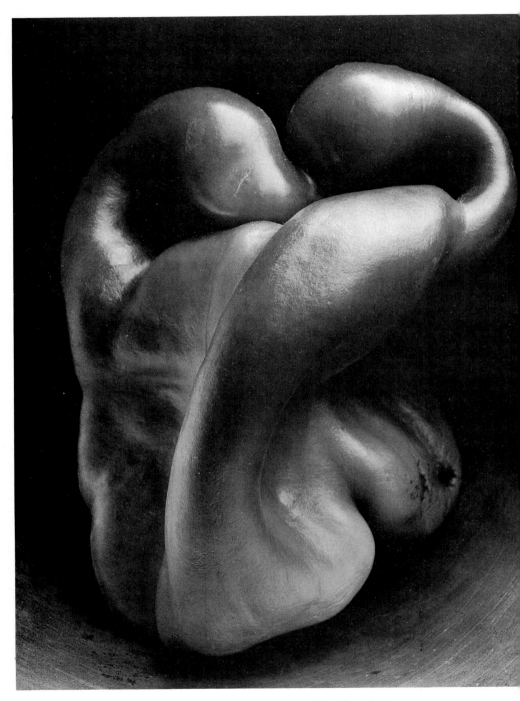

Food for thought? 'Pepper No.30' by Edward Weston.

THE DEADLY DIET OF DEMOCRACY?

Unlike food snobs, politicians who do not wish to alienate voters often pretend to have uncultivated palates. In the American presidential campaign of 1840, the Whigs claimed their candidate, William Henry Harrison, survived on wholesome 'raw beef and salt', whereas his patrician rival, Martin van Buren, tickled his taste-buds with 'fancy French cooking' and such effeminate foods as strawberries, celery, and cauliflower. They also criticized van Buren, who was fighting for re-election, for appointing a Frenchman as the presidential chef. How could such a refined aristocrat care about the common man?

Harrison got the job, but his manly diet did not save him from getting pneumonia at the Inauguration. The briefest functioning president in American history, he died thirty-one days after taking office.

Unlike the upper-class, whose meals are unexciting and un-original, members of the upper middle class will sometimes flirt with foreign foods: snails, pâtés, exotic fungi, and unpasteurized cheeses (the more unpronounceable the name the better). Which ethnic cuisines are socially acceptable depends upon the moment: Mexican is out, so is Chinese (except for Szechuan), Japanese is in. Though non-Anglo-Saxon Americans may cook spicy meals for themselves, most lower-middle-class WASPs avoid any sug-gestion of a strong flavour. They go for the bland, the mild, and the soft, and they steer well away from almost anything piquant. Garlic is not even to be considered. While these gastronomic expressions of class distinction remain valid, they are now being partly undermined or rewritten by the growing movement of middle-class foodies, of which more in Chapter 25.

One way to flatter your guests is to offer them rare and expensive foods. In medieval times, lords displayed their rank by spicing their dishes with pepper, cloves, sugar, and exotic herbs. At the time, spices were so costly they were stored in locked cabinets, often next to the household's finest plate. In 1377 a bull went for the same price as two ounces of cloves. Their price was kept so high

because Arabs monopolized the spice trade. They managed to
keep their source so secret that the ignorant English believed they
came from 'Paradise', then thought to be somewhere in the
Middle East. Spices were used both to flavour and to colour dishes:
food was dyed red with sandalwood, and purple with turnsole.
The most prized colouring agent of all was saffron, since the
stigmas of 75,000 crocus plants are needed to make one pound of
the spice. Mixed with egg yolk and flour, it was painted on roasting
fowl and meat to make the flesh appear golden. A man who could
serve such gilded food was, by implication, noble and rich, and the
shiny dishes reflected his glory.

Foods only remain exclusive so long as the majority of folk are
excluded from using them. Once their price has dropped and they
become generally available, they are no longer of any use to the
wealthy. The rich ditch them from their diet and look for new
types of rare food. Once Europeans had broken the Arab monopoly and the lower classes began to season their own food,
spices stopped serving a snobbish function for those at the apex of
the social pyramid. In reaction, the cuisine of the English and
French aristocracies gradually switched from a heavy use of spices
to an emphasis on the elaborate preparation of dishes. The story
is the same with sugar: once treasured by the nobility as a spice,
condiment, or substance for making fantastically ornate table
decorations, it is now regarded by the wealthy as a proletarian
staple, to be avoided for health reasons, while sugar sculpture is
no longer thought a worthy art but a curious form of high kitsch
practised by talented but obscure artisans.

Of course, if a common food becomes rare for one reason or
another, then the rich can appropriate it for themselves. Oysters
and salmon were so plentiful in the last century that they were a
standard part of working-class fare. London apprentice boys even
rioted in the 1850s because they were sick of being served the fish
so often. But since pollution and over-collection have diminished
the supply of both foods, they have been re-valued. Today, a
whole smoked salmon from Scotland is a special Christmas treat
and Dublin Bay oysters are specialities of upmarket seafood
restaurants. But the circle is about to turn yet again, for fish-
farmers have recently begun to breed a Scandinavian type of
fresh-water salmon on an industrial scale. The days of smoked
salmon as a luxury item are numbered, and that number is low.

The only way to ensure that a high-prestige food does not slip down the social scale is to control its total supply. And the only person in Britain who can do that lives in Buckingham Palace. By law, all white-feathered swans and all sturgeon found in British waters belong to Her Majesty the Queen. (Formerly, the British monarchy also exercised the right of royal pre-emption over other animals, such as deer, and conger eels in the Channel Islands.) Though Elizabeth II's predecessors were not renowned as gourmets, their taste was impeccable, for swan is said to be the most tender and delicious of all web-footed birds, while the flesh of sturgeon has always been highly esteemed. The royal right to swans was most likely established by King John at the turn of the twelfth century. County sheriffs had to provide their sovereign with a number of the birds whenever their high lord requested. Henry III was particularly fond of the fowl, and for his Christmas feast in 1251 at York he summoned his sheriffs to provide him with 125 of them. The monarch could grant others the right to sell the bird, and from the late thirteenth to the mid-seventeenth century swan was the most expensive kind of poultry in the kingdom. The flesh of young cygnets was said to be extraordinarily good, so long as they had been fattened on oats, so removing any fishy taste from the meat.

TO PREPARE SWAN, ENGLISH STYLE

Cut its neck, collect the blood. Skin it, cut off the neck, feet, and wings. Roast and baste with lard. Serve with chawdron sauce.

To make chawdron sauce: cut the swan innards into small pieces. Clean and boil in water. Mix the liquid from the cooked innards with bread, ginger powder, and galingale. Strain this mixture, and mix it with the swan's blood and a little salt. Strain the innards and add to the mixed blood. Bring the sauce to the boil, and add vinegar to taste.

Also, the neck of the swan may be stuffed, and served as a separate dish, which was known as 'Puddyng de Swan Necke'.

Elizabeth II also displays her distinction and dispenses her grace by giving dead deer to her most senior servants. Cabinet ministers receive two animals a year from the Queen's Herd, at the beginning and end of the hunting season, respectively. Mere Ministers of State only receive one. The deer, cut into large chunks and transported in raffia hunting bags, are delivered to the ministers' local butchers, who carve them up into cookable pieces. Royal venison might be an impressive dish for one's guests, but some politicians, surprisingly, haven't the stomach for it. The wife of one ex-minister confessed to me that, after trying some of the first animal, they let their butcher keep the rest for himself.

Culinary class means knowing how, and how not, to behave in the appropriate social setting. Imagine, for example, that you are invited to dinner by the Puke and Pukess of Pork. You do not wish to go, but your partner bends your arm. You wish to make sure that you will not be invited back. Therefore:

After unfolding your napkin, look around the floor ostentatiously. If your host asks what you are doing, say, 'The ring for my serviette must have slipped under the table.'

Refer to the first course as the 'starter' or the 'appetizer'.

If soup is served, tilt the plate and spoon *towards* yourself.

Do not break the French bread with your fingers. Cut it with a knife.

Do not call the next course the 'meat' or the 'main course', but the 'roast', the 'entrée', or the 'joint'.

Do not make a small heap of salt at the side of your plate. Sprinkle it all over the food vigorously.

Drink the water in your fingerbowl (with any luck your hostess will be so polite she will feel obliged to follow suit).

Ask her what you are having for 'sweet', 'afters', or 'dessert'.

Use your spoon to cut up and eat your pudding. Regard your pudding fork as part of the table decoration.

In between your remarks about politics and religion, compliment your hostess on the food.

When the person on your right passes you the decanter of port, pour yourself some and then give it back to him. When you notice that the decanter is not moving from his place, remark on how abstemious everyone else is being.

On rising from the table, carefully refold your napkin.

Remember: do not expect witty, clever conversation from your hosts. The only thing exceptional about them is their inherited status and their wealth. Nothing more.

HOW TO GET ON IN SOCIETY

Phone for the fish-knives, Norman
 As Cook is a little unnerved;
You kiddies have crumpled the serviettes
 And I must have things daintily served.

Are the requisites all in the toilet?
 The frills around the cutlets can wait
Till the girl has replenished the cruets
 And switched on the logs in the grate.

It's ever so close in the lounge dear,
 But the vestibule's comfy for tea
And Howard is out riding on horseback
 So do come and take some with me.

Now here is a fork for your pastries
 And do use the couch for your feet;
I know what I wanted to ask you -
 Is trifle sufficient for sweet?

Milk and then just as it comes dear?
 I'm afraid the preserve's full of stones;
Beg pardon, I'm soiling the doileys
 With afternoon tea-cakes and scones.

John Betjeman, 1951

That should do the trick: the Puke and Pukess will not be inviting you again for a meal.

Upper-class dining rules may seem restricting and over-formal, but they are freedom itself when compared to the etiquette of Victorian dinner parties:

Very soon after the last guest has arrived, the servant ought to announce dinner, and the host, after directing the gentlemen whom to take in, should offer his arm to the lady of the highest rank in the room, the gentleman of highest station taking the lady of the house. . . .

The gentleman who takes you into the dining-room will sit at your right hand. Take off your gloves, and put them on your lap. Before you, on your plate, will be a table napkin, with a dinner-roll in it; take the bread out and put it at the side of your plate. Lay the opened table napkin in your lap, on your gloves, and then listen gracefully, and with attention, to your companion, who will do his best to amuse you till the soup is handed round.

The lady of the house should be at leisure to give her whole attention to her guests. If a clergyman be present, he is asked to say grace; if not, the gentleman of the house does so.

The present fashion of giving dinner parties *à la Russe*, is far preferable to the old mode of having the joints, etc., on the table; but it supposes that you have a sufficient number of waiters, as otherwise it would be impossible and ridiculous.

The table, then, is laid thus: in the centre is some exquisite ornament – an alabaster stand crowned with pineapples, beneath which hang clusters of grapes; or a frosted-silver tree, with deer, etc., beneath it, holding on its branches glass dishes filled with the most picturesque fruit. Round it the dessert dishes are placed; then small dishes of preserves, sweetmeats, etc. At the house of a nobleman, with whom we occasionally dine, the table – a round one – is encircled by small silver camels, bearing on their backs silver baskets, holding tiny fruits or sweetmeats.

On each plate a bill of fare is placed, so that the guests may see what will be handed round, and may be prepared to select, or wait for, whatever dishes they prefer.

Soup is then handed; wine is offered after it.

Now I must just say (as this book is written for those who do not profess to know much of society) that you should eat your soup from the *side* of your spoon, not take it from the point; that you should make no noise in eating it; that you should beware of tasting it while too hot, or of swallowing it fast enough to make you cough.

You must begin, or appear to begin, to eat as soon as it is put before you; not wait for other people.

Fish follows the soup. You must eat it with a fork, unless silver knives are provided. Break a little crust off your bread, to assist you in taking up your fish, but it is better to eat with the fork only, which you may do if it be turbot or salmon.

Put the sauce when it is handed to you on the side of your plate.

If you do not wish for soup or fish, decline it with a courteous 'No, thank you', to the servant.

After soup and fish come the side-dishes, as they would be called, if they were on the table – the oyster or lobster patties, quenelles, etc.

Remember, that for these you use *the fork only*; as, indeed, you should for all dishes which do not absolutely require a knife. You must use a knife, of course, for cutlets of any kind, although they *are* side-dishes. It is proper to eat all soft dishes, as mince, etc., with the fork only.

Do not put your hands on the table, except to eat or carve (the latter is not required at a dinner *à la Russe*). Do not use your handkerchief if you can help it; if you *must* do so, let it be as inaudibly as possible.

Meat, chicken, or turkey are handed after the made-dishes. Then follow game, puddings, tarts, jellies, blancmange, etc.

For the partridge or pheasant, of course you use the knife and fork; all sweets are eaten with the fork, or spoon and fork, as you like; but the spoon is only required for cherry-tart, or anything of that nature, custard, etc.

Ladies scarcely ever eat cheese after dinner. If eaten, remember it should be with *a fork*, not a knife.

You should *never*, by any chance, put a knife near your mouth.

Anon, *Modern Etiquette in Private and Public*, 1872

If you think Victorian etiquette mind-bogglingly detailed, however, consider the traditional Chinese manner (among their many, many other rules of mealtime behaviour) of serving fish at table:

If the fish is dried, turn its head towards the guest. If it is fresh, turn its tail towards the guest.

If it is summertime, turn the belly of the fish to the left; if it is winter, to the right.

The reason why: winter is the reign of Yin, not Yang, and Yin corresponds to the Below; the belly is seen as the lower part of the fish, and so is Yin. Moreover, during winter, the belly should be the best-nourished part, the fattest and most succulent. The belly is placed on the right-hand side since you should eat with your right hand and should begin by eating the best part of the fish. Since summertime is the reign of Yang, the rules are reversed.

Or let us go to Dagestan, a region of the southeastern Caucasian highlands, east of Azerbaijan. The year is 1900. You are invited to dinner by men of rank. You must follow these rules:

You are invited into the best room. You will be allowed to sit before everyone else. Repeatedly invite the hostess to sit down with you and your host.

You must taste a little of each of the numerous dishes laid out before you.

If taking food from a communal plate, take the piece nearest to you. But if the nearest is, say, the biggest or best apple or apricot, offer it to your host, or to a child.

Start eating from the near edge of the plate. Lift the spoon to your mouth without bending your head.

Do not hurry. It is impolite to display appetite, however hungry you might be. Chew food thoroughly. Do not stuff your mouth, blow on food to cool it, take large bites, or eat with your mouth open.

Do not ask for anything. That would imply discontent with what was served.

Do not mention the quantity of the food or compliment the host on any of the dishes.

Your host constantly invites you to eat more. Do not refuse directly. Instead say, 'Do not worry, I am eating . . .' or 'Yes, everything I need is on the table.' Never forget the key rule: restraint. As the local Kumykhs say, 'A wolf, even when hungry, pretends to be full up.'

In Dagestan, worthy people do not grab leftovers. Show that you are up to the same standard.

Make edifying conversation. Do not joke constantly, laugh loudly, or talk in too animated a manner. Food is a serious business, only gained after much hard work labouring under the sun. In the words of the local Laki people, 'If you do not make your brains boil in summer, your pot will not boil in winter.'

If your host invites in local singers or a storyteller, afterwards present each performer with a small gift of appreciation.

Finally, contrast the manners of Victorian and modern Britain, China and turn-of-the-century Dagestan with those of Japan. One evening, your host invites you to dinner:

You must refuse. If your aspiring host persists and repeats the invitation several times, then you know his/her offer is genuine and you may accept.

A basic rule: do not make demands on others until they force you to. So when your hostess asks what you would like to have for the upcoming dinner, say that anything will do. If she urges you to answer the question in a more positive manner, choose a very simple local dish. You should not be surprised if you arrive at the house and find, not just the humble food you requested, but a sumptuous feast of different dishes served with your hostess's best utensils. You should, however, act as though you were surprised.

Do not expect to be shown around your host's house. Unlike Western ones, Japanese homes are private places. On arrival you will be taken to a room specifically set apart for outsiders. Do not stray beyond its boundaries. Regard the fact you have been invited to a home, and not to a restaurant (the more common course), as compliment enough.

In a small dinner-party of five to six people, everyone will participate in the same group-based conversation. The aim is to keep the communal party spirit going. Breaking off from the main conversation to talk about a separate topic to those on either side of you is a sign of great discourtesy and lack of respect to the other diners and, above all, to your hostess.

It is very difficult to decline alcohol that is offered to you without causing offence, so maybe best to drink a few glasses of milk before you go. Even a little alcohol can help Japanese shed most of their apparent inhibitions. They joke more, laugh more loudly, and start to sing and clap hands. You should be just as animated. Do not, however, under any circumstances, get too drunk. You must be able to regain your sobriety as soon as the meal finishes.

The people of highest status are allowed to dominate the conversation, especially at a dinner-party of businessmen or company employees. Others merely play the role of bit-part actors. Functioning as the supporting cast, they are not meant to launch into monologues, but only to make the occasional witty or light remark. They feed the star performers with lines, and not vice versa. The honoured guests, as the principal actors, can speak for longer, change the conversation more often, and even gently belittle members of the supporting cast from time to time. They can interrupt, while others must listen until they finish. The bit-part actors may feed the lead's self-importance by asking him questions he can answer in an authoritative manner. They should express exaggerated interest or surprise at his comments.

In other words, the dinner-party is staged like an improvised play where everyone knows the groundrules but makes up the script as they go along. Guests and hosts work together to produce a flawless, highly enjoyable performance. Since there are no rehearsals, each production is a one-off, and treasured as such. You can only improve with practice.

Imagine, then, the problems that arise when an ignorant foreigner comes to dinner in Japan, or in Britain or Dagestan. He/she literally does not know how to act. She lacks the necessary social graces. Since her hosts will be too polite to reveal just how clumsy and awkward her performance is, she will leave thinking she has finally learnt how to conduct herself in a different culture. Her hosts will be left exhausted, for they have had to work doubly hard, covering up her mistakes and making up for her deficiencies. Like actors in a miscast play, they have been forced to make twice as much effort because the lead does not know her lines. Or, to use the simile of one observer, they are like Fred Astaire trying to dance gracefully with a 200-lb woman who has never danced before.

16

RECIPES OF POWER

The British have little to be proud of. What is worse, it seems at times some of them do not even know it. For they appear content, even pleased, with their cuisine, even though it is one of the most unhealthy and impoverished in the industrialized world.

John Bull is all too good a symbol of this sorry state of affairs. His hat is too small, his shirt is made of cheap bunting, and his face beams ignorant self-satisfaction. But despite his evident delight in the food of his land, his unimaginative daily diet is slowly killing him. High in cholesterol and low in sophistication, it has given ol' JB a red face, a big belly, and a level of blood-pressure that would make a life insurance salesman blanch. All he has really got to be smug about is the bloody roast beef of England.

Continental visitors to Britain look askance when they later recount what they have been made to eat. They cannot believe that such a famous nation does not have a cuisine to match its political status. How could Britain have become Great on such a bad diet? Was it the irritations of dyspepsia and colic that made the British such truculent, and successful, colonialists?

It would be nice to think that so many people left Britain to rule other countries as part of their search for finer, more varied cuisines. The depressing truth is that the British took their bad taste with them wherever they went and only sampled local fare to the extent it could be adapted to Anglo-Saxon palates. The earliest settlers in America turned their backs on local foods and only started to use them when their value had been realized by cooks back home. During the British Raj, colonial officers did not ask their experienced Indian cooks to display their broad culinary talents; all these white masters wanted were repetitions of their home diet and, unaware of their own short-sightedness, they would complain if the cook could not reproduce their favourite sauce. For special occasions they would not demand some rare Indian delicacy, but dishes like 'Sind Club ham in gin', or its even more wasteful variant, which involved marinating the meat in champagne. Reducing the rich variety of the different Indian cuisines to a few bastardized dishes, the British came up with the meagre list of kedgeree, mulligatawny soup, chutney, and curry. For some reason, old colonials tended to believe that the hotter the curry, the more authentic it was. Perhaps it is not surprising that 'cock-up' – originally an Anglo-Indian term for a European gentleman's breakfast – now means a bungled failure.

The British cannot tout their style of cooking as a praiseworthy part of their cultural contribution to the world. They may be happy with their deadly diet, but they know there are no political gains to be made out of lauding suet pudding or bangers and mash. These dishes may be robust old favourites, but they are certainly not subtle culinary creations. English propagandists cannot trumpet the cause of their cuisine: the competition is too stiff. For if there is one national cuisine that the British and the Americans have long looked up to as a consistent standard of culinary excellence, it is the French.

In fact, most of the French, for most of their history, have eaten just as badly as the English. French cuisine as we know it today is very much a fabricated product of the nineteenth century. A series of dedicated and successful chefs, such as Carême, Dubois, and Escoffier, helped to refine French taste by progressively simplifying dishes and using fewer ingredients, with more discrimination. They wanted to draw out the 'natural' flavours of food by adding fewer spices and using lighter, more varied sauces. These learned professionals lectured widely in France and abroad, while thousands of their trained disciples spread the message further by getting jobs in other countries. At the same time, the more literary-minded gourmets produced philosophies of gastronomy and toured the provinces in order to rediscover the forgotten treasures of regional cooking.

The efforts of both the cooks and the writers found a receptive market among large sections of the upper classes and bourgeoisie, who, unlike their English counterparts, held good cooking in great respect, were ever vigilant about standards, and loved to participate in animated discussion about recipes and quality. To members of all these three groups French cooking was, like French literature, a source of national pride and prestige. Authors, playwrights, and poets reflected this culinary interest in their works; it was not just Proust who lingered on the delights of the table, but Balzac, Flaubert, Maupassant, Zola, Colette, and many others.

Dumas *père* wrote a formidably long *Grand Dictionnaire de Cuisine*, while his son even went so far as to include a recipe for mussel, potato, and truffle salad in his play *Françillon*.

Thanks to the propagandistic work of these chefs and gastronomes, most sophisticated Britons and Americans of the time tended to agree that French cuisine was one of the world's finest. They had little option, for, besides bull and abundance, they had almost nothing to offer as a gastronomic counter-argument.

EPICUREAN EXCURSUS

I became aware that I was eating something particularly delicious, soft-boiled eggs embedded in a layer of meat jelly, seasoned with herbs, and discreetly iced. To please Marambot I smacked my lips.

'First rate, this.'

He smiled.

'The two essential ingredients are good jelly, which is not easily procured, and good eggs. How rare they are, really good eggs, with reddish yolks, and the proper flavour. I keep two poultry yards, one for eggs and one for fowls for the table. I have a special method of feeding my layers. I have my own ideas on the subject. In an egg, just as in chicken, beef, mutton or milk, you recover, and you should be able to taste, the extract, the quintessence of all the food that the animal has consumed. How much better people would fare if they paid more attention to that point.'

'I see you are an epicure,' I laughed.

'I should think so. So is everyone who isn't an idiot.'

Guy de Maupassant, *Madame Husson's Rose-King*

Basque nationalists would understand the French strategy very well, for they have been playing the same game ever since their political movement started in the late nineteenth century. If the name of the nationalistic ploy is to show that your particular society is as culturally rich and distinctive as the best of them, then promoting the variety and finesse of your style of cooking fits the bill perfectly. As one Basque recently wrote, 'There is no community of people with history without a cuisine.' Since Basque nationalists most definitely see themselves as a people, and as one with a history, then they must also have a cuisine. It has also to be said that the Basques are lucky, for the dice are already loaded in their favour; local gastronomes seem never to tire of extolling the range of Basque foods, from the variety of fish caught off the Biscay coast, to the hard cheeses and succulent beef of the Pyrenean foothills, to the vegetable cornucopia of its southern region known as 'the Garden of Spain'. Jingoistic gourmets are able to boast of such dishes as hake in parsley sauce (no flour, of course); elvers fried with garlic; *chilindron* (Navarran lamb stew); wind-dried sausages; and *menestra* (a delicate vegetable stew). The natural flavours of the food are not blitzed by spices, but are gently drawn out by cooking that is slow, careful, and patient.

Maintaining a high standard is so important to most Basques that cooks almost expect to have their meals constructively criticized by their spouses and children. Saying there is too much salt in the salad or that the bass is slightly over-cooked is not taken as an insult but as a gentle corrective against making the same errors next time. Basques like to brag about the refinement of their palate, and the claims made by some make fishermen's tales appear very models of precision and verity. One chef revealed that some of his friends allege to have developed such an acute discrimination for different tastes that they can tell, when eating beef, which pasture the cow grazed.

The more socially minded nationalists can also make mileage out of two traditional Basque institutions: the *sidrerias* ('cider-shops') and the gastronomic societies. The shops make their own cider and let their clientele drink as much as they want for a fixed charge, sing as much as they want, and grill their own meat on the charcoal fires. The societies can be just as informal, for they are private male clubs where groups of friends cook for one another in the communal kitchen. Given the culinary ability of most Basques, the societies are a clever way of having a cheap, good meal in company you know you will enjoy. Nationalists like to claim that most Basques believe in egalitarianism and that both the shops and the societies are exemplars of this ideal. They are seen as traditional but popular social institutions, ones manifesting the popular democratic nature of Basque culture. The fact that no member of the Basque *haute bourgeoisie* would enter a cider-shop, or that the more established societies tend to be meeting-places for the relatively well-to-do, is quietly passed over.

To the nationalists, Basque cookery is yet another example of how their noble society has added to the cultural richness of the world, and why they should be taken seriously as a people. I have yet to meet a nationalist who did not rate the food of his region highly. Though Basque politics is fractured into a spectrum of parties, none of them ever raises a finger against spending money on the promotion of the local cuisine. In fact, they normally cheer when a crew of chefs are sent abroad as cultural ambassadors for their region. Most Basques are openly proud that the most garlanded restaurant in Spain is a Basque one in Madrid. Even Herri Batasuna, the revolutionary socialist radical separatist party associated with the gunmen, does not criticize the place though most of its clientele are, given its prices, the very biggest of big businessmen. This is one den of high capitalism the Party does not want to see die.

Some Basques underline the distinctiveness and the distinction of their cuisine by denigrating that of other Spanish regions: the Valencians, they say, eat nothing but rice; the Riojans are notorious as eaters of whole roasted garlic; and it is best not even to talk about what the Andalusians regard as food. This kind of gastronomic put-down is a world-wide strategy used by the people of one nation to sneer at those of another. For instance, until very recently, ignorant Britons used to claim that Chinese hosts, wishing to impress their banqueting guests, would employ little boys to push shaven-headed monkeys through a hole in the centre of a table, so that the host could slice off the roof of the animal's skull. The guests would then feast on the warm brains with long silver spoons. Inscrutable Orientals might not care about the feelings of a poor ape, while the British, so the story-teller implied, only slaughtered their animals humanely.

Those who feel the need to put foreigners down poke fun at them on the basis of one particular food in their diet, downplaying just how much is common to both of their cuisines. Little Englanders brand Germans 'krauts' (after sauerkraut), French 'frogs', Italians 'macaroni', and Spaniards 'onions'. In a similar fashion, the French call the British *Les rosbif*, while poor whites in the Deep South used to label Afro-Americans 'coons' because they hunted

MARINATING MUSSOLINI
(The Flavour of Fascism)

To Filippo Marinetti, Futurist poet and leader of the Italian avant-garde, the future lay with the future, and not with some glorified version of the Italian past. So down with out-of-date ways! And up with electricity, aeroplanes, machines, velocity!

The new age promised by *Il Duce* demanded a new cuisine. Out with staid recipes and tired culinary formulae! In with new harmonies, unexpected flavours, and gastronomic surprises! Down with Bollito, Ragu Bolognese, and Fettucine alla Marinara! Long live 'Drum Roll of Colonial Fish', 'The Ox in the Cockpit', and 'Raw Meat torn by Trumpet Blasts'!

If, Marinetti argued, 'our virile proud dynamic and dramatic peninsula' was to advance, then habits had to change. 'Since everything in modern civilization tends towards the elimination of weight and increased speed, the cooking of the future must conform to the ends of evolution.' In other words, pasta – that staple of the nation's diet – had to go. A barbaric and piggish food, it weighed down the body and benumbed the spirit, establishing a dictatorship of the stomach and bringing on a seductive sense of indolence that neither plebeians nor intellectuals could resist. It was a waste of time to struggle for the health, agility, and freshness of Italian intellectuals if this gut-rot blocker was allowed to bar the way: 'Today we need to remake the Italian man, for what point is there in having him raise his arm in the Roman [Fascist] salute if he can rest it without effort on his bulging stomach? Modern man must have a flat stomach, under the sun, to think clearly.'

Not everyone was convinced. In Naples they protested in the streets. In Aquila the women signed a petition in support of their beloved food. In Turin a conference of chefs tried to debate the issue: it ended in violence.

Enraged magazine editors attempted to discredit Marinetti by fabricating photos of him eating spaghetti. The Duke of Bovino, Mayor of Naples, declared pasta celestial food: 'The Angels of Paradise eat nothing but vermicelli in tomato sauce.' This merely confirmed Marinetti's suspicions about the monotony of life on a cloud. Better to be a Futurist with your feet on the ground and your fork stuck into 'Steel Chicken' or 'Roars of Ascent'. Patriotism required nothing less.

and ate racoons. The logic underlying these gastronomic slurs seems to be, 'If you and your compatriots dare to eat differently from us, you cannot be up to our standards. We know what is fitting and proper to consume. You lot do not, and therefore you are, in some sense, inferior.'

It is said the Chinese are the only people in the world with no food taboos, and that they will eat anything with four legs but a table and anything that flies but a kite. Unfortunately, some foreigners are too culturally blinkered to appreciate this culinary versatility. When in 1885 the Chinese community of Tacoma, Washington State, invited several local businessmen to dinner, the hosts laid on a ten-course ethnic meal, all of whose ingredients had been carefully selected to give the least possible offence to Western tastes. At the end of the banquet, 'the Chinese competed in expressions of humility and gratitude for the presence of their guests, in expression of wistful hope that the little dinner might strengthen the bonds of friendship and commerce that bound east and west.' Despite the extreme courtesy and culinary considera-tion shown by their hosts, at least one of the diners did not appreciate the meal. Regretting the absence of shoulder of fricas-seed rat from the menu, he discoursed on the delights of 'parboiled mouse, two months old, its teeth extracted, its tail pomaded with glue, its ears nicely set, the whole immersed in a sputtering, crackling lake of dragon's lard, dotted like an archipelago with ambrosial isles of waxed insects, tanned sealskins, swans' rudders, cormorant filets and jackass corns.'

The onset of war reveals just how rapidly such nationalistic attitudes can be learnt (and unlearnt), and how provocative they can be. After Pearl Harbor, Japanese food suddenly became unpopular in the United States; Americans did not want to share the tastes of people prepared to launch murderous attacks on their troops. The reverse had happened in the previous war when Italy joined the Allies. Until then, middle-class Americans had held the diet of Italian immigrants in disdain. Now that they were fighting side by side against a common foe, women's magazines started to run articles on 'Spaghetti, food of the ally'. Instead of raising their noses, Anglo-American mothers began to realize that pasta and tomato sauce was a good, nourishing dish to make when short of meat. In other words, thanks primarily to the forging of a military alliance, Italian cooking became the first immigrant cuisine to be accepted and taken up by the American well-to-do.

Turning a national cuisine into a political tool either for raising oneself up or putting others down may be a time-honoured tactic (the Nazis criticized Jews for using garlic), but what are its chances of survival in an industrialized world where food is increasingly uniform? How do you poke fun at others when they eat almost exactly the same as you? At times, it seems as though the only remaining important difference between European and American foods is the preservatives used. But while Common Market legislation may allow additives different from those tolerated by the US Food and Drug Administration, I really cannot see Europeans getting annoyed if an American shouts in their direction, 'Hey you! E394!'

17

JUST DESSERTS?

Men win the bread, women make it, so the old theory goes. The husband provides the cash, and his wife the meals. According to these old-fashioned stereotypes, a woman who wants to be a good wife and mother has to be able to cook. As one of the North of England women interviewed by the sociologists Nickie Charles and Marion Kerr said, 'I think it's awful if she can't cook. I mean, a fella can't do a proper day's work and not come home to a decent meal.'

What is surprising is that, in our post-industrial society where much of the economics underpinning this conventional separation of the sexes no longer holds good, most women still do the shopping, cooking, and clearing up. Despite feminists' sustained efforts to change attitudes, Charles and Kerr's research shows that even though a wife may have a job, and even though her husband may be unemployed, she still ends up doing most of the cooking. Emancipated young couples may decide to share all domestic tasks but when the first child arrives, the woman usually becomes a full-time mother while her partner deserts the kitchen and retreats into the exclusive role of breadwinner.

As a general rule, fathers only put on the chef's hat to make 'fun meals' on festive occasions: in Britain the Sunday breakfast, in the United States barbecues, and in Spain picnic *paellas*. Unless they are particularly interested in cooking, they almost never make a 'proper meal' for their families. Husbands can choose to cook when they are in the mood; wives are forced to do it day in, day out. The North of England women interviewed did not necessarily disagree with this sexual allotment of tasks. While most think men should be *able* to cook but should not *have* to cook daily, some declare the kitchen their exclusive dominion and bar their husbands from entering. Others would like a little help from time to time and lay the blame on their partners' mothers: 'It's women that bring men up and they bring them up to be bloody useless, don't they?'

A dutiful wife is meant to cook what others want, not what she herself desires. And if all that is left after serving a roast are the burnt and crusty bits, then that's all the meat she is going to eat. She is not supposed to enjoy the meal, but to take pleasure from watching others tuck in. Her job is to prepare dishes that will be savoured, both as good food and as a sign of her love for them.

Of course it is men, not women, who define what 'good food' is, and what they want is something hot. To the unreconstructed male, any dish not made from fresh ingredients, any meal that relies on tinned or convenience foods is a cheat, an insult. Their wives are meant to have put thought, effort, and time into their cooking. And those who do not are seen by their husbands as bad and selfish spouses. Greeks living in Turkey used to call any dish that did not take all day to prepare 'prostitute's food'. For if the woman had not been busy cooking while her husband was away at work, what exactly had she been up to?

Good cooking, according to folk wisdom, keeps your man from straying. 'I mean,' one wife admitted, 'if you didn't cook, if you didn't give them what they liked and wanted, they'd go and buy their own or go to somebody else, I suppose.' In unemancipated households, Wifey serves Hubby the right foods to keep him happy in his role as breadwinner. Besides, after putting in so much loving care, she does not wish to see the fruits of her labours regarded as fodder fit only for the bin. Unlike Basque women who *expect* comments on their cooking, their English counterparts are hurt if they receive too much criticism. For many of them, praise from their partners is the sweetest ingredient they know.

Men are trained to have 'hearty' appetites, while women are meant to be 'dainty'. As a female friend of mine remembered,

> When it came to the seconds, my mother would automatically say to my father, 'Have some more. It needs finishing off.' He would help himself, clearing all the dishes while me and my sister looked on hungrily. I used to feel resentful that there he was finishing off all the food, and he was so overweight anyway. How could he possibly still be hungry?

Many of the North of England women interviewed thought it 'natural' to serve their husbands and sons larger helpings of food and the choicer cuts of meat. This might seem 'natural' and sensible when men are employed in physically arduous tasks. It does not appear so logical when they are overweight and work as sedate clerks in offices while their women are busy cleaning, cooking, and wishing they had as many arms as a Hindu god in order to cope with their energetic offspring.

Some British husbands, unmoved by the arguments of feminists, think it their right to control absolutely their wives' tasks and the times when they should perform them. These domestic dictators, tyrants writ small but just as terrible, expect over and above everything else a hot meal ready for them when they come in, even if they arrive home in the middle of the night at the stale end of a four-day drinking bout:

> She'll have my tea ready when I go into this house, not when she feels like it. Going to bed and all this. She does nae work. I work. She should be up for me.

Wives and mothers who express themselves through the meals they prepare can also get their own back though the medium of food. The popular stereotype of a murderous wife is of one who kills her husband by giving him a poisoned dish. In Almodovar's film, *What Have I Done to Deserve This?*, the infuriated wife kills her mate by clobbering him with a hambone; and in the Roald Dahl story *Lamb to the Slaughter*, an aggrieved woman brains her husband with a deep-frozen joint and then serves the murder weapon up to a hungry detective.

While most aggrieved wives' impulses may be less murderous, they can be almost as deadly in effect. The anthropologist Mary Weismantel, who worked in the Ecuadorian Andes, gives the case of the young wife, burdened by infants, whose husband deserted her at the local fiesta.

> After a difficult trip home carrying both sleeping babies up steep slopes in the dark, the wife was very angry indeed. When her husband arrived home many hours later, drunk and sleepy and ready for bed, she informed him that he must be very hungry; as an obedient wife, she had prepared a nice dinner for him. Almost unconscious, he forced himself to sit upright long enough to eat two enormous bowls of soup under her reproachful eyes. The meal over, he crept off to bed, but his ordeal had only begun. The next day found him in an extremely delicate physical state, such that the three very elaborate meals she prepared for him, which he dutifully consumed, resulted in several hasty exits from the kitchen to the

bushes outside. She appeared to enjoy cooking for him very much
that day, smugly playing the virtuous wife in front of her in-laws,
who watched with some amusement and did not interfere.

Feeding one's male mate and other children is bad enough, but
women have also to act, and most important, *look* the part played
out in a hundred glossy magazines. If you can't slip your uncorseted
body into an hourglass shape, he'll leave you before the sand runs
out. Time is not on your side; the biological clock cannot be
reversed. The only prospect you face is a constant struggle against
flab and bodily decay until he finally relaxes into post-menopausal
quietude. It is enough to turn a nation of women into Jane Fonda-
clones pelvic-thrusting to disco muzak. Thanks to the advertising
industry, slimness has come to connote fast cars, sexy clothes,
sophistication, and good times in exotic settings warmed by a
tropical sun. In contrast, Flab is Boring and fat people are not
taken seriously. So women are forced to diet, even if they are
surrounded by food and forced to think about it every day. They
have, at one and the same time, to give others food and deny it to
themselves. It is like a tightrope act on a high-tension cable and
some fall at the first step, as my mother – never a small woman –
confessed:

> You must remember that a mother always finds it extremely
> difficult to diet because the mother has bought the food – the father
> has paid for it, of course – the food has cost money, food is left on
> the plate by a child, the mother invariably eats it, the mother will
> always pick at the food, that is general more or less.

Those who can withstand waste face other, persistent temptations. For those on a diet food becomes foe not friend. Those old
companions, chocolates and cream cakes, turn into traps to avoid
at all costs. Once forms of succour, they are now the enemy. The
meals a dieter makes remain a source of pleasure for others but
become a potential source of guilt for herself. How can she, for
example, sit down with her brood at her biggest weekly performance, the Sunday dinner, if all she is going to put on her plate is
a leaf of lettuce and two raw carrots? To keep up the idea of her
family as a sharing unit, she has to eat the beef and two veg along
with the rest of them. No wonder the food, laced with guilt, tastes
so bittersweet.

Weakened by hunger, the dedicated dieter may succumb to the

insidious pleasures of food pornography. A photographic style identified by the feminist commentator Rosalind Coward, these glossy illustrations in women's magazines portray sumptuous meals in suitably suggestive settings. The room is elegant and tastefully decorated; the table is perfectly laid; the prepared dishes glisten and shine, inviting to be devoured – in sum, a repast fit for a king, and one even a cat like you or me can look at. Cropped close-ups may show a fat piece of gilded chicken, a larger-than-life cream tart with a hyper-real texture, or a slice of sponge cake, its dark chocolate filling threatening to ooze over the edge. Either way the message is not understated, but shouted: 'Eat me! Eat me!'

NAUGHTY BUT NICE

If the ads in women's magazines advocated self-indulgence in alcohol or cigarettes as flagrantly as they do for chocolate, they would be banned. As one slogan put it, 'If chocolate is your downfall, you might as well enjoy the trip.'

Chocolate is 'wicked', 'dangerously irresistible', and some cannot resist. Their willpower weakens, their diet goes by the board, and they succumb to the hedonistic temptations of these super-fattening foods. An unhappy few, unable to regulate their intake, get locked into compulsive chocolate eating. In the words of one chocoholic, 'It's that lovely cloying that sticks to your mouth and all around your teeth.' 'It just makes me feel comfortable,' said another. 'After I've had a nice fill of it, I really feel relaxed, almost like an orgasm.'

Chocolate is so tempting because it is not an ordinary food like meat, vegetables, bread, or fruit, and it is not normally eaten at mealtimes, but between meals, or at their very end, as the fitting finale to a feast. Chocolate is not part of our daily routine, it is an escape from it. Like alcohol and cigarettes, it is an exciting supplement meant to enrich our lives, but which destroys our health. While bottles of whisky are essentially male gifts, chocolates are *the* clichéd present from a man to the woman he wants to sugar up. For if she does not have the self-control to reject these calorie-rich confections, will she ever be able to resist *him*?

These photos have as little to do with reality as the bodies of women presented in 'girlie' magazines: they are just as manicured, air-brushed, and touched-up. For dieters, these sensual shots of forbidden fruit are fodder for their fantasies, calorie-free food for thought. But they do not, in fact, dull hunger; they feed it and aggravate its pangs, reminding the viewer of past pleasures and increasing her guilt when she finally surrenders. If she gives in to food, her body will proclaim her defeat; if she keeps to the diet, she is continually reminded of the dangerous delights that await her when she comes off. It is damned if you do and damned if you don't, and the only winners are the advertising agencies, for their clients sell both food and 'slimming aids'.

Dieting is not just big business (more money is spent each year in the West on slimming aids than is needed to feed all the world's hungry), it is also becoming a way of life and one, moreover, with strong religious overtones. Today's diet books, charged with evangelical earnestness, strive to convert guilt-ridden readers with their promises of permanent redemption: 'Yes! You too can be saved.' The missionaries of this nutritional creed do not preach a calorie-counting regime meant to occupy you for a few weeks, but a new life trajectory designed to keep you busy till (a suitably postponed) death. By following their word, you can mortify the flesh and sanctify yourself by the continuing exercise of self-denial. Those with sufficient moral strength will emerge from their cocoon of fat purer, more virtuous, and more 'whole'. The only sins they might commit along the way are those of pride and self-righteousness. And, so far, neither has been declared a health hazard.

Anxiety about dieting starts young. In San Francisco, a staggering 70 per cent of nine-year-old girls are already so concerned about their bodyshape that they have started dieting. The British statistics are not so alarming, but are still very worrying: before they are ten years old, 25 per cent of English girls have started skipping meals and deliberately eating less. Of course, the danger is that this may blossom into full-blown anorexia nervosa. Confirmed anorexics look like walking cadavers: they have cut their food consumption to almost starvation levels, they have stopped menstruating, and they indulge in frantic, continuous exercise. Their skin sprouts a downy body-hair, while their hands and feet turn blue and go numb as the blood stops circulating to the extremities. It is a serious condition and it can be fatal.

Anorexics are most commonly adolescents from the upper social classes. Some research shows that they tend to have been excessively compliant, selfless girls, more concerned with pleasing others than developing their own personality. Their mothers are often submissive, conservative types with little self-esteem. As a whole, their families are usually overprotective, resistant to change, and try to avoid conflict at any cost. Family members strive to preserve the myth that they are a perfectly harmonious single unit. Like the different components of a well-run cuckoo clock, they all work together (sacrificing their characters as they do so) in order to keep the system ticking over, making the appropriate sounds at the right time.

In this sort of domestic hell, refusal to eat is a dramatic assertion of autonomy. By rebelling at mealtimes, the daughter withdraws from the family circle and all it stands for; by leaving her plate untouched she gives herself a much-needed sense of control and shores up her brittle self-esteem; and by stopping her periods she tries to suppress her emerging sexuality and the worries that brings in its train. This is a strong form of passive aggression, one that leaves those around her impotent and frustrated.

Some analysts see anorexia as the ugly product of the increasing pressures Western women have to bear. On the one hand they are taught to conform to an image of 'femininity' which stresses daintiness, dependence, and self-sacrifice. On the other, they are now told to be successful, assertive and high-achieving. Combining both roles without any hitches, they strive to be '110% Women' able to keep their husbands, raise their families, and pursue productive careers at one and the same time. If this all sounds too much (and it is), then anorexia is an easy exit, an adolescent cry for freedom from overbearing parents who expect their daughters to become wonderwomen. In these circumstances the real question is not why some become anorexic, but why more do not.

Curiously, many women respond to anorexia with envy, and regard the condition as almost desirable. According to them, anorexics practise an extreme version of femininity, in the sense of self-denial and silent suffering as they masochistically subjugate the flesh. They are seen to possess the self-control that so many women desire but fail to achieve. On top of that, this modern-day ailment is also one that carries with it clear overtones of spirituality; anorexics claim their sense of touch and hearing is heightened, and that the world seems gloriously, unbearably vivid as their experience moves ever closer towards the ecstatic. In these terms anorexia is the twentieth-century equivalent of tuberculosis, with the same sort of romantic fascination and the same sort of love-death.

Many anorexics, however, admit they are *not* in control of their own condition. They have become anorexic because they have not known when to stop dieting. At a certain stage, the ailment itself takes over and then they complain of some internal alien – for instance, 'the little man who dominates me' – dictating their behaviour. At this point they move off into another world where they are forever preoccupied with food and hyperactivity.

Eating disorders, such as anorexia nervosa, bulimia, compulsive eating, and laxative addiction, make up a sorry list of the female condition in the industrialized West of the late twentieth century. It is difficult to talk about these modern ailments without sounding like an outraged orator railing against the ills of this world. But, when viewed collectively, these different syndromes constitute a damning indictment of our contemporary society, with its bizarre obsessions and nightmarish consequences.

Even if we cannot drastically reduce the incidence of these afflictions immediately (though that is no excuse for inactivity), we should at least recognize them for the cultural oddities they are: things that Western women feel forced to do to themselves and that the majority of women in this world do not. They are not a problem for others; they are *our* problem.

18

MEAT AND VEG TOO

Meat is strength. Meat is power. Meat is life. It is the very king of foods. It gives us might, increases our potency, adds edge to our aggression, heats our passion, augments our sexuality, and turns us males into macho men. Edmund Kean, the great actor of the last century, knew its qualities well. He ate beef if he had to play a murderer, pork for the role of a tyrant, and mutton for the part of a lusty lover. Consuming the fresh flesh of dead animals is meant to feed the animal-like side of our human nature and give a gory zest to our otherwise humdrum days. Without it we are but enfeebled characters forced to trace out bloodless lives. Bread might be the staff of life: bloody meat is the very stuff of it.

Meat is such a valued food that at mealtimes it is the centre around which everything else is arranged. The 'main course', the heart of most European meals, is so called because it is the one with meat. Most cooks put the chop or the steak on to the plate first and only then add the vegetables. If they hope to be congratulated for the meals they prepare, it is above all the meat they want to be praised for. Meat is so central to our ideas about nourishment that the very word can stand for all food in general, as in 'our meat and drink'.

Animals eat meat raw. Ripping and tearing at a carcass, they devour the wet flesh and paint their teeth red with the blood. In contrast, humans cook their food, so changing its colour from vivid red to dull brown and evaporating the liquid. This simple culinary transformation is taken as a mark of civilization. Only monsters in horror movies prefer their meat uncooked. Some businessmen, however, deliberately exploit the associations of rawness and bestiality by ordering the only raw meat dish in the whole repertoire of Western cuisine. As one British entrepreneur admitted, of power lunching with a vengeance,

> You take the guy you're negotiating with to a fancy restaurant for a business lunch and then order steak tartare. It totally unnerves the other guy seeing you eating this raw meat with blood dripping out of it, and actually does make a difference – it can just give you that edge.

145

Men need meat to fight, so soldiers deserve more if they are to do their job properly. Red-blooded males cannot be expected to enter battle and kill unless they are filled with the right juices. In the Second World War, American generals gave their troops a diet Dracula would have envied. In the Navy, men breakfasted on prunes, cornflakes, and one-fifth of a pound of bacon. For lunch they had cream-of-tomato soup, half-a-pound of pot roast with potatoes and spinach, followed by chocolate cake. And come dinner-time, they were served a half-pound hamburger, spaghetti, salad, and pudding. Eating two-and-a-half times more flesh than the average civilian, these servicemen were, in the phrase of one publicist, 'the greatest meat-eaters in the world'. Is this why they won?

All these fancies about the supposed effects – whether sexual or military – of turning carnivore are enough to make vegetarians go beetroot purple. Unlike their blood-thirsty opponents, they have seen through the mask of meat ideology and seek to dispel the myths that still fool others. Meat-eaters might seem tough, but vegetarians have a full battery of arguments to attack their all too pregnable position.

Perhaps first on the list comes ignorance, for the English language cloaks the reality of killing animals in euphemisms. We don't eat cowmeat, pigmeat, or sheepmeat, but beef, pork, or mutton. The suffix 'meat' is only added to types of flesh we do *not* normally eat, like horsemeat and dogmeat. The anatomy of the animal is similarly camouflaged. We do not cook 'pig's thigh' or 'cow's arse', but ham and rump steak. Zealous vegetarians bent on challenging the gastronomic *status quo* try to reawaken our consciences by referring to 'slaughtered nonhumans', 'scorched corpses of animals', 'murdered chicken', or 'putrified game peppered with lead balls'. They deliberately violate our sense of reality by bluntly calling things for what they are. And to a certain extent, this verbal trick works. Could you, for instance, really walk into a smart restaurant and ask, without any embarrassment whatsoever, for a 'partly cremated portion of a dead lamb's rib-cage'?

To vegetarians, meat is not life. It is death, decay, and corruption. To them, a roast joint on the Sunday dinner-table is not a succulent, fortifying foodstuff; it is a dangerously high-cholesterol piece of a dead animal, dripping in its own fatty juices. What life it had is now gone, and, as far as vegetarians are concerned, those meat-eaters who think that the rotting flesh of a once-animate creature can vitalize the person who eats it are employing the same logic as cannibals. Opposed to the consumption of these dark, heavy, morbid foods which pass slowly through the gut, strict vegetarians laud fruits, nuts, and grains, which they associate with lightness, sunshine, and eternal youthfulness. Vegetarians don't want to feed off death and decay. They want to promote life.

Even if one were to believe that meat provides vigour, vegetarians see it as an overly masculine energy that stimulates the wrong sort of feelings. Ferocity and unbridled sexuality are not emotions nurtured in the vegetarian soul. Trouble is, lusty meat-eaters tend therefore to see vegetarian males as 'feminine', weedy, and probably impotent, if not gay. These attitudes may even be projected on to vegetarians' pets. When the Scottish anthropologist Nick Fiddes asked one couple about their visit to her Italian aunt, they said:

> *Her:* Yes, I mean, even the dogs were vegetarian . . . she was that bad about it. She had a strong belief in it rather. The dogs were perfectly healthy though; the two dogs were terrific, and were 100 per cent vegetarian. She did not let them have meat.

> *Him:* God, their street-cred must have been absolutely the pits. Can you imagine going out with the lads, you know, 'Come on, let's go and ravage a few cats.' 'I'm sorry, I'm not into cats; any mushrooms we can ravage?' Woof!

Once again, the English language is on the carnivore's side. According to the American *Heritage Dictionary*, 'vegetable' connotes 'passivity, dullness of existence, monotony, inactivity'. 'To vegetate' means to do nothing, while 'cabbage' or 'vegetable' are insulting terms for those with severe mental handicaps. Vegetarians try to go against this linguistic grain by reviving the original meaning of 'vegetable', for the word comes from the Latin *vegetabilis*, or 'vivifying'. When the Metaphysical poet Andrew Marvell told his coy mistress about his vegetable love for her, he was not implying that he was not going to do anything, but that his amorous feelings towards her would continue to grow and grow. This is the sort of life-enhancing emotion that earnest vegetarians wish to arouse. Reacting against the carnivores' caricature of their lifestyle, they try hard to present themselves not as boring deadbeats but as lively souls. To them their culinary style is not a load of old lentils served up day after day, but a cornucopia of rich and imaginative dishes that promote the right kind of health and do not stimulate a passionate bellicosity that threatens to destroy the world.

Next on the vegetarians' list of meat-eaters' sins is their sustained disregard for fellow sentient beings. Animals are not footballs that can be kicked around until they puncture. They have feelings like us. To ignore this by treating them cruelly, or even slaughtering them, is to debase and brutalize ourselves. Compassion is the highest morality we can uphold. It is the ultimate ethic. There might still be people who believe that *Homo sapiens* is the apex of all creation and that animals are merely one of God's gifts to humankind, placed on this earth to serve our needs and help satisfy our desires. But most of us – vegetarians hope – have learnt enough natural history and have a sufficient smattering of ecology to know just how wrong-headed this arrogant attitude is.

Committed vegetarians also reject the idea that hunting is a civilizing behaviour, a way for males to assert their self-appointed place at the top of the animal hierarchy. Vegetarians do not see hunting as in any way 'natural'; and, as a counter-argument to meat-eaters' barbaric notions, they can point to the long-held conception of hunting as a later development of the human race. According to this view, early man and woman lived in a state of nature, surviving on a diet of fish, milk, herbs, and berries. Some push this idea even further and see the original humans as akin to Adam and Eve, cohabiting harmoniously in Eden with all the other animals, snakes included. Whether or not most vegetarians would wish to go this far, their message is clear: we are not here to dominate this planet; we are here to share it with others, animal others.

To vegetarians in the last century these arguments had great moral power. With the rise of industrialized methods of raising and killing animals in recent decades, they have gained even more force. For the details of modern intensive methods of rearing animals are enough to put most people off their meaty meal. In batteries, chickens are crowded into cages where they peck viciously at one another. Those at the bottom of the pecking order are slowly done to death and then eaten by their stronger neighbours. The survivors are taken to the slaughterhouse where they are strung upside down and then shocked senseless by an electrical charge. (Some remain conscious.) Their throats are slit by automatic blades, their blood is vacuum-sucked out in a Bleed Tunnel, and their feathers are loosened by scalding and removed by mechanical pluckers. Singed, decapitated, gutted, injected with additives, they are then packed ready for sale to us. As one British farmer confessed, 'If God's a chicken, we're in trouble.'

The fate of baby cows is even worse. In Holland those calves which are to be reared for their white veal are wrenched from their mothers in the first three days of life and squeezed into stalls less than 60cm wide and 140cm long. Their liquid diet is kept low in iron and certain vitamins so that their prized virginal flesh will not discolour. Since the food they are given also lacks fibre, the calves nibble at their crates and hair. They are not given any bedding lest they start to chew that too. After fourteen weeks of this imprisonment, it is time to go on the one trip they ever make in their lives. Though this veal-crate system has been banned in Britain since 1990, most of the veal served in English restaurants is imported from Holland. Remember that the next time you order veal escalope in white wine sauce.

Some vegetarian attitudes have infiltrated the camp of the opposition, for the majority of modern meat-eaters do not wish to be reminded of exactly what it is they are eating. We have learnt to become squeamish. Nowadays, the work done in slaughter-houses is hidden from the public gaze, and even their function is veiled by the French term *abattoir*. More and more people feel queasy when they walk past the massed racks of dead hare, shot-filled pheasant, and decapitated deer strung up outside the windows of rural butchers. People who take pride in knowing how to skin and clean a freshly killed rabbit are fast becoming the exception. Gone are the days of British banquets when the whole cooked animal was laid out in front of the guests, and the only fruit in sight was a roast apple wedged between its jaws. The only heads to be seen at todays' dinners are those of the consumers, not that of the to-be-consumed.

These days the smell of blood emanating from the mounds of raw meat in butchers is too off-putting for some. Instead, sensitive carnivores have chosen to take their custom to the meat stalls of supermarkets. In these cleverly constructed environments, there are no clots of blood, guts, or gristle to be seen. No worries here about getting out of the way as a delivery boy brings in a dead animal lolling over his shoulder. The lights are bright, the floors are sawdust-free, and the general tone is one of conspicuous hygiene. Cleaned, unrecognizable bits of a dismembered carcass are set in plastic, hermetically sealed trays. If it was not for the label stuck on the cling-film, you would not be able to tell what kind or cut of flesh it was. It is just one more packaged product, like the boxes of detergent or cornflakes on the nearby shelves. And, like many breakfast cereals, these flesh-foods are increasingly sold as prepared and processed items, as 'coated nuggets', or 'sweet-and-sour bites'. Shoppers are not meant to think of the animal the meat once came from, but of the meal they are going to make.

The giant hamburger chains have also adapted to the change in their clients' sensibility. They now use much less red and more pastel shades in their decoration and advertising, and the most attuned to shifts in the market have decided on green. Even if they cannot, by definition, become vegetarian, they can at least pretend to be ecologically aware.

The third charge against meat-eaters is that of bad economics. Raising cattle is a highly wasteful use of natural resources, compared to the returns offered by arable agriculture. Animals eat far more grain and soya than they produce as food. A chicken that will yield a kilo of meat has to be fed three kilos of grain. The ratio is even worse for turkey and pork, and worst of all for beef – a cow needs sixteen kilos of feed for every kilo of meat it produces. These animals are literally 'protein factories in reverse', grossly inefficient grain convertors, gobbling up an important share of the globe's diminishing resources. Third World countries, striving to gain foreign currency, are forced to export their grain as feed for Western cattle. As Mahatma Gandhi put it, 'The cattle of the rich steal the bread of the poor.' If we stopped eating meat the surplus grain could be used to feed the malnourished (over *1.5 billion* humans go hungry and about 500 million of those have only just enough to keep themselves alive.) An acre of land given over to feed for cattle produces enough protein – in the form of meat – to keep an adult alive for less than 250 days. The same plot of land sown with edible soybeans would provide ten times that amount of protein – in the form of vegetable matter. Chew on that, carnivore.

The fourth error of meat-eaters is their cultural blindness. Blinkered Western carnivores usually brand vegetarians as whole-food fanatics, as gastronomic marginals. But when the issue is looked at from a global perspective, it is the beef-eaters, not the fruit-and-nut nibblers, who emerge as the weirdos. Outside of the United States and a few other affluent countries, steak and prime ribs are seldom eaten. Most people throughout the world keep cattle for their labour-power, not for their flesh. The unusual idea of raising livestock specifically for consumption was developed only in relatively recent times by members of the British upper class, who had the means to indulge their carnivorous fancies. That is why the French used to call the English 'beef-eaters', and why so many European languages use the loanword 'beefsteak' and lack their own term for the cut. On the Continent, most cows are still reared for their milk rather than for their meat. Since their carcass is so tough when they die, the flesh is only good for stews or pot roasts. Surplus male calves are not normally fattened up but are soon slaughtered and sold as milk-fed veal.

Beef is the highest-status food in the United States. In the words of one native anthropologist, steak is to meat what Cadillac is to cars. And Americans, who learnt their love of beef from the British, are prepared to pay for it. Steak is the most expensive meat in the land. It is much more costly than, say, tongue; yet, if you think about it there is always a lot more steak to a cow than there is tongue. Though its price has risen over 500 per cent in the last sixty years, its per-capita consumption has remained remarkably steady. This national taste for beef is not just highly developed and relatively resistant to inflation. It is also very particular, as nowadays their use of beef is effectively confined to hamburgers, steaks, or roasts. The other, highly edible, parts of a cow are converted for use in hot dogs, pet food, and feed for cattle. When it comes to meaty mealtimes, carnivorous Americans know what bits they want. The rest they push aside. In other words, members of this highly affluent society can afford to be as choosy as they wish. And since their country is the most powerful in the world, they can pretend their eating habits are the norm, and not the cultural peculiarity they in fact are.

The fifth complaint about meat-eaters is their smell. Amorous vegetarians claim that, close up, the carnivorous objects of their desire turn out to be obnoxious characters whose reek betrays their gastronomic tastes. The Chinese have long argued that our meaty, milky diet makes us Westerners stink of the stuff. As one English journalist recently confessed, the kindest remark his Peking wife could make about his body odour was that he smelt like a musty Alsatian. Less polite vegetarians aim below the belt when they gripe about meat-eaters' farts. Abstainers from flesh say all they themselves produce is hot air, as quickly forgotten as it is produced, while carnivores let off far more offensive effluvia. Not surprising really, when you consider what their guts are full of.

The more mystically inclined of vegetarians try to raise themselves above this fray and carry their gastronomic creed to a higher plane where universal abstinence from meat is thought sure to usher in the New Utopia. To get to this stage, true believers have somehow to bypass the fact that Hitler, Himmler, and Frankenstein were all strict adherents to the faith. Undaunted by that disturbing detail, most vegans (members of the vegetarian avant-garde who keep away from meat, fish, dairy produce, eggs, honey, and leather products) regard their ascetic lifestyle as a spiritual adventure whose dietary code releases animals from suffering and themselves from a sense of guilt. Unpolluted by 'strong' foods like beef, they feel more healthy, more whole, their outward personality is more receptive to the interior life of the spirit, and they come to enter the cosmic unity which encompasses all humans and animals. The world is at one, and at peace.

To bloody-minded meat-eaters, this sort of visionary babbling only proves their prejudices about veganism as a pseudo-religion of grains and seeds preached by a bunch of nuts and flakes. Plastic sandals and pacifism aren't for them. Militant defenders of their steak-eating habit may think world harmony a fine and dandy principle but they don't see why individuals have to act like weeds in order to help achieve it. Men like this (for here we are talking, above all, about men) see little wrong in grouse-shooting or deer-hunting, and they savour the flavour of roast pheasant all the more because its carcass has been left to putrefy for several days before the feast. Killing may be an unpleasant act, but it is at times necessary and even 'natural'. To ignore this is like looking into a mirror and refusing to admit what you see. They do not understand what is unethical about rearing an animal, slaughtering it humanely, and using its flesh for food and its skin for shoes or woolly jumpers. When it comes to the gruesome details of modern factory farming, however, even the most dedicated of meat-eaters prefer to change the topic, or simply sigh in a vague gesture of impotence against the organized forces of the industrialized world.

The more knowledgeable of carnivores know that the argument for vegetarianism for the sake of one's health is not as damning as it at first seems. The medical case against high cholesterol is strongly suggestive but it is not conclusive, and some recent, highly controversial, epidemiological studies even seem to indicate that a meaty, milky diet may be good for you. In a similar fashion it is easy to show that the ecological argument for vegetarianism is slightly flawed. Only 10 per cent of the earth's surface (excluding those areas covered by ice) can be cultivated practically. Another 20 per cent, or 3 billion hectares, is non-arable land on which animals can graze and browse. In this way, as the geographer Calvin Schwabe has argued, animals can convert highly scattered or otherwise inaccessible plant life into high-protein food. As much as 60 per cent of all animal-protein produced in the world today comes from animals left to wander on such non-arable land. These animals exploit these areas for us: it would be inefficient if not impracticable to harvest these plants in any other way.

Moreover, unwavering meat-eaters are not the band of Henry VIII clones that some vegetarian polemicists imply they are. Attitudes have moved on since the days when Argentinian gauchos stuck to their steak diet and viewed vegetables as food fit only for animals. Today's carnivores are not, on the whole, greedy characters more concerned with the amount of flesh on their plate than its type or quality. As the sociologist Julia Twigg has detailed, most Western carnivores are in fact very discriminating consumers who carefully grade different kinds of meat (and other foods) into a generally recognized hierarchy:

red meat (steak, game, etc.)
|
veal, lamb, mutton
|
white meat (chicken, turkey, and other fowl)
|
fish
|

eggs
|
dairy produce
|
fruit, vegetables, and cereals

Bloodiness is the principle that organizes this system, at least in its upper reaches. As the traditional seat of the passions and the very essence of life, it is blood that endows meat with much of its potency and energizing quality. It is for that reason that red meat, oozing gore as you cut into it, goes at the top of the table. Soldiers needed it, sportsmen were fed it, and even today astronauts are given it in their last meal before take-off. In Victorian times and later, red meat was thought so 'strong' that invalids were told to stick to a diet of boiled chicken, steamed fish, and poached eggs. Academics were also advised to keep off this potent food, otherwise the blood might rush to their heads, and it would not be books they would end up thinking about.

Though white meats are thought to be as full of protein and nourishment as beef and game, they are seen as effectively bloodless, and thus less stimulating: they do not shake up the emotions the way a T-bone steak is meant to. That is why they were the traditional choice of meat for ladies. Even today, most meat-eating women still prefer white flesh to red, and very few females of my acquaintance boast of a love for beef. Keeping chicken meat perfectly white is so important that poultry manufacturers (to give them an honest name) have to ensure that all the blood is sucked out of their carcasses. Broilers must be raised on deep litter, not in batteries where the wire would blister and so discolour their breasts. Since white meat is now seen as 'light' food and thus potentially less damaging to one's health, lamb and mutton are increasingly presented as though they were white, not red, meats. It is intriguing that so very little of the sheep meat produced in the United States is mutton. It appears – unless American sheep are a distinctly different breed from those reared elsewhere – that the States has some of the oldest 'lamb' for sale on this planet.

While red meat is thought fortifying, there are some crimson-fleshed creatures that even the most hearty of human carnivores won't touch: uncastrated animals, carnivores, and omnivores. There is, however, no good nutritional reason why we should abstain from the meat of boars or bulls who died with their testicles on. People in other countries eat this kind of meat and do not complain about the taste. It is just that in our culture they are thought 'too strong', as though consuming the flesh of these untamed and occasionally aggressive males would turn the eater into a ferocious savage bent on rape, murder, and general destruction. Spanish hunters always carry a sharp knife in their belts, for if they shoot a wild boar they must cut its spermatic veins as quickly as possible; otherwise, they claim, the testicular blood will pollute its flesh and render it inedible.

Humans are predators but they (or at least the people of the industrialized West) do not kill other predators for consumption. They do not eat the flesh of animals that eat other animals. Like bulls and boars, their meat is said to be 'too strong'. But, as with the case of bulls and boars, this is more a statement of our own cultural attitudes than anything else, for some peoples have no qualms about eating carnivores. In Russia, for instance, foxes are a delicacy. One reason for our taboo might be that we feel a need to make a clear distinction between ourselves and other sorts of animals. As Nick Fiddes has argued, those we eat are 'natural victims', while those with a predatory nature seem disturbingly akin to us. We grant ourselves the right to kill our prey, and we accord carnivores the right to kill theirs. Hunters are usually proud of their ability and they often express respect for the skill of other predators. We might fear the damage done by foxes, but we still call them 'cunning.' One of Fiddes' interviewees put it this way:

> Well . . . a fox is a sort of special animal, isn't it? It's OK with sheep and cows and things because, like, they're just waiting there and not doing much. I don't mind the idea of that because, it's sort of like that's why they're there for us, isn't it? But a fox sort of like lives its own life. I mean, I can see why we have to hunt them to keep them down, but it wouldn't be right to eat them.

Predators share affinities with humans. Killing them might be justifiable. Eating them would hint of cannibalism.

People in Britain were so uneasy about the salmonella and 'mad cow' scares of 1988 and 1989 for similar reasons. Poultry and eggs, the public learnt, were being contaminated with salmonella because chickens were being fed the only partially sterilized carcasses of other chickens as a protein supplement. In effect,

CATERING FOR CARNIVORES

Other peoples aren't as fussy as urban Americans or Western Europeans. Their tastes are broad and they do not let prejudices about carnivores impoverish their cuisine. A few examples of their imaginativeness:

Mice in Cream *(an Arctic recipe)*

Skin, gut, and wash some fat mice without removing their heads. Cover them in a pot with ethyl alcohol and marinate for two hours. Cut a piece of salt pork or sow belly into small dice and cook it slowly to extract the fat. Drain the mice, dredge them thoroughly in a mixture of flour, pepper, and salt, and fry slowly in the rendered fat for about five minutes. Add a cup of alcohol and six to eight cloves, cover, and simmer for fifteen minutes. Prepare a cream sauce, transfer the sautéed mice to it, and warm them in it for about ten minutes before serving.

Bear's Paw *(a Chinese recipe)*

Pack the washed paw of a bear in clay and bake it in an oven. Allow it to cool, crack the clay, and remove it. This will also remove the hair. Simmer the paw in frequently changed water until its gamey smell disappears. When the paw meat is very soft, continue to simmer in a minimum of water with shredded lean ham, shredded chicken, and sherry until a thick sauce results. Slice the paw and serve it in this sauce.

Ndomba Snake *(centre-south province, Cameroon)*

Cut off the head and tail and bury them. Gut and cut into pieces. Grill each piece lightly so that the scales fall off when scraped with a knife or machete. Wash the pieces. On banana leaves previously waved over a fire, place *citronnella* leaves, then the meat, and lastly salt, large and small leaves of *basilics*, pepper, bark from a garlic tree, and onions. Wrap the banana leaves into a packet using banana fibre as string. Place this packet on a bed of banana leaves in a *marmite*. Half cover with water. Once cooked, it may be eaten with any starchy food as accompaniment.

modern methods of factory farming were turning passive animals into carnivores, cannibals of their own species. The slightly later outbreak of 'mad cow' disease (bovine spongiform encephalo-pathy) was caused by feeding cattle the remains of sheep, some of them infected with the spongiform disease 'scrapie'. Once again, a vegetarian animal had been forced to become carnivorous. And once again, the meat produced had been sold to customers who do not believe that they should eat animals which eat other animals, even if they are not diseased.

The uncastrated and the carnivores are considered bad enough, but the carrion-eaters and the omnivores are thought easily the worst. Carrion-eaters do not hunt, they feed off the dead, and therefore they cannot be respected in any way. We do not eat vultures, and we let hyenas have the last laugh, all the way to the corpse. But these exploiters of decomposing protein live far from us. Rats, however, are a different matter. As I write, there are hundreds beneath me running the courses of the Oxford sewers. In larger cities they run in their thousands. These hated, feared rodents do not stay meekly in the wild – they invade and adapt to almost any environment, living off whatever they can find, wherever. They are promiscuous omnivores that put putrefying flesh on a dietary par with grains and poisons their bodies have learned to digest. They are not food to be salivated over, but vermin to be exterminated. In fact, their meat is said to be similar in taste to partridge or pork.

Westerners consider rats so disgusting that when people have to eat them, whether in a siege or during a famine, it is taken as a sure sign that their predicament has become desperate. To my knowledge, the only case of Englishmen unashamed to cook rodents is that of the early Jamaican planters, who ate rats that had been fed on sugar in the canefields. These sweet animals had not feasted on rotting flesh and human garbage. Though still rats, they were not *dirty* rats.

As the number of vegetarians rises rapidly in the West (at a rate of 20 per cent a year in Britain), meat-eaters have started to act like a threatened majority. But if the nutritional warnings have not yet swayed them, it is unlikely the ethical arguments will move them either.

Many of these unreconstructed carnivores, however, are not inadequates sheltering behind some Rambo-like idea of meat's

---

ENTRECOTE A LA BORDELAISE
(From *Larousse Gastronomique*)

The tastiest rats are those which live in wine cellars. Skin and de-gut. Rub with a thick sauce of olive oil and crushed shallots. Add salt and pepper. Make a fire of broken wine barrels. Grill the prepared carcass over it. The rat can be served with a *Bordelaise* sauce, made according to the recipe of the great French gastronome Curnonsky: cook half a cup of a red Bordeaux and six shallots in a small pan for a few minutes, until it has reduced by a third. Add bay leaves and thyme. On a gentle flame add butter, stirring from time to time. After five or so minutes, strain the sauce. Just before serving, add three ounces of chopped beef marrow with the juice of a lemon.

---

powers. To them, their chosen diet is a matter of taste, for no other food has the same texture as meat. Vegetables can be just as tough or as tender as cooked flesh, but they are not something to get one's teeth into. They do not provide anything to chew on. Nut cutlets, festive loaf, and couscous patties are all delicious, but they do not promise the same masticatory enjoyment as a lamb chop or a steak *au poivre*. Meat-eaters want something more out of their mealtimes. They want bite.

19

OFFAL!

When I asked a visiting American academic at lunch whether she ate kidneys she turned her head to one side and sniffed, as though I had suggested she were the sort of strict Hindu who drank her own urine. When I went on to ask her if she liked brains, she looked at me as if I were insane. There seemed little point in enquiring whether she preferred her testicles fried with breadcrumbs or cooked slowly in a spicy tomato sauce.

Instead, I told her about the time in Sulfa Bay my host offered me a flying fox, commonly known as a fruit bat, with a stick up its arse as handle and grilled gently over an open fire. With its large eyes looking down on me, and its fearsome jaw bumping against my left eyebrow, I contentedly nibbled the meat off its ribs and abdomen. When I came to the guts – uncleaned, of course – I stopped. My host, seeing my hesitation, said quickly, 'It's OK. The shit doesn't stay. All it eats are berries.' He was right. As I told my lunch companion, they had a rather rubbery consistency but otherwise tasted fine. She got up and left.

This exaggerated squeamishness about eating offal seems to be a peculiarly middle-class American trait. Their disgust for some organs is so great that Congress recently passed legislation effectively banning the sale of lungs, spleen, and certain other viscera. The more pragmatic British are not so fussy. They make liver and kidneys a standard part of their diet, while tongue remains an old favourite for many. Sweetbreads and brains are considered slightly more exotic, tripe is losing popularity, testicles are thought mildly perverse, and the only time most English people come across eyes is on the dissecting table during a biology class. On the whole, they are thankful that udder, which tastes like chewy tongue, is a regional dish confined to a small cluster of towns in industrial west Yorkshire and east Lancashire.

Despite the apparent breadth of British taste compared to American fastidiousness, the inventiveness of French cuisine makes even the English look pernickety and unimaginative. In the late seventeenth century, as French cooking was on the rise, creative chefs in search of new recipes came to revalue previously

159

denigrated offal. Innards were too useful to be ignored or fed to the cat and a variety of dishes were invented, which included ingredients such as tail, lungs, palate, udder, mesentery, spleen, and intestines; tripe was particularly useful as a carrier for other tastes in dishes which would otherwise lack substance. Though French cuisine is no longer quite so comprehensive, even today the sight of the varied produce on sale at a butchers in a Parisian public market would be enough to make my American acquaintance gag.

Why has offal so often had to play pauper to meat's king? Why is it so frequently despised? From the beginning the term itself, which comes from *off-fall* (the bits that fall out when an animal is cut open), was extended to mean 'putrid flesh, inferior fish, refuse in general, dregs, offscouring, or scum'. By definition offal is the remainder, what is left when the good stuff has already gone. The stomach of cows has not fared much better in common parlance: 'a load of old tripe' is not a butcher's bargain but a derogatory term for an unconvincing argument. It is the sort of phrase to put you off the real thing before you have even had the chance to try it.

While muscle meats carry clear connotations of strength, viscera cannot bear such associations, for their function is to help maintain the body, not support it physically or articulate its parts.

GEED
(Spiced Bull's Penis)

First scald the penis and clean it. Boil for ten minutes, remove, and slice. (A bull's penis may weigh one pound or more.) Brown a chopped onion, chopped cloves of garlic, and coriander in oil. Add the penis and fry. Mix the ingredients together and add a chopped tomato, pepper, cumin, saffron, and salt. Cover the pot. Cook over a low flame for two hours, adding a little water from time to time to prevent burning. Serve hot. Season with *hilbeh* (fenugreek seeds that have been soaked in water for two hours, then drained and mixed with a tomato purée and a little *zhug* – a spicy mix of ground black pepper, caraway seed, cardamom, dried red peppers, garlic, and fresh coriander).

Offal comes from a once-living being, but it lacks the vitalizing qualities granted to flesh, and its status is even lower than that of secondary meats like bacon, sausage, or pork pie. Moreover innards, with the exception of tripe and dry liver, are not chewy like meat. They do not offer much resistance to the teeth. Most sorts of offal have a soft, mushy texture (lungs are not even that, but spongy), which does not appeal to steak-loving men. Such blood-crazed *machistas* want beef, and they regard sweetmeats as exotic and effete.

Since people have become so squeamish about eating bits of animals, it is offal's bad luck to be so instantly recognizable. Brains *look* like brains, and lungs could not be mistaken for anything else, while bulls' balls are still testicles – only larger than life. The usual culinary solution is to cut the stuff up and stew it or to disguise it with a sauce. The rural Welsh cook tripe in milk with onions and parsley, and serve it with a white sauce. Eighteenth-century British cooks mixed sweetmeats, cockscombs and sheeps' tongues into 'Bombarded Veal', a decorative dish of minced meat hemispheres surrounded by veal fillets, mushrooms, and artichokes. Another way out is to transform the offal into something else. Thus oxtail can be made into soup, and the muscle meat attached to pigs' heads turned into 'headcheese' or 'shield of brawn'. But problems may still arise at the purchasing end of the chain. The story is told of the young Nebraska woman who asked her butcher for an inexpensive cut of meat which could both serve as a main dish and later be used to fill sandwiches. When the man suggested beef tongue, she exploded. 'I am not about to put something from a cow's mouth into my mouth!' Instead she bought a dozen eggs.

The way to forestall this kind of reaction is to rename the produce or mask the ingredients of a dish by giving it a special name. In the British countryside, a cooked mixture of an animal's tongue, heart, brains, lungs, and liver, together with fried, plaited (and cleaned) intestines, is known as 'pluck'; coagulated blood wrapped in guts is that old favourite, black pudding; and London butchers sell testicles under the name of 'lamb's fry'. In the United States, offal in general are called 'variety meats', lungs become 'lights', the spleen 'melt', and testicles 'mountain oysters'. Just as imaginatively, the French politely dub the scrotal sack *animelles* or *rognons extérieurs*.

UDDER TIMES

In case there is not a tripery near your home which could prepare the udder for you, follow these instructions:

Drain the elder of any remaining milk, otherwise the udder's flavour will be tainted. Here best to imitate the example of the tripery in Denholme, a hill village above Bradford: that is, give the elder 'a bit of a bashing' to remove the excess liquid (the tripery uses a machine for this). Then, starting at 10 a.m., gently simmer it for six hours or more, until you think it sufficiently tender. Turn the heat off, cover the pot, and leave. Next morning, boil the elder again for two hours, remove from the pot, rapidly cool in very cold water, and 'dress' it by removing any excess fat and remaining skin with a stiff brush. Finally, as a cosmetic gesture, trim it with a knife to remove any bruised bits or teat-holes and give it shape.

You will now have a compact lump of light-coloured, flesh-toned udder, about a quarter of its original weight. The exact colour, depending on the breed of cow, may be pink, yellow, or brownish-hued. It will smell faintly of tongue, its texture is almost as soft but slightly chewier.

Udder should be eaten fresh and kept cool. Best to keep it under water, at freezing point, in a bowl in the fridge. It should keep for a week.

One way to prepare it: dice the elder into half-inch cubes. Marinate for thirty minutes in a well-seasoned vinaigrette with freshly chopped parsley and spring onion. Serve as an aperitif. One unknowing taster thought it pâté.

Despite these culinary tricks and verbal manoeuvres, offal is still seen as the cuisine of the poor, not food to be proud of, and certainly not a dish to set before a king. It is more appropriate for times of low budgets and high unemployment. While country folk may relish a food that comes free every time an animal is killed, cooked innards are just what the urban poor want to leave behind when they are given the chance to rise above economic squalor;

it is too strong a reminder of the hardships they once endured, when off-cuts and offal were all they could afford. Perhaps it is for this reason that viscera are particularly despised in the United States, where social advancement is the only common creed and people are ranked primarily in terms of their wealth. For European immigrants on the make, to serve their guests sweetbreads was like waving a culinary banner of poverty and social failure. During the Second World War, the only way the government could persuade people to eat kidney was by publicizing its preparation and consumption in the United Kingdom, a country then still regarded by Americans as one of high status.

Of course, there is no intrinsic reason why viscera should be valued so lowly. Calves' and lambs' kidneys do not, as some people claim, taste or smell of urine. American gastronomic conservatives, or the downright timid, may try to justify their learnt fear of offal by speaking of 'germs' and possible infection, but there is no medical reason why the innards of a properly reared animal should be more dangerous to the body or harbour more infection than red flesh. Nutritionally, offal is often a far better source of vitamins and protein than muscle meat. Blood has twenty times more iron than steak and weight for weight provides 20 per cent more protein. Sadly, however, it has to be stated that offal concentrates chemical additives as well as essential nutrients. If you do not like your liver or your kidneys flavoured with pesticides, antibiotics, probiotics, steroids, or heavy metals such as copper, then it is best to patronize an organic butcher, if you can find one.

Other, less polluted societies have not been so blind to the potential worth of offal. Famous French chefs may have been very imaginative in their creation of offal-based dishes, but they still cannot match the diversity displayed by the uncredited cooks of the world's other cultures. Chinese are prepared to pay more for liver than for flesh, and Yoruba value offal more highly than carcass meat: they flatter guests by offering them body organs rather than steak. The Ancient Romans made spicy sausage out of pig uterus; Russians make kidney soup; Yemeni Jews prepare a piquant dish of bull's penis; and people in the Caribbean cook oxtail in red wine with hot peppers. Argentinian gauchos look forward to their *fiestas de huevos* ('egg' fiestas) when the cattle are rounded up for branding, vaccination, and castration, and fresh testicles are the order of the day. Various native American groups went much further. They used to eat dried buffalo lung, buffalo blood jelly congealed with stomach rennet, moose nose, and the upper intestines of a buffalo filled with chewed grasses, tied up and left in the sun to ferment.

OLD ENGLISH
Neat's (Ox's) Tongues, Very High Flavour

Having cut away the useless parts at the roots, and removed the gullets, rub the tongues all over with coarse sugar or real West Indian molasses, and let them lie twenty-four hours; then take

> *Juniper berries* 1 oz
> *Black pepper, ground* $^1/_2$ oz
> *Sal prunelle (potassium nitrate)* $^1/_2$ oz
> *Treacle* 1 lb

Mix, and rub with it three days, turning them daily; then add

> *Bay salt* 9 oz
> *Common or rock salt* 12 oz

Rub three days, and turn the meat daily for a week, when you may dry it and smoke with beech and fern or grass turfs. The above proportions are for one fine tongue of eight or nine pounds.

From *The Art and Mystery of Curing, Preserving,*
and Potting all kinds of Meat, Game, and Fish,
by a Wholesale Curer of Comestibles, 1864

If there is one body organ that has been singled out by different peoples of the world, it is the liver. Ancient Greeks and Maoris saw it as the repository of the emotions; Tongans called it the seat of courage; Aztecs read omens from the livers of slaughtered animals; and several groups in central Africa have regarded it as the site of the soul – men who ate it enhanced their spiritual being. Native American Omaha thought buffalo liver gave a man a clear voice and a courageous spirit, while on extraordinary occasions, the bravest warriors of the Dakota tribe still warm strips of dog liver in order to take on the wisdom and valour of this esteemed animal. In the film *Dances with Wolves*, the Sioux show their regard for the white protagonist by cutting out the liver from a freshly dead buffalo and giving him it to eat, raw.

FRIASE DE VEAU LYONNAISE
(Mesentery with Onions)

Mesentery (the membranous fold attaching parts of the intestines to the back wall of the abdomen) should be well soaked, then scalded for a few minutes, and allowed to cool. Cook in a stock of flour, salt, lemon juice, onion, clove, and bouquet garni. Drain and dry well. Cut into thin slices, season and sauté in very hot oil. Add two finely sliced onions previously sautéd in butter. Sauté the two together for several minutes in order to mix them well. Serve garnished with chopped parsley and sprinkled with hot vinegar.

Escoffier

American fur trappers of the last century ate buffalo liver and kidneys raw, but only after adding a little zest by pricking the gall bladder and squirting the organs with the green juice. Unlike the city-slickers on the East Coast with their fancy tastes, these 'mountain men' relished 'prairie butter' (the roasted marrow of buffalo bones) and were not fussy about the type of flesh they ate. In the words of one, 'Howsomeever, Meat's Meat! And what sort does not matter a whit, long as it's some kinda meat.' They also made a soup of marrow mixed with blood. One visitor who saw them slurping this rich and nourishing soup said it made them 'shine with grease and gladness'.

Cowboy diet was not so varied. Down on the range they flavoured their otherwise dull days by making that well-known dish 'Son-of-a-Bitch Stew', a mixture of the choicest parts of an unweaned calf together with its tongue, brains, liver, heart, sweetbreads, and the marrow gut between the stomachs, plus onions, chilli, salt, and pepper, the whole perfectly complemented by the distinctive taste of the last ingredient: the rennin-curdled, milky abomasum – the calf's fourth stomach.

Modern middle-class sophisticates, secure in their social position, do not have to worry about the association of innards with indigence; they can praise and cook once denigrated peasant cuisine without any guest thinking their hosts have gone into the red. Serving up calf mesentery at a dinner-party implies their taste is so discriminating that they do not have to bother about the dish's social origin. And, if fashionable metropolitan heirs are busy revaluing the same foods and offering them at modern prices, then the host can even appear trendy, as one who keeps up with the culinary avant-garde. Thus guests may end up boasting to friends of the gourmet dishes they were given – ironically the very same dishes their grandparents would have been ashamed to be seen eating. Brains on toast and cold tripe with salt, pepper, and vinegar may have dropped out of favour with the British working class since the end of the last war, but they are now to be found in expensive London restaurants as *cervelles au beurre noir* and *tripes à la mode de Caen*.

It seems a new baptism requires a new name.

20

FIRST CATCH YOUR MAN

When man is cut, he is cut in a different way from bullock or sheep or pig or goat. Cut out the navel, then cut the fingers at all the joints, then the wrists, then the elbow, then the shoulder, then all toe and foot joints, then the knee, then pull out his stomach, then cut out the neck, then cut out the legs. Then cut everything into pieces. Give the legs to the chief [it is up to him if he takes both or not]. The rest of the body is divided among the naml *[different lodges within the village].*

When you cook man, it is very yellow, very greasy and very sweet. It cannot be cooked like normal meat. It tastes better if hung for a couple of days. Put the meat in a lap-lap *[grated tuber pudding wrapped in banana leaves like a long, flat packet and cooked in an earth oven].*

You must be very careful when eating human flesh because when you eat man, if any bit of meat sticks in the middle of your teeth, if you use a toothpick to remove the bits, someone from another village will shoot you [in other words, subsequent misfortune will be attributed to the breaking of this taboo]. You make a drink from nesu, *a special kind of sugar cane, and use it to clean out your mouth if human flesh is stuck. This is the only way you can get rid of bits.* Nesu, *once drunk, cleans you out generally so that now you can go to your wife or to your garden. If you do not drink* nesu, *your wife, your garden are taboo to you.*

The body is cut up in this special way as a mark of respect. If the body is cut up like an animal, the meat is taboo. If eaten, the spirit of the dead man will spoil the village by making the people of that village go to places where people of other villages can kill them.

Dictated to me by John Peter Anahapat, a Big Nambas chief, of
Malakula Island, Vanuatu, on 11 December 1978

Anthropophagy – the eating of humans – may be a worldwide occurrence, but it is above all a Western obsession, a topic of endless fascination for civilized Whites. Parents scare their children with legends and fairy tales of man-eaters; journalists thrill their readers with the latest report of cannibalism; globetrotters titillate their friends with tales of exotic roasts that looked suspiciously familiar. Though it has been conclusively proved that the son of Nelson Rockefeller died by drowning off the coast of Irian

Jaya, rumours still persist that he was eaten by the villagers he was staying with. Over twenty years after his death, his mother continues to receive so much mail about the event that one of her secretaries has to spend all her time just dealing with the correspondence.

Stories about cannibalism go the rounds and then keep coming back. They have a perennial hold on our imagination. One planter in the South Pacific told me the tale of the geologist touring in the jungle who, at a feast, was handed a cooked human hand. Nervous, not wanting to be impolite yet uncertain what to do, he nibbled at the tendons, with the unintended consequence of making the fingers claw and close over his face.

Though reports of cannibalism come from all corners of the globe, there are relatively few authoritative accounts by trustworthy eyewitnesses of anthropophagites in action. The vast majority of accounts depend not on observed events but on stories told to Westerners. Now, because all colonial regimes made cannibalism illegal, its practice was necessarily secret. In consequence, expatriates could impute any mysterious disappearance to the possibility of cannibalism and so help perpetuate the idea of 'those bloody man-eaters up in the bush'. As the American anthropologist Bill Arens has argued, most 'reports' of cannibalism made by travellers or foreign residents are grossly exaggerated or unfounded. Their popularity tells us more about Western sensationalism than about the manners of non-European peoples. As astute missionaries knew, putting 'cannibal' in the title of their books widened their market and increased sales or donations from fervent Christians. Weighty tomes like *On Brown Humanity* or *Thinking Black* could not compete with the racily entitled *Cannibals and Convicts* or *In Cannibal Land*.

Calling others cannibals, however, is not an innocent tactic but a time-honoured political strategy for raising oneself up and putting others down. In Sierra Leone today, accusing an antisocial, selfish chief of eating human flesh is still a powerful tactic for getting him out of office. More generally, imputing others of cannibalism is a spectacularly effective way of exaggerating the cultural gap between Them and Us: by highlighting the apparently odd and downplaying what is common, Other Peoples can be made to seem very different. For just what kind of persons eat fellow humans as part of their ritual diet? Should we even regard them as fellow humans? The Vatican did not think so. In 1503 Pope Alexander VI (Rodrigo Borgia) issued a papal edict permitting the enslavement of man-eaters, but of no one else. In the minds of many Westerners the monstrousness of Bokassa, dictator of the Central African Republic, was confirmed on his fall from power by the evidence left in his fridge – human limbs as titbits for whenever he felt peckish.

Time and again, European colonial officers and missionaries bent on domination used cannibalism as an excuse for asserting moral superiority over their supposedly indiscriminating, carnivorous charges. Putting Whites in the pot revealed their moral blackness and their need for conversion to Christian ethics, hygiene, and diet. Such pagans had to be saved from their own devilish customs and weaned from human flesh to the body and blood of our Lord.

Though the idea of cannibalism has a universal appeal, it appears that ritual man-eating is not a worldwide occurrence. Most of the credible reports come from North America and the Pacific Islands; sub-Saharan Africa and South America come next on this grisly list. Only two dependable cases have been described in the Mediterranean area, and there are no good accounts at all from anywhere in East Eurasia. It seems that neither Russians, the Chinese, nor any of their neighbours used to do it.

In English, 'cannibal' has become a pejorative term signifying 'bloodthirsty savage', an uninhibited character with the tastes of a vampire. And many Westerners still think of cannibal banquets as wild and unstructured gatherings where crazed natives filled their bellies with the rarest of meats. But, in truth, the seemingly dramatic facts of eating one's own kind mask the mundane anthropological reality that cannibalism is merely a socially defined process or ritual like any other. Different peoples may have different reasons for consuming human flesh, but they always go about it in an organized manner. In some societies cannibalism is not an isolated act but part and parcel of their way of life. Though the ritual is elaborate and lengthy in some places, simple and perfunctory in others, it is always carried out according to certain rules. A feast of human flesh is not a riotous free-for-all but a communal meal shared by kith and kin. To cannibals, the idea of unregulated man-eating – consuming anyone, anywhere, any time, anyhow – is as horrific as it is to us. If one is going to indulge in human meat, one must do it in the ritually prescribed manner.

The Hua of the New Guinea Highlands were not cannibals because they wanted to be, but because they thought they had to be in order to survive. They believed that life depended on *nu*, 'vital essence', the source of fertility and growth. In order to be fit and active, Hua constantly strove to top up their levels of this precious substance. People had *nu* and so, since its supply was limited, Hua were *obliged* to eat their dead: a man ate the corpse of his father and a woman that of her mother. If adults did not consume the flesh of their parents, they, their children, their animals, and their crops would all become stunted and feeble. These rules had to be observed properly: a man who ate a woman's body would be polluted by the wrong kind of *nu* and so weakened.

Travel writers have constantly asserted that cannibals come to appreciate a particular part of the human anatomy as especially tasty. Some say it is the inner thigh, others the rump, yet others the upper arm. Though they cannot agree on which bit is the favourite, they all state the flesh is sweet; monkey, they claim, is the closest meat to it. (I'd like to know how they made the comparison.) Certain 'nutritionist' anthropologists have recently argued that societies practised cannibalism because they were short of high-protein foods. But humans do not bear much meat: for forty people to eat adequately, they would have to consume eight fatty adults a month. And how could such a small band of men, women, and children be consistently able to find, and then able to kill, that number of humans every thirty days?

Some anthropologists distinguish between endocannibalism, eating a member of one's own group, and exocannibalism, tucking into the cooked corpse of someone outside one's group. The exocannibalistic Big Nambas of northern Vanuatu ate only their enemies, men killed in raiding parties on other villages, or offered as victims by a warring village suing for peace. The endocannibalistic Yanomami of southern Venezuela burn their dead, crush the charred bones into powder, and then mix the ashes with boiled plantain soup. The living drink this mix in order to see their departed friends and relatives in the world beyond. Sharing this loving cup is one of the most intimate of acts. To the Yanomami, it is the supreme way to display friendship and bind alliances.

(I imagine it would taste like the contents of an ashtray tipped into a thick pea soup.)

Too often, the Western image of Black cannibals is a chauvinistic one. In so many Victorian engravings, man-eating males bent on satisfying their desires fill the foreground while their womenfolk, off in the bush, patiently await the end of the meal. Of course, women in cannibal cultures have seen no reason for fulfilling Western prejudices. Why should they be excluded from the feast?

The Gimi, who live in the New Guinea Highlands, believed that cannibalism was the special prerogative of women, who had in fact invented the practice. Adult males who ate from cadavers were considered 'nothing men', people of low status and little strength. When a Gimi man died, his body was left on a bamboo platform in his vegetable garden to decompose. His bereaved female relatives would crowd around their late kinsman, caressing his limbs, kissing his corpse, beating their breasts, and wailing for hours on end. Finally unable to contain their sorrow, they would secretly steal the body and eat it.

This physical incorporation of men by women *can* be regarded as equivalent to the female appropriation of male reproductive power. Following this cultural logic, such women would no longer have need of men; they could reproduce without recourse to sex. To correct this blurring of the gender lines and to regain their dominant position, men would give the female cannibals pieces of pork corresponding to the particular parts of the corpse each of them had eaten. The pork took the place of the male flesh, which was expelled on excretion. The released male soul, thus freed from its captivity inside female bodies, could then go forth and fertilize the soil, plants, and animals of the Gimi's territory. This particular kind of cannibalistic ritual, set in motion by women but finally controlled by men, was a way of temporarily mixing up the difference between the sexes and then categorically reasserting it. In this way men and women knew where they stood – on either side of the sexual divide.

Cannibalism plays many different roles in different societies. Precisely what meanings it is given depends upon each particular culture at a particular time. For the Huron of southern Canada in the seventeenth century, cannibalistic ritual fulfilled a variety of functions: it was a socially approved means of invigorating themselves, of securing peace, of demonstrating tribal strength, and of

venting otherwise dangerous feelings. According to the eyewit-
ness account of a captive Jesuit priest, once the Huron had selected
a particular prisoner of war as their next victim, they started to
treat him like an esteemed guest. He was given food to eat and a
pipe to smoke, while the chief wiped the sweat from his brow and
gently cooled him with a feather fan. Forewarned of his approaching death, the condemned man attended a farewell feast held in
his honour. Before the meal began, he addressed his audience,
telling them he had no fear. Then he sang and danced with several
others. The torment began that evening when the prisoner was
made to run the gauntlet between two rows of excited young men
armed with firebrands. They repeatedly burned him as he ran up
and down, and the crowd imitated his shrieks. If it looked as
though he might die too soon, his assailants relaxed and revived
him by giving him some water to drink. At dawn he was tied to a
tree, burnt some more, then decapitated. The people feasted on
his body later that day.

The Huron believed they had to satisfy desires expressed in
dreams. Once these urges had been revealed, it was fatally
dangerous to frustrate them. Thus the Huron thought that for
their own sake they had to act out their desires, even if they might
only do so symbolically. A captive was often given to those who
had lost relatives in war, and these mourning kinsfolk might
decide to assuage their grief and exact revenge by having him
tortured and eaten. Though his tormentors raged as they burnt,
they were not angry at their victim, rather, solicitous and caring.
He was taken to represent the relative who had died, and so they
called him 'uncle' and spoke to him in friendly terms as they
continued to burn his body. Since the captive was meant to
replace the life that had been lost, killing him ritually was
symbolically equivalent to performing the funeral rites for the
deceased kinsman, whose corpse had been stolen by their enemies. By torturing him the tormentors gave vent to their violent
feelings, and by eating him they ritually devoured them.

For his part, the captive on the whole bore his ordeal with
patience and did not once insult his killers. His exemplary endurance of the pain proved the power of the Huron and their
neighbours. At a time when their way of life was increasingly
threatened by European encroachment, the stoicism of such
victims demonstrated the unbending strength of the locals, a

strength that could be maintained even in the face of death. And by consuming the flesh of these admirable captives, the Huron fortified themselves. It invigorated them. Two supernatural beings, the Sun and the God of War, witnessed these torture rituals, and a dying victim who had bravely withstood the persistent physical torment become one with them. He was absorbed into the local pantheon. He had indeed died well.

The Hua, the Gimi, and the Huron all had compelling reasons for practising anthropophagy. Ritually eating humans kept them strong, relieved their emotions, and reminded the advancing Whites they were a foe to be reckoned with. But cannibals do not necessarily have to justify their actions. They do not always feel forced to supply a meaning, whether it be nutritional, psychological, or military. In the last century, warring Fijians ceremonially ate their opponents. But they never advanced any special motive for doing so. It was merely something they did, as good Fijians.

To Westerners, cannibalism borders on the unthinkable. It becomes almost a definition of humanity, for can one be more uncivilized than a man-eater? White cannibals are considered either criminally insane (and therefore to be confined) or desperate people driven to drastic measures in order to survive (and therefore to be pitied). Conditions of starvation such as potato-hungry Ireland, besieged Leningrad, postwar Berlin, or Nazi extermination camps are thought of as extremes where the usual rules had to be broken. They were exceptional periods that demanded abnormal behaviour. In all these cases cannibalism was a shameful but excusable act.

Some medieval Catholics saw Holy Communion in terms of cannibalism and were disgusted by the practice. Seventeenth-century Christians, in contrast, argued that eating the flesh of God was such an extraordinary event it could not be compared to ordinary anthropophagy. One of the reasons for fasting before Communion was to purify the stomach and guts before receiving the Host. It was thought this heavenly manna was so full of power and grace that whoever ingested it was strengthened in body and spirit, and cleansed in soul and flesh. This divine substance provided a foretaste of paradisiacal happiness, acting as a pain-killer and even estranging martyrs from their bodies at moments when the torments they were undergoing became insupportable. As far as these Christians were concerned, eating this 'living bread' could not be equated with the disgusting habits of distant foreigners. *They* were divinely inspired Christians acting on their faith, the others were despicable cannibals driven by their instincts.

The only Western group who practised cannibalism as an occasionally necessary, though still unlikable, act were British sailors. Until the end of sail Victorian seamen accepted that the only way to survive when adrift in a small boat was the ritualized drawing of lots. The castaway who pulled the short straw could only hope that his end would be as painless as possible. In 1884, however, the mariners' agreed-upon rules clashed with the morals of the English legal system in the celebrated trial of the survivors of the *Mignonette*. When the small ship sank in a storm in mid-Atlantic, four of its crew managed to escape in a dinghy. But with no food, no water, and no boat in sight, their plight rapidly turned desperate. The youngest among them, a lad, became feverish and delirious. After nineteen days in the cramped dinghy, having had only a turtle to feed upon, the other three, all highly respectable seamen, agreed to kill the boy before he died. After stabbing him, they drank his blood, cut out his heart and liver, and dismembered the corpse. They immediately felt invigorated and survived on his meat until they spotted a boat five days later. The British high court judged two of them for murder. Since public opinion was so strongly in their favour, the pair of seamen expected to be pardoned. Instead, to their horror and dismay, the sentence of death passed on them was only commuted to six months' imprisonment. To the worthy judges, maritime morality, whether or not legitimated by years of practice, could not prevail over legal ethics.

The only recorded example of a modern Oriental group who committed anthropophagy is the Japanese army in the Second World War. In the officers' mess, human for dinner was said to have been treated as a festive occasion, while other ranks might be served only a broth made from the flesh. The practice became so widespread that the army had to put out an 'Order Regarding Eating the Flesh of American Flyers'. Soldiers were allowed to consume the enemy, but those who ate their compatriots were executed. When it came to the crunch, however, the troops were told to chew on anyone. In their harangues, desperate generals emphasized that if cornered with no supplies or ammunition, the troops would have to fight 'even with rocks and would be forced to eat even their own comrades killed in combat and the flesh of the enemy'. Sweet meat for tough times?

Cannibalism is one of the most physically repugnant acts we can imagine. The Uruguayan rugby players stranded in the Andes when their plane crashed only ate their team-mates because the strong-minded medical student among them said that if they did not consume their late friends, their bodies would consume themselves, as their starved hearts – desperately seeking energy – would start to feed on their own cardiac muscle. The survivors found that slicing up chunks of human flesh into slivers made it easier for them to forget where the meat came from. Roasting it slightly on a fire improved the flavour greatly; it tasted like beef but was softer to chew. Over the weeks they were stuck up in the mountains, their cravings for new tastes and textures led them to try marrow, livers, brains, blood clots, small intestines, and even putrid lungs. None, however, touched the genitals, and when one tried to eat a tongue it stuck in his gullet. They discovered that rotten flesh tastes like cheese. Rationing themselves to a small handful of meat per person per day, they ended meals with a spot of toothpaste each, as a pudding. Once back at home after seventy-two days away, these men – who had committed the unthinkable and turned one of our most taboo acts into a virtual way of life – had to start to live with the memory of what they had done.

The Uruguayans were not alone in finding human meat difficult to stomach. While many travel-writers have claimed that some man-eaters have a gourmet relish for the taste, not all cannibals like what their customs enjoin them to do. Gillian Gillison, the anthropologist who lived with the Gimi, has argued that they did not object too strongly to the colonial authorities' prohibition of cannibalism because of the Gimi's 'ever present and deeply felt ambivalence toward the practice'. Members of the Bimin-Kuskusmin told their resident anthropologist, Fitz John Porter Poole, of their horror and disgust at their own acts. Many stated that they had been unable to bring themselves to eat human meat, had thrown it up, fainted, or secretly hidden the piece they were handed. In the eleven acts of funerary cannibalism Poole witnessed, he often observed the extreme reticence and ambivalence of participants about what they were doing.

The descendants of man-eaters are understandably very touchy about the practice. The Christianized people of Vanuatu, generally proud of their distinctive traditions, have learnt to regard the cannibalistic practices of their forefathers with great shame. The man who gave me the recipe which heads this chapter was careful to emphasize that though his late father had eaten some of his enemies, he had never touched the stuff and would never think of doing so.

If cannibalism is seen as a cultural extreme, as an outrageous breaking of Western moral codes, then it becomes easy material for jokes. It is used as a further means of scoring the racial divide. Laughing at Blacks' gastronomic immorality bolsters a White sense of racial integrity. My personal favourite of the genre (because it is one which reflects back on ourselves) is the South Sea Islander's reply to Randolph Churchill's almost inevitable question. No, he answered, he had never eaten a white man, only an American.

Since cannibalism epitomized a European conception of diabolically different peoples as yet untouched by Western ways, then that image seems outmoded now in our world of development programmes and international aid. Except for very few isolated pockets, ritual man-eating has been effectively eliminated from our planet. Today the sons and grandchildren of former cannibals receive Western education and run their own countries, without the overt interference of colonial authorities. They no longer have any need for man-eating rituals. To us, anecdotes about anthropophagy appear *passé*, as the cultural difference between the First and the Third World is no longer seen in such extreme terms. Jokes about cannibalism have a dated ring about them and seem of a piece with the sepia photographs taken by travellers in past decades. In the 1950s, a Western producer could still make a film which climaxed in Spanish peasants eating the American protagonist. But these days such an ending would be laughable to audiences and the latest film to put cannibalism on the big screen, *Eating Raoul*, was seen by critics as a fine example of low camp.

Today anthropophagy has become a source of black humour for those Westerners who wish to snigger at their own cultural past. It is a way for us to snort at the ignorance and racist prejudice of our imperialist forefathers. (The implicit assumption is that we are not like that any more; we know better.) The cannibal tales of

Biggles and his like-minded contemporaries in real life are now just material for jokes. Popular magazines no longer include cartoons of topeed adventurers sweating it out in a bubbling pot. And if they do include them, the laugh is on the old-fashioned Whites, not the Blacks.

The study of cannibalism informs us as much about the acts and attitudes of ourselves as it does about those of other peoples. And what it reveals is not flattering:

> We walked for about three hours without seeing any signs of a village. Then we heard, faint in the distance, the sound of a tom-tom. Soon we were within hearing of a chanted song. We advanced with caution, until we reached the edge of a village clearing. From behind a clump of bushes we could watch the natives who danced there. The dance was just the ordinary native hay-foot, straw-foot around the devil-devils in the center of the clearing, now slow, now gradually increasing in tempo until it was a run.
>
> What interested me was the feast that was in preparation. On a long stick, over the fire, were a dozen pieces of meat. More meat was grilling on the embers of another fire. On leaves nearby were the entrails of the animal that was cooking. I do not know what it was that made me suspect the nature of this meat. It was certainly not much different in appearance from pork. But some sixth sense whispered to me that it was not pork.
>
> The savages had no suspicion of our nearness. . . .

(After an hour of waiting, a porter is ordered to throw a radium flare into the fire.)

> As they stooped down close to the flame to see what had been thrown there, the flare took fire and sent its blinding white light into their faces. With a yell they sprang back and ran in terror directly towards us. When they saw us, they stopped so quickly that they almost tumbled backward. Then they turned and ran in the opposite direction. The half-minute flare had burned out; so they grabbed the meat from the fire and carried it with them into the bush.
>
> My boys sprang into the clearing. I, with my camera on my shoulder, was just behind them. When I came up to them, they were standing by the fire, looking at the only remnant of the feast that was left on the embers. It was a charred human head, with rolled leaves plugging the eye-sockets.

I had proved what I set out to prove – that cannibalism is still practised in the South Seas.

Martin Johnson, 1922

This Yankee adventurer had fulfilled his journalistic mission. Capturing the natives with his camera and colonial metaphors, he had shown that long-pig remained on the menu in the villages of the Melanesian archipelago of Vanuatu. He could now report back to his readers, satisfying their fascination for that most degraded of savage customs executed by primitive peoples, 'a custom which at once inspires horror in the civilized mind' – cannibalism.

21

UNMENTIONABLE CUISINE

'Outrage over Queen's guest. LOCK UP YOUR CORGIS MA'AM' ran the
Daily Star headline on 20 November 1989. In pithy prose and one-sentence
paragraphs, 'the paper that gives it to you straight' warned its unsuspecting
readers that Her Majesty was about to give lunch to the president of a dog-
eating nation, South Korea. Revelling in its scoop, the popular tabloid
revealed that Koreans bludgeoned two million cats and dogs to death every
year, purely for the sake of tickling their taste-buds. Members of this
unfeeling nation caged labradors, hanged puppies, and scorched their
carcasses with blowtorches before cooking them. Such barbarity could not
go unchallenged. Luckily, the International Fund for Animal Welfare had
already planned a 'pooch picket' to be held outside the gates of Buckingham
Palace; animal-lovers were to march on Downing Street bearing a pets'
petition; Paul McCartney, Brooke Shields, and other stars had pledged their
support. President Roh Tae-Woo, they hoped, was to be given a lunchtime
he would not forget.

England is notorious as a paradise for pets ruled by animal-lovers.
Dogs, who top the national list of beloved beasts, are elevated to
the status of pseudo-humans and treated as honorary members of
a family. (Just look at the homes corgis are invited into.) Unlike
ordinary animals, the pampered pooches of Britain are given
personal names and a host of special privileges. They are kissed,
caressed, patted, stroked, fondled, tickled, scratched under the
ear, and, after having cleaned themselves thoroughly, are even
allowed to lick the face of their owners. The English adorn their
cosseted creatures with rings, ribbons, bows, bells, and winter
coats; they pander to their eating preferences; they wash, sham-
poo, perm, comb, and delouse them; they inoculate them against
disease and care for them when ill; they even let them sleep with
them. When the animals finally pass away, their owners bury
them in pet cemeteries and put portraits of their late beloved up
on the wall; and should their doting masters, by mischance, die
before their pets then they leave them money in their wills.

Granted the freedom of most cities, these adored (for once the adjective is not hyperbolic) mutts are allowed to wander the streets at will, and – a privilege denied to humans – can foul public places as and when they please without fear of being charged. Dogs can walk about with their heads high; the Brits have to keep theirs down to prevent themselves from treading in the stuff. Even a sacred cow in India would be envious of a British dog, for the only services it is ever made to provide are barking at intruders, herding sheep, chasing foxes, sniffing out drugs, or collecting game for men who like to shoot fat birds dead.

'Love me, love my dog,' intone the British, as newly-wed males are forced to learn when they realize the matrimonial bed is to be shared with the wife's cocker spaniel. In this sort of triangular relationship the bottom line seems to be, 'If you cannot accept my bestial best buddy, then I won't accept you.' These ever-faithful, four-legged friends act as surrogate siblings for only children and provide companionship for lonely adults (and lower their blood pressure in the process). For the more sensually inclined (or starved), lap dogs warm the thighs and heat up the groin, while social inadequates bolster their sagging egos by making their mastiffs props for their personalities – it is not Rottweilers we have to worry about, but their owners. Some might say we do not cook dogs because they are carnivorous and eat filth, but the fundamental reason is that we have raised them to the rank of honorary humans. Dishing up the house pet at dinner would be like feasting on your sister. We are not cannibals: we do not eat Rover.

Farmers may come to love their animals and give them individual names. But, unlike dogs, they are not allowed into the house and are deliberately reared for the pot. Some Spanish villagers, who personally raise a pig every year, resolve this dilemma by eating sausages made from the animal but refusing to touch its chops. Chewing the ribs of an old acquaintance is too much for them, while a cooked tube of minced pork in a plate of haricot beans seems a long way from the animal they once cared for.

Lavish concern for one's pets is a peculiarly Anglo-American attitude. People in other countries would be shocked at the extravagance and wastefulness of transatlantic cuisine, for more than 13 million dogs and cats are destroyed every year in US city pounds and shelters. Putting that another way, at least 6 million kilos of potentially edible meat is garbaged annually in the United

States alone. If we stopped restricting our meat menu to expensive cuts of beef, lamb, pork, and veal and started including dogmeat in our diet, then food aid to the malnourished could rise dramatically. In America, for every 1 per cent increase in national beef production, the amount of food sent to the Third World decreases by 10 per cent. In other words, since it takes 10 kilos of marketable grain to produce one kilo of beef, wouldn't it be better to eat less beef, more dog and send the surplus grain to the needy? We might not wish to gorge on Trigger, but should we exclude the possibility of cooking any stray mutt? Just because a family makes one particular pet special does not mean we have to spare the whole species.

A CHINESE GOURMET'S DINNER

First Course
Shredded and stir-fried fillet of dog, with shredded bamboo shoots and black mushrooms, garnished with finely shredded lime leaves.

Second Course
Double-boiled soup of the bones and meat scraps, plus the penis and testicles, if it is not a bitch.

Third Course
Braised paw and muzzle, with sliced ginger in a brown sauce.

Fourth Course
Steamed ribs, cut in thick slices, sandwiched with slices of ham and black mushrooms, served hot in their own juices.

Such statistics and arguments do not trouble most pet-owners. They are so fixed in their own convictions that the dog-eating habits of other countries are not seen as evidence of Anglo-American cultural blinkers, but as excellent grounds for differentiating themselves from foreigners. 'We wouldn't do that,' runs the logic of the dog-loving nations. The apocryphal story of the

English diners who asked the waiter in a Hong Kong restaurant to feed their poodle, only to have it served up an hour later, is still bandied about as though it were true, as though it were yet another example of just how damned perverse those inscrutable Orientals can be. The same strategy is used in America: when a sizeable number of Vietnamese refugees were settled into a small Kentucky city, rumours were soon spread that cats and dogs were disappearing from around town. It doesn't matter whether any of these yarns are true or not, so long as there are still sufficient people who believe in them and are happy to pass them on. The aim of such tales, besides their value as entertainment, is to justify our continued distance from Chinese, Vietnamese, and others. Such people could never be our friends. If they do not know how to treat their pet hounds, they wouldn't know how to treat us. You could never dine at their houses, because you couldn't be sure about what exactly you were being served.

'A dog's dinner' may be a right mess in Britain, but a dog for dinner is something of a delicacy in many countries. Filipinos barbecue them, American Plains Indians boil them, Europeans living in the Alps smoke their hams, Cameroonians bake them wrapped in banana leaves, and Spanish villagers who have taken you into their confidence will admit they have heard dog is very good cooked in a stew with just a small chilli added. In Nigeria, those who like to get their canines into a bit of hot dog rename the edible object of their desire a '404 station wagon', because of its supposed resemblance to the French Peugeot. The head is a 'gearbox' or 'loudspeaker', the tail a 'telephone', the legs '404 wheels', etc. The water in which the dog is cooked is dubbed 'penicillin' because of its claimed medicinal qualities. Until American colonialists imposed their particular ideas about cuisine, Hawaiians used to raise and force-feed their own mutts. Vegetable-fed dogflesh was greatly appreciated, but the tastiest of all was said to be puppy suckled by a woman. The Chinese, of course, are well-known as breeders of black-tongued chow for the table. According to the food-writer Paul Levy, who knowingly ordered 'fragrant meat' (as it is called) at a Macau restaurant, the young flesh he ate looked like pork, 'was chewy, and had a very strong, though not disagreeable, flavour, like mutton, venison, or goat'. Calvin Schwabe, the world expert of tabooed meats, says its taste is similar to that of lamb or mutton.

DOG A LA BETI
(As Made by the Ewondo of Cameroon)

Ingredients: one dog, salt, small-leaved basil, skin of a garlic plant, pepper, 'Odjom', citronella, onions, sweet bananas ('Odzoe beti' variety), banana leaves.

Only castrated male dogs are eaten. The dog is tied to a post for a day and hit with small sticks, to 'shift' the fat in the adipose tissue. After killing, it is cut up into chunks. The skin is scorched over a fire and then scraped with a knife. The bowels are emptied, cleaned, and rolled up. The pieces of meat are washed and scraped several times, until there is no trace of blood or dirt left in the water. The stiff main veins of the banana leaves are skinned, and then softened over a fire. The leaves are placed in a criss-cross fashion in a big pan. The pieces of meat are mixed with all the condiments in a separate pan.

This seasoned meat and some sweet bananas of the 'Odzoe beti' variety are placed on the prepared leaves. The leaves are tied together with banana fibre to make a packet. This packet is braised in a pot whose base has been covered with banana leaves. Water is added only up to the mid-point so that it cannot penetrate the packet during the cooking.

Cooking the packet takes eight to nine hours. Once done, the food is served immediately. It is a noble dish reserved for the elders of the village.

The sweet bananas absorb the fat exuded by the chunks of meat in the course of its cooking. Bananas so prepared are considered succulent.

(The other nine recipes for dogmeat in J. Grimaldi and A. Bikia's *Le Grand Livre de la Cuisine Camerounaise* involve very similar cooking procedures, but different assortments of spices and condiments. Under the entry for 'Cat', the authors are terse: 'Cat is prepared just like dog.')

Warning: some dogs have trichinosis. Before eating they should be cooked thoroughly. Wear rubber gloves when handling the guts.

None of this cross-cultural data would interest a British dog-lover, proud of his bulldog breeding. It would not amuse him; it

would give him apoplexy. Barristers would claim self-righteous
rage as a mitigating circumstance for his murderous designs on
anyone who thought of stir-frying their Towser. He would not be
responsible for knifing the dog-eater; he had, after all, been grossly
provoked. When an Illinois columnist suggested (with Swiftian
irony) that substituting dogflesh for other meats in the American
diet might indirectly alleviate the Ethiopian food crisis, he received a flood of angry letters and phone calls from across the
country. At the British food conference where he later discussed
the affair, an American attacked his 'sad and decadent' idea that
'starving Africans should go to the dogs'. It was rumoured the
critic had pursued her prey to the conference, so that his views
would not go unquestioned nor Britons get the wrong idea about
Americans.

CAT IN SAUCE
(Navarre, Spain)

Skin and gut the cat, wash it well. Cut into pieces and place
them in a pot together with two finely chopped cloves of
garlic, some sprigs of thyme, and a cup of vinegar. Leave to
marinate overnight.

Next day, add a kilo of chopped tomato, a tablespoon of
ground red pepper, two apples split in half, half a chopped
onion, and a cup of oil. Bring to the boil, then lower the
heat, and simmer until the meat is tender. Strain the liquid
and then return to the pot. Bring it to the boil for a short
period, then serve.

English promoters of horse steaks would not fare much better
in blinkered Britain than American advocates of real hot dogs
have done in their country. Yet the arguments in favour of eating
our way through a stables are as strong, if not stronger, than those
for letting a food company empty the dog pound in one go. For
horsemeat is good, with a flavour between that of beef and
venison, and a slightly sweetish aftertaste that is esteemed by
some connoisseurs. Unlike most beef, this meat is lean, tender,
and does not toughen with age. Unlike dogs, horses have no
unsavoury habits like eating their peers' droppings. Since they are

not fed the mashed up bits of other animals, there is no fear of BSE. Horse must also be the only form of flesh in England today not pumped full of 'feed supplements' that read like the ingredients for a chemical time-bomb, although it is perhaps best to keep your hunger at bay when offered a plateful of racing thoroughbred. Gourmets, however, appreciate the rump from a horse used for riding more than the same cut of meat from a beast of draught. Horses for courses?

The Anglo-American taboo against eating horse is not a geographically specific example of a more general phenomenon but a cultural peculiarity when compared to the gastronomic customs of many of the world's peoples. In areas where there is sufficient forage horses are not a luxury animal and their meat is properly appreciated. In Mongolia and other parts of Central Asia, for instance, horse is the most popular form of flesh and mare's milk is highly prized. The Chinese and Japanese eat it, as do the Belgians, Dutch, Germans, Italians, Poles, Icelanders, Russians, and, of course, the French. In Sweden more horsemeat is sold than lamb and mutton put together. And, until recently, 'kicker', as it was locally known, was an established part of Yorkshire fare.

While horsemeat is good, the flesh of donkeys (especially donkey foals) is said to be even more flavourful. But at least one British aristocrat was not so sure. When Paris was besieged in the Franco-Prussian War, the well-heeled kept up their protein intake by eating a zebra, a yak, two buffaloes, two wapiti (a large North American deer), two camels, and two elephants from the city zoo. Though Lady Dorothy Neville joined her hosts in their feasts, she later confessed, 'Well, I rather enjoyed the donkey although it was a little dry, but I never partook of it further, it made me stink.'

Though the French are usually regarded as more sophisticated than the rough and ready English, insular Britons like to point out their neighbours' lack of true refinement by muttering darkly about their predilection for horsemeat. In fact, in France, horse ranks low on the gastronomic snob scale, is eaten mainly by the urban working class, and is now on the decline as its price has risen relative to that of other meats. Frenchmen have not forgotten the origins of the horse-eating habit in the philanthropic campaigns of the last century to improve the diet of the poor. According to recent statistics, the French eat over 15 kilos of beef, and less than 1.2 kilos of horse, per capita every year.

Horses are to be loved, not digested, no matter how good Parisian workers may say they taste. Adolescent girls who spend pleasure-filled days with a hunky male between their thighs do not want to see him end his days on a plate. When British Guardsmen learnt that their aged, but trusted, steeds were being shipped across the Channel, they offered to buy the animals to save them from such an unseemly fate. But even old gee-gees snatched from the clutches of the horse-butchers and allowed to die a natural death are still carted to the knackers' yard and made into meat for dogs. (When was the last time you saw a horse cemetery?) So the unadmitted truth of the case appears to be that Britons are not against their favourite mounts being eaten. Rather, they are prepared to see their aging mates end up as food for the dogbowl, not the table. Or, perhaps more accurately, they just do not want to know what happens.

Recent historical evidence suggests, however, that this aversion to eating horse is not as unshakeable as it may seem. In the Second World War, a horseflesh shop did good business in the smart London borough of Chelsea; locals quickly learnt to make horse-liver pâtés and jellied tongues. In the United States during the oil crisis of 1973, the price of beef rose so much that prime horse steaks suddenly became a cheap, nutritious option. Stocks of the meat sold as fast as the public could buy them. But the crisis ended, horsemeat became more expensive, and Americans returned to their usual diet. Seven years later, a meat-packing company introduced a willing public to economical 'horseburgers' and 'Belmont Steaks'. This experiment, initially very successful, only failed because of pressure from bodies such as the American Horse Protection Association on the powerful beef lobby. The message, however, is clear: when the price is right, inhibitions about eating mares and stallions are put aside, even in the land of rodeo and the cowboy.

So long as the nuclear family continues to split into sub-atomic groupettes of ageing singles, lonely widow(er)s, childless couples, or one-parent or one-child families, there will remain a need for household pets as animal-life-long companions. And while that need remains, urban Westerners will most probably persist with their strict taboo on carving up cats and dogs. What, for instance, would Her Majesty the Queen think if 'Corgi' were not the name of a toy car manufacturer, but a famed speciality of the Ritz?

Unlike the near absolute prohibition on preparing Puss or Pooch for the pot, the aversion to chomping on horsesteak is mainly kept in force by lack of opportunity: if butchers put the meat on sale at a low price, there would be takers for sure. But protests would also be mounted (on horseback?), mainly by those with incomes that allow them to survive on beef. If such a gastronomic change is unlikely in the immediate future, we can at least content ourselves by chanting that old bit of horse-sensed doggerel,

> A four legged friend, a four legged friend,
> He'll never let you down.
> Tender and tasty right up to the end,
> A one, two, three, four legged friend.

22

GOBBLE, GULP AND GO

Saudi pupils in private British schools spend their art classes painting the stuff. The black bourgeoisie of some African cities eat it with knives and forks. Yap Islanders, in the North Pacific, watch commercials for it on American-donated televisions, though they are hundreds of miles away from the nearest outlet. The rural economy of countries like Costa Rica has been turned upside down for the sake of its production and export to the United States. Modern artists have acknowledged its place as a key icon of modern life by making sculptures of it. With billions sold annually, it is now the most popular way of eating beef in the USA. The once humble hamburger, the epitome of fast foods, has become such a fitting symbol of contemporary American culture that it is almost a cliché. And the archetypal temple of its consumption is found behind the golden arches of any McDonald's sign.

McDonald's did not invent fast food. It simply realized its sales potential and skilfully exploited it to the full, and to great profit. Now the fourth largest retailer in the USA, 96 per cent of American consumers eat at McDonald's in any one year, and more than half of the country's population live within three minutes' drive of one of its 9,300 restaurants. Its 20 per cent share of the fast-food market is more than that of the next three chains combined, and, as the largest buyer of beef in North America, it sells more than 600,000,000 pounds of hamburger meat in its restaurants every year. It also has one of the largest advertising budgets in the nation, while Ronald McDonald vies with Santa Claus and Mickey Mouse as American children's most familiar fantasy character.

In the process of becoming the nation's greatest cooked food retailer, McDonald's has also turned itself into one of the greatest employers. It now has a staff larger than the entire American steel industry, with over half a million people on the payroll at any one time. Seven per cent of the whole US workforce got their first job behind the golden arches. Since turnover of staff is so high, it has been estimated that by the year 2000 over half of its customers will be former employees. At that rate, it seems McDonald's is influencing not just the eating habits of the country, but the work habits as well.

Of course, a McDonald's outlet is not a 'restaurant', but a smoothly functioning assembly line manufacturing a uniform and reliable product. There are no chefs, not even short order ones, and no real cooking. It is what businessmen call 'a food management system'. And this standardization is the key to McDonald's success. Everything is rationalized: the product, the service, the cooking, the seating arrangements, the location of the outlets, and the technological hard- and software are all designed or planned according to the golden principle that there is only 'one best way'. Just in case any budding McDonald's managers have ideas of their own, they are ironed out in courses taught at the chain's Chicago seminary, Hamburger University, which awards its own degrees: Bachelor or Master of Hamburgerology.

What this means is that on entering a McDonald's you will always encounter the same product, the same setting, every time. The layout never differs; each suburban restaurant has its identical arches, brown brick, plate-glass windows, and mansard roof. Every detail has been carefully thought out: the size of the counters, the number of tills, the space between each one, the standing room round the tills, the distances between tills and tables, the size of the tables, and the number of chairs and their position. This ensures the maximum use of production space, sufficient room to queue, and the right standing-to-sitting ratio. So that people do not linger in fast-food outlets, the hard, immovable chairs are deliberately designed not to provide prolonged comfort. That way, the clientele get fast food and the management get a fast turnover.

The staff are always young (though by law McDonald's cannot discriminate against age, only the youthful can stand the pace of work). Their dress is as uniform as the outlet's architecture. Employees have to wear McDonald's hats, ties, and shirts, together with dark trousers and shiny black shoes. The way they do their job, store and unpack the materials, as well as cook, wrap, and present the products are all tasks carefully prescribed down to the smallest detail in the staff manual. They are not caterers but 'attendants'. Instead of preparing food, they operate machinery, according to the designers' instructions. Even what they can say is standardized. If you ask for a 'Big Mac' in the United States, the trained response

FAST-FOOD FACTS
The Nutritional Low-Down

Many of the products sold by McDonald's, Burger King, and other chains are among the most highly processed foods available. They tend to be low in nutrients, high in calories, and high in fat as well. A Big Mac is 550 calories, of which 45 per cent is fat, and over one-third of the fat is saturated. When in 1987 McDonald's ran a series of advertisements in the United States showing, for example, a bottle of milk, a potato, and some fresh minced beef with the slogan 'What we are all about', the Attorney-General for Texas threatened to bring a case against the company. As he said, 'Fast-food customers often choose to go to McDonald's because it is inexpensive and convenient. They should not be fooled into eating there because you have told them it is is also nutritious.' McDonald's stopped the series.

Fast-food chains tend not to say a lot about how their products are made or what goes into them. Their recipes are prized trade secrets. But if you made a beefburger according to the following rules, you would not be far wrong:

> Flake or grind 30 grams of beef shin (including gristle, sinew, and some fat). Mix this with 16 grams of beef mince, which includes heart, tongue, and more fat. To this add 19 grams of rusk and soya flour, as well as 16 grams of pre-chopped beef fat. Blend with 20 grams of water, 2 grams of salt and spices, 1 gram of monosodium glutamate, and half a gram of polyphosphates and preservative. Stir in 10 grams of 'Mechanically Recovered Meat'. (To make MRM, strip every bit of useful tissue from the remains of the carcass, and then grind the bits into a fine slurry.) Cook.

To be fair, McDonald's *are* trying. Their American outlets now sell low-fat milk-shakes, salads, frozen yoghurt, and fat-free sorbets, as well as the ubiquitous burger. In the United States at least, it seems that market pressure is forcing change behind the golden arches.

is, 'Will that be with fries, Sir?' As you pick up what you ordered, the next comments on their Pavlovian programme come out: 'Have a nice day, Sir,' and finally, 'Come in again.'

In this sort of homogenized environment, you know what you are going to get. There is nothing unpredictable: no nasty surprises, nothing to upset you, or to make you feel gauche and awkward. You know where you are, in a familiar setting that offers comfort, security, and reassurance. No need to worry about your table manners, or lack of them, as the vast majority of items on sale are easy-to-eat 'finger-foods'. Among the very few foods that require cutlery are some of the breakfast items, and at that hour of the day everyone is too bleary to notice, or care, how you hold your knife and fork. The drinks are well-known, soft and mostly sweet, so there is no need to be anxious about such etiquette as, for instance, choosing the right wine. And, as there is no table service, there are no waiters to put you down. You can relax. You are among your equals.

McDonald's food is as streamlined as the rest of its package, for the chain prides itself on both the cleanliness of its outlets and the consistent quality of its industrially-produced hamburgers. In fact, before McDonald's, there was no standard formula for the composition of a hamburger. When you choose something at one of their eateries, there are no 'weird' flavours or unexpected tastes to surprise you, nor are you going to bite into something odd that might crack your teeth. The food is neither tough nor overcooked, simply 'perfect every time'. It is basically infantile fare, the sort of stuff kids relish and undiscriminating parents put up with. A Big Mac – that edible commodity scientifically designed for the mass market – might taste bland and unexciting to some, but that, it appears, is what the majority wants. You pay for what you get. And remember, at McDonald's you do not have to pay very much.

People do not go to these outlets for a gastronomic experience. They go there to have a quick bite and to get away from their home/their office/the street. They are not gourmets with individual tastes and the time to linger over courses, but utilitarians with a no-nonsense approach to their mealtimes. Though certain commentators regard a Big Mac as 'the taste of democracy', others see it as more an example of the Lowest Common Denominator than of the Highest Common Factor. When a visiting British sociologist asked some of his American colleagues why they ate at a nearby McDonald's, they appeared embarrassed by the question and tried to justify their lunchtime choice in terms of convenience and speed. They were vaguely apologetic, as though they did not want to be associated with its unpretentious, low-budget style. Others plainly feel the same way. When the chain tried to open outlets on Madison Avenue and in Hampstead, London, residents

---

MEALS BETWEEN WHEELS
(The Fastest Food on Earth)

If you are going on a long journey and you do not like roadside fare, do not forget that you have a stove up front of the steering-wheel.

Car-engine cooking is for those galloping gourmets who cannot stomach McDonald's and cannot do without their favourite dishes, done to a T, on a V6. Treble-wrap the ingredients in aluminium foil, wedge it in the right spot, and off you go!

M40 Tuna Wiggle

1 bag frozen green peas
1 can light tuna in oil, drained and flaked

At home or on the road, thaw peas enough so they can be separated. In a mixing bowl, or clean hubcap, mix the peas and tuna. Dump the glop on a sheet of foil. Fold into a neat package with no protruding flaps. Repeat twice so food is securely wrapped in three layers of foil. Place in a secure position on the engine, such as the fuel injector housing. Since the 'wiggle' makes a relatively soft package, you can also wedge it into a gap between two warm parts of the motor.

Drive approximately 55 to 1,000 miles. If you are leaving London, get to Oxford and find it is still underdone, then keep on going till Birmingham.

Warning

Do not place, check, or remove food with the engine running. *Come back with the same number of fingers you started with.*

in both cases successfully argued that they would attract the 'wrong sort of person' into the neighbourhood. It seems the McDonald's version of democracy is not for everyone.

McDonald's is not, on the whole, in the business of selling food as food but as 'an edible part of the entertainment industry'. Since its products are so simple and so predictable, it has to present a visit to one of its outlets not as a gastronomic event, but as an 'experience'. As one fast-food ad candidly put it, 'We'll help you make a meal of it.' The 'McDonald's experience' is targeted primarily at families, especially children. Their outlets, according to their inhouse slogan, are meant to be all about 'food, folks, and fun'. Their advertisers, working hard to glamorize the standardized consumption of a mass-market product, try to put across the message that eating at McDonald's is informal and pleasurable. The atmosphere is presented as emotionally warm, almost playful, and determinedly casual. Something special is meant to happen when parents and children visit a McDonald's: the usual arguments, as well as the usual hierarchy, are set aside. (They are, after all, eating in a very public place and do not wish to be observed squabbling.) Unlike a meal at home, where children might complain about what they are given, at a McDonald's each member of a family can choose what he or she wishes to eat. Moreover, Father cannot play authority figure as convincingly as usual: since there are no place-settings, he cannot position himself at the head of the table. Instead of being authoritative and burdened with responsibility, Mum and Dad are meant to relax, secure in the knowledge that their kids can enjoy themselves in a safe environment. It is a carefree home away from home.

By offering the same style and the same foods, at pretty much the same prices, almost wherever you go, or whenever you go there, McDonald's erase the differences between 'this place' and 'that', and between 'now' and 'then'. The irregularities of space and time are smoothed out under the market pressure of a remunerative uniformity. The only concessions to foreign tastes are the sale of wine in their French outlets and beer in their German ones. To many Americans, the predictability of the McDonald's ambience is so reassuring that when abroad they prefer to eat there rather than risk the local restaurants. And this applies even when they visit countries with famed cuisines, such as France.

When entering a new country, there is often no need for McDonald's and its competitors to spend a lot of money glamorizing their products, as they are already perceived as glamorous. For foreigners who regard the United States as an exemplar, a Big Mac embodies the trumpeted ideals of the country it comes from – in other words the American Dream of power, freedom, efficiency, and ease. When a fast-food chain opened its first outlet in Japan, demand was so heavy and so sustained that the cash registers burnt themselves out. And when in 1987 McDonald's opened its first outlet in the Soviet Union, after twelve years of negotiations, the world's press lined up in banked rows to record the popular event. One of the first satisfied customers told reporters, while licking his fingers, 'It's like the coming of civilization.'

Directors of McDonald's have found that, when starting up in a new market, it is easier – and more profitable – to change people's eating habits than to adapt to them. So, as the fast-food chain spreads its corporate net further and further around the globe, the hamburger comes to symbolize not just American culture, but American cultural imperialism as well. In the Ecuadorian capital of Quito, for instance, middle-class parents despair as their fashion-conscious children reject local dishes and demand hamburgers. The more politically conscious try to combat this gastronomic form of Americanization by boycotting fast-food outlets. Instead of lusting after imported recipes they stick to a diet of shrimp ceviche, meat or fish stews, lentil soups, fried potatoes, marinated onions, rice, and hot pepper sauce. In Ecuador and other countries, Big Macs are not to be found on the menus of the ideologically sound.

But there is hope. For the inhabitants of one small Caribbean island have seen McDonald's open in their capital and then – remarkably – close. While murky politics played a role in this failure, a major cause of the closure was that beefburgers are simply not for the Barbadians, whose healthy local diet has helped produce three Mr World bodybuilders and a long string of outstanding cricketers. As their leading nutritionist said, 'There was always the worry about the multinationals, comin' in with a big fanfare and then shortchangin' us. . . . We Barbadians ain't hamburger eaters. We doan like that fatty stuff.'

23

THE WHOLE TRUTH?
NATURALLY!

In the 1960s and 1970s people worried about sex. Were they getting enough of it? Were they doing it right? Were they doing it with the right person? These lusty concerns, however, were relatively short-lived as the appearance of herpes and then of AIDS quickly pushed them into the background. These days, people worry less about their sex lives than about their health. Once-bestselling love manuals now fill remainder shelves, and many sex shops, in London at least, have closed down. In this decade, ambitious authors have to become instant experts in nutrition if they want to make the big time, while an astute shopkeeper does not stock naughty nighties, but royal jelly and organic vegetables.

Though people are just as narcissistically concerned about themselves as ever, the focus of their anxiety has shifted from the genitalia to the body itself. As Rosalind Coward has argued, instead of fretting about how to make love properly, they have become obsessed with keeping to the right kind of diet. By following the dictates of tomes like *Live to One Hundred*, people can postpone death and avoid the degenerative diseases associated with that now obscene stage in life, old age. This is not a pact with the devil but an agreement with your body. Some believe in megavitamin therapy, others stick to a mucus-less diet, and yet others follow the dictates of colour therapy. 'Your Body, Your Temple,' the ads proclaim, and while the anxious are only too ready to worship at the shrine, they are keen to ensure they make the right food offering. Faddism has become fashionable, and food, not sex, is today's Public Worry Number One.

This switch would be all very commendable if it weren't that people's ideas about health foods and nature are often as vague, woolly, and mystically inclined as their earlier notions about sex. To the amateur nutritionists of the 1990s, 'nature' is not a violent, dangerous place where everybody and every animate thing has always to compete merely to stay alive. Stressing ecological interdependence over Darwinian struggle, they do not think of nature as 'red in tooth and claw' but as endlessly beneficial, its products wholesome and virtuous. Not surprising, then, that these starry-eyed traditionalists are hostile to technology, scientific development, and commercial exploitation. In their eyes these disruptive forces have fractured the harmony of nature, bringing disorder where once there was order. Modernity, in a word, corrupts.

When people today state that they prefer to eat healthy foods, what they are really saying is that all additives are bad and that any industrial process of refining or preserving edibles is highly suspicious, if not downright detrimental. As far as they are concerned, foods should be produced as 'naturally' as possible, with the minimum of human intervention. They know that only 2 per cent of additives are preservatives and that all the rest are only added to make the food appear to be something it isn't. Any sort of added chemical is taboo to them, and their list of prohibited ingredients is almost as long as the Vatican catalogue of banned books. Pesticides, insecticides, herbicides, flavourings, flavour modifiers, preservatives, antioxidants, emulsifiers, dyes, bleaches, colours, humectants, anti-caking agents, surfectants, stabilizers, sequestrants, milk-boosting hormones, moisteners, non-nutritive sweeteners, thickeners, thinners, propellants, release agents, buffers, bulking aids, and angel dust are only the most notorious of their invidious inventory. Best to have done with the lot and get back to basics – whatever 'basics' are.

GASTRONOMIC GUIDELINES FOR THE BUDDING NATURALIST

1. Do not eat anything you cannot pronounce. Propylene glycol alginate, for instance, is not a secret ingredient in motor oil but a stabilizer used in bottled salad dressing. But does that make it sound any better?

2. If you discover a bug in your food, cheer! Insects and other animals do not eat food that is plastic or doused in chemicals. If you bite into an apple and find half a worm, it *must* be organic.

While damning the modern, the more radical of New Age nutritionists extol the supposed virtues of the ancient, the archaic, the folkloric, the traditional, and the primitive. The seed of the Guarana berry, for instance, is marketed as 'Jungle Elixir': 'For centuries, the Brazilians have revered the bright red berries of the guarana as sacred fruit and have used them as food, folk medicine, and as a tonic. . . . It's the Life Force of the Amazon!'. The underlying assumption is that foods produced by technologically simple societies are good simply because the producers lived, or live, closer to nature. This attitude seems to be so wilfully ignorant of the facts that it is no exaggeration to say it borders on racism.

Many non-industrialized societies, both in the past and today, have highly sophisticated, subtle, and complex cultures. The Australian Aborigines, for example, previously thought to be one of the least evolved societies on earth, turn out to have kinship systems so intricate that anthropologists are still trying to understand how exactly they operate; the religious beliefs of the West African Dogon are so complicated they can be justifiably compared with those of the major world religions; the artistic objects produced by many African groups and by the people living along the northwest coast of America are far too subtle even to be considered as primitive; the terraced irrigation systems found throughout Southeast Asia are genuine marvels of engineering skill and social organization. Just because the cultures of these peoples have evolved in different ways from ours does not mean that they have not developed. Only Westerners who view the world through the narrowest of blinkers could regard the members of such societies as uncivilized, or even primitive. Rather than seeing themselves as 'closer to nature', people in traditional societies normally see nature as the archetype of disorder and they strive constantly to keep it in its place – beyond the village boundary.

Food scientists, like non-Western villagers and unlike modern-day romantics, do not see nature as soft, kind, and forever harmonious but as potentially dangerous, insufficiently predictable, and difficult to control. As far as they are concerned, pesticides and processing were invented for good reasons: to ensure harvests, increase their yields, and guarantee the hygiene of the food produced. As they point out, natural foods may not contain quite what the customer expects, for bacteria acting on edibles can produce deadly toxins, while food that has not been tinned or frozen is much more likely to decay. Anyhow, scientists can argue, preservatives have been used in food for over two thousand years: does not that make them (or some of them, at least) 'traditional', if not 'natural'? In this debate the choice is between the types of risk one is prepared to accept: between the technologists' fear of causing illness by unleashing nature, and the romantics' concern about doing the same by taming it. Most of us, wishing to avoid extremes and stay healthy at the same time, hedge our bets by trying to follow an unsteady middle course.

THE GUIDE TO GOOD NUTRITION
(To Be Updated Annually)

Protein
Good in moderation but too much makes you fat. Red meat is for vultures, so best to stick to fish (and do not overdo that either). If you must eat steaks and chops, do not barbecue them, grill them.

Carbohydrates
No longer thought to be fattening, but do not cover them in high-calorie/-fat sauces.

Fat
The killer. Forget croissants and only keep olive oil in the kitchen. It does not matter if you cannot tell the difference between margarine and butter: ignore them both.

Sodium
Is salt really so bad? Maybe not for you. Best to ask your doctor.

Sugar
Not for children or adults, but only for the infantile and suicidal. Give up soft drinks and take up wine (but not more than two glasses a day for women, or three a day for men).

Timing
Eat three times a day, at meals and not between them.

'Nature' is such an ambiguous word – the *Oxford English Dictionary* lists twenty-six different definitions of the term – that food manufacturers can easily exploit its intrinsic vagueness for their own, highly profitable ends, as what is 'natural' to them may not be 'natural' to you. They also play the same game with the word 'light' ('lite' in the USA). Light foods are usually those reduced in calories, but since the term has no legal definition, it may just mean that a food is low in sodium, alcohol, or caffeine, or simply that it has a light texture. 'Light' foods are seen as 'Clean, Green, and Lean', and are bought by people who want convenience, taste, and healthiness all in the same food. What most consumers do not realize is that 'light' foods can also be highly processed products loaded with artificial flavourings, colourings, stabilizers, and preservatives. By saving on calories you stock up on chemicals. Though buying 'light' products is meant to show your concern for health and nutrition, it also shows the size of your pocket, as these foods are almost invariably more expensive than the standard product. You pay more for less and are meant to feel virtuous, not gullible, in the process.

Advertisers make the most of public credulity, and so make a healthy profit for their clients. As G. W. Post, the founder of General Foods, said, 'You cannot just manufacture cereal. You've got to get it halfway down the customer's throat through advertising. Then they've got to swallow it.' Some tricks of the trade:

The Stretched Meaning

'Nature's way of moving your bowels' is the slogan of All-Bran, the British high-fibre breakfast cereal. But in nature it is very difficult to find a foodstuff as high in fibre as concentrated bran.

British cheese may be promoted as having 'natural colour', but is it 'natural' to dye Red Leicester with beetroot juice?

British milk is sold by the slogan, 'Full of natural goodness', but how natural is the stuff the Brits drink, given that it is pasteurized – a scientific process only invented late last century?

Ice-cream may be sold as being made of 'only natural ingredients'. But is it 'natural' to make a small amount of ice-cream seem larger by pumping it up with air?

The Sneaky Diversion

Milk shakes can be advertised as 'low fat' though they are also high in sugar.

Instant coffee is marketed as 'low sodium', though it has never had sodium in it. Vinegar is sometimes promoted as 'low fat' though the truth is vinegar has no fat.

Eggs can still be called 'natural eggs' even when they have been laid by battery hens in Black-Hole-of-Calcutta conditions. Ninety per cent of English people think 'country fresh' means free-range. They are wrong. To food producers, 'fresh' does not mean 'collected this morning' or 'pulled out of the ground five minutes ago' but 'not rotten' or 'this food was fresh when something was done to it to prevent it from deteriorating'.

The Floating Modifier

In X's Natural Chocolate-Flavoured Chocolate-Chip Cookies, the 'natural' modifies the 'chocolate flavour', not the 'cookie', which may contain as many chemicals as a school laboratory.

In Britain, Crosse and Blackwell claims its 'Healthy Balance' baked beans contain '25 per cent less added sugar and salt', without explaining what they are 'less' than.

The Selective Truth

A high-fat food can still be sold as 'low fat' when all the manufacturer has done is to remove a fraction of the fat.

In Britain, Farley's Low Sugar Rusks contain as much sugar as digestive and other sweet biscuits. Smaller print on the box explains that the rusks contain 'less sugar than Farley's original rusks'. Imagine how much they contain!

The Ambiguous Adjective

Just because something is marketed as 'special minced beef' does not mean that it is especially good. It may mean that it is especially high in fat, that it is especially low in quality, or that the graphic artist was feeling in an especially mischievous mood on the day he designed the label. The same rules apply for 'selected' or 'quality'.

The Misleading Negative

'Free from artificial preservatives' the package states. But that does not mean it is also free from artificial flavourings or colour. Chances are, it is full of them.

In Britain, one kind of commercially produced wholemeal loaf is marketed as 'Bread wi' nowt taken out'. Maybe nothing has been taken out, but the important question is, what has been added in?

Margarine manufacturers sell their product as having 'no cholesterol'. That is quite true, cholesterol has never been included in these lumps of hydrogenated, highly processed vegetable oils.

'No added sugar' may mean that a sweetener other than sugar has been added, and that additive may be as much a cause of concern as sugar.

The Best Defence
Be assertive, do not bother with defence. Anheuser-Busch's Natural Light Beer claimed to be natural, but it still contained numerous additives.

Nutrify It
The packet might say 'Now with added vitamins/fibre/minerals!' but it could still be loaded with sugar and a cocktail of chemicals. If a well-known brand of breakfast cereal were not sprayed with a chemical goo, it would be more nutritious to eat the packet than the cereal.

The name of this particular game is, 'Put back in what processing took out and charge extra for the service.'

The American public, according to one advertising analyst, has lost all trust in 'natural' as a label, while in 1988 British Trading Standards officers found that 79 per cent of cases of food products using 'natural', 'not artificial', and similar phrases were grossly misleading. They could regard only 9 per cent of product labels and 6 per cent of advertisements as probably legitimate. Since food manufacturers think putting 'natural' on their labels is sufficient excuse for a hike in prices, the only truly consistent meaning of 'natural' is 'value-added'. It's a rip-off, naturally.

Some people are not fooled. Large sections of lower-income groups are deeply sceptical about 'natural' or 'light' foods and they see the recent obsession with a proper diet as yet another example of the vanity and pomposity of the financially secure. Some know that many of the wealthier, and on the whole more educated, people who scorn red meat and white sugar for seaweed cakes and apple juice do so partly out of a sense of group allegiance. And that is one group the unpretentious poor do not wish to join. To many of them, well-marbled prime beef, refined white flour, and heavily sweetened puddings remain foods to be valued, not ones to be avoided. Some of the American poor perceive this dietary difference in ethnic terms. As one Hispanic told her researcher, 'Yeah, "eating right" sounds like "eating White".'

Others, especially young males, deliberately maintain a hamburger-and-fat habit as a way of sneering at danger. No muesli, tofu, or escarole salad for them. They are not wimps – just, perhaps, nutritionally suicidal. Others ignore the advice of nutritionists because they cannot believe that what is good for them can also taste good. They do not want to suffer their meals but to enjoy them, and they are not taken in by claims about 'natural' or 'light' food.

The disquieting truth is that maybe – just maybe – these sceptics are not completely misguided. As health professionals are forced to admit, the human body is a fabulously complex organism, and nutrition, despite all the work done in the last decades, is still an inexact science. There may now be an emerging consensus about what foods and cooking methods to avoid, but no one can yet be 100 per cent sure about the constituents of the perfect diet. Cholesterol, for instance, seems to have been almost conclusively identified as a major cause of heart disease. But two very recent studies, carried out in Wales and Boston (USA) have suggested quite the opposite. Further research, it is hoped, will determine whether these surprising results are due to the influence of extraneous factors. The immediate consequence, however, is that people are confused and unsure who to listen to. Since nutritional scientists often disagree over their findings, and since a number of them work for food manufacturers, the general public is left wondering which way to turn, while scare articles in the press ensure the level of anxiety is kept high. All they can do is cross their fingers and hope they are following the advice of the right 'expert'.

It is like a game of 'Believe It or Not', in which two players ('the nutritionists') manipulate a number of pawns ('the public') about the board. When the pawns are moved to a marked square, one of the cards from the 'Dietary Data-Base' is revealed. Typical examples:

1983: The Royal College of Physicians in London recommends halving the national intake of sugar. One expert claims a high white-sugar diet is directly related to gallstones, diabetes, heart disease, hernia, varicose veins, appendicitis, ulcers, diverticular disease, and cancers of the lower gut.

1986: The US Food and Drug Administration categorically state that the only danger of eating sugar is the possibility of tooth decay.

1975: A Californian study reveals that those who cut their salt intake by 30 per cent show a 6.5 per cent drop in blood pressure.

1986: The results of a World Health Organization survey state that though the Japanese consume a lot of salt, they have the lowest rate of heart disease in the world.

1986: The results of a Royal Society of Medicine survey state that salt might perhaps exert a small influence on blood pressure, but the effect is insignificant compared with being overweight or drinking too much.

There is a very large, ever growing number of these cards. The game has no clear winners and no obvious end. The aim is simply to keep on playing.

The days – only a decade or so ago – when people worried mainly about sex now seem positively innocent by comparison.

24

EATING THE OTHER

Ethnic eating-out is one of the great pleasures of modern urban life, a justified source of pride in the multiracial societies we now all inhabit. When Europeans cannot afford to visit other countries, they can at least sample their evocative cuisines by indulging in a good meal. Just like those cannibals who gobbled up others to strengthen their own identity as a group, Westerners who today dine on ethnic or regional meals are indirectly reminding themselves of what is their own 'national cuisine'. By eating the Other, they re-find the Self.

The irony underlying this sort of gastronomic tourism is that all too often the food purveyed as exotic and foreign is not as authentically 'other' as most consumers would like to imagine. Many dishes now popular in the United States and thought of as examples of foreign cuisines were in fact invented in America itself. Rather than representing the cooking of some other country, these foreign-sounding recipes are American concoctions that suit the tastes of the American market. Though chilli con carne has a Spanish name, Latin Americans are categorical that it has nothing to do with them. One Mexican dictionary even defines the dish as 'a detestable food with a false American title which is sold in the United States from Texas to New York'. (It appears the dish was invented in the Texan city of San Antonio in the 1870s.) Vichyssoise, though revered as a French dish, comes from the New York of the 1910s; curry cannot be found on any menu in India, bar tourist haunts; and *cioppino* might sound Italian but the word has no meaning in that language, while the dish itself, a seafood stew, was not thought up in Siena or Sicily, but San Francisco.

Chop suey may seem quintessentially Chinese but it was unknown in the People's Republic until restaurants there had to start catering for American tourists. It seems the dish comes from the days when Chinese labour was brought in to work on the building of the US railroads. To keep these hard workers happy, their employers got the railroad-gang cooks to make them food they would like. Though the cooks produced a dish which makes a nonsense of Chinese culinary principles, for it jumbles flavours rather than separating them, it still had enough savouriness and crunchiness to remind the labourers of home cooking, while the familiar ingredients of tomato and egg have made it acceptable to mainstream American tastes.

The food served in some ethnic restaurants can be just as 'inauthentic' as any of these dishes. For if immigrant restaurateurs want to draw Westerners into their establishments, they are often forced to adapt their recipes. It is hard to imagine a Chinese eatery that served items like 'chicken's blood porridge' and 'soyed pig's bowel' pulling in the crowds. Italian restaurateurs in London have to remember that Britons brought up on gravy and square loaves prefer thicker sauces with pasta dishes and do not like their pizzas with the traditionally very thin layer of dough. In the United States, mass-marketeers have had to omit dishes using unfamiliar spices, fermented foods, too much garlic, offal, or uncooked meat. The majority of Westerners only wish to flirt with the Other; they do not want the downright Unfamiliar.

Though the rise of tourism and travel overseas is often given as a major cause for the rise in popularity of ethnic restaurants, a more fundamental reason is their cheapness. At the lower end of the market, only ethnic restaurants can compete with the fast-food chains for value. For newly arrived immigrants without many skills to offer, opening up an eatery is often the easiest way to get on the first rung of the economic ladder. The financial success of these establishments normally relies on an astute entrepreneur managing a family-staffed business. Since he and his kin are prepared to work long hours for initially low wages, they are not obliged to charge high prices. And for members of certain social groups, especially students, a faintly exotic meal with friends in an Indonesian restaurant is greatly preferable to meeting up in a family-oriented fast-food joint like McDonald's.

Ethnic restaurateurs may have to alter their recipes to meet local demands, but they and their families are often far more resistant to modifying their own diet. Though immigrants are usually forced to change many of their traditional ways if they wish to be accepted by the nationals of their new home, food is frequently the site of the migrants' last stand. In many cases it is a cultural core the incomers try to maintain against the culinary temptations of the host cuisine. Vietnamese women in the United

States who do not have enough time to prepare elaborate ethnic meals tend to buy dishes at Vietnamese take-aways rather than make them badly, in a hurry, at home. Paradoxically, Greek-Americans in Philadelphia have actually broadened their traditional diet because local stores always have on sale foods only available in certain seasons or regions in Greece, while the more developed US kitchen technology enables them to make otherwise very time-consuming dishes. Similarly, Hungarian-Americans have turned once-festive foods into their staple fare. Thanks to their higher incomes, a beef or veal goulash is no longer something special, but an everyday dish.

Usually it is the first generation, especially the women in charge of family meals, who hang on hardest to their ethnic foodways. It tends to be their children who adapt first to the new foods, which they subversively bring back home. The upwardly mobile among migrants normally drop those traditional foods regarded as of low status by members of the host culture; they are not going to let taste obstruct their aspirations to class. The Illinois Germans, for instance, know their blood sausage is repugnant to most of their neighbours. They do not offer it to non-German guests if they want to underline their degree of assimilation. Sometimes, incomers continue using the distinctive sauces of their culture yet give up many of their ethnic foods because they are too expensive in their new homeland. Some compromise by restricting their traditional foods to one particular meal of the day (usually supper), or one meal of the week (usually Sunday lunch). Researchers studying Italian-American foodways found the format of their evening meals alternated: one day it was Italian (pasta with a tomato- and meat-based sauce), the next day American (meat, potatoes, and vegetables); on Fridays, like many traditional Catholics, they had fish. Even when an ethnic group's diet appears to have been completely Westernized, it may still contain traditional aspects, like the native Americans who rely on bought foods but continue to serve overlarge portions at mealtimes. Though their foods may have changed, the enormous amount customarily eaten at any one meal has not.

Given the recent reappraisal of ethnic, regional, and migrant cuisines, previously denigrated foods are now eaten and sold with pride by their traditional makers. Soul Food is no longer sneered at, Creole cooking is now chic, and in northern Michigan the

PIE IN THE SKY
A High-Flier's Guide to Airline Cuisine

Migrant chefs only have to worry about modifying their recipes to the taste of one culture – that of their host community. Your problem at 30,000 feet is serving food that will be acceptable, appetizing, and interesting to as many passengers as possible, no matter the countries they come from. The rules in economy class include:

Make the meat/fish and the vegetables familiar in taste and texture. So, no octopus or offal. Serve rice or potatoes rather than millet or maize.

Exclude all pronounced tastes. If you are going to dish up curries, make sure they are mild.

Make the mode of cooking as commonplace as possible. So, serve roast or casseroled meat rather than boiled.

Remember, appearance is everything. The food may provide some nourishment, but its main job is to titillate the bored and distract the anxious from worrying about their luggage/a bomb/the level of alcohol in the pilot's blood. So, make the food look pretty on the plate.

Make token gestures to the cuisine of your destination, ones which will not upset the other passengers. On planes bound for the Middle East, garnish the fruit salad with a mint leaf; on flights to Sweden use a bit of dill.

Give secular names to the foods associated with religious holidays. Rename simnel cake, normally served at Easter, and Christmas cake 'festival cake'.

In first class, serve French-based cuisine. Arrogantly assume it is so universally prestigious that the rich will not demand anything else.

Do not worry. You cannot always get it right. One Scandinavian airline trying to reassure its Islamic passengers on flights to the Middle East painted a picture of a pig with a black cross over it on the lid of their meal trays. Muslim passengers, however, did not interpret the sign as meaning 'No pork', and, suspicious of the meat's origin, chose to go hungry until their destination.

Cornish pasty – introduced by the tin-miners of the last century and developed by later Finnish immigrants – has become a symbol of the region's new self-respect. These hand-sized meat-and-vegetable pies are served to tourists in a deliberate attempt to advertise the quality of local life. And by buying them in great numbers, visitors validate locals' ideas about the worth of their own culture. Pasties have become pastries to be proud of.

Some food writers try to pigeonhole other cultures according to their own ghastly good taste. They think of cuisines as something static and hermetically sealed. But this jam-jar approach to foreign ways of cooking ignores the fact that the world turns and people with it. In today's world of mass transit and accelerating change, any sense of culinary purity has given way to one of gastronomic promiscuity while hard-to-answer questions about the supposed 'authenticity' of a dish seem increasingly irrelevant. Different peoples around the globe might retain characteristic foods, flavours, or modes of cooking, but, more than in any other time in world history, they also share much that is common. Anyone wishing to study cuisine in a contemporary South Pacific village would have to mention not only yams, taro, and wild honey but white rice, tinned fish, and hard tack as well. Hamburgers, processed cheese, and a variety of other products manufactured by the Western food industry are now bought by the locals of almost every nation on the planet, while in Europe and North America even the smallest grocer stocks a host of foreign foods, spices, and sauces. If the contemporary British middle classes, for instance, can be said to have an identifiable style of cooking, it is one that mixes traditional English dishes with recipes for Italian pasta, Indian curries, and Chinese sweet-and-sour. At times it begins to feel as though our persistent flirtation with the Other has led to a semi-permanent engagement.

Of course, some people thrive on this cultural jumbling. One establishment in suburban Cincinnati recently advertised itself as 'The Italian restaurant with the Spanish name hosted by the Jewish couple with the Greek partner featuring American steaks, French onion soup, Ecuadorian ceviche and Swiss fondue.' Dare you ask for couscous?

25

HOW TO WORSHIP FOOD

*In the bland, boring days BF (Before Foodie-ism) only an educated
minority trained their palates in the finer pleasures of gastronomy. Compared to the broad and cultivated tastes of this select band, the greedy
majority simply revelled in their favourite foods while revering French
cuisine – usually from afar – as the unsurpassable height of the culinary
arts. To most of them, 'gourmet' was a foreign word for a mildly eccentric
person one did not dare invite to dinner, and 'good food' meant tried-and-
trusted dishes with ingredients of high quality cooked according to a time-
honoured recipe. Such people did not bother with a shelf of cookbooks, as
their mothers had taught them almost all they needed to know. Anything
new or exotic they approached cautiously, sampled suspiciously, and then
left aside.*

Those days have gone. Epicures, once egregious, are now every-
where, while delicatessens have become as numerous as supermarkets. These days it is not just OK, but almost *de rigueur*, for
members of the aspiring middle classes to be foodies: to be
knowledgeable about food and to cultivate an aesthetic sensibility
towards it. Psychobabbling about your sexuality has become
démodé; instead foodies score conversational points by name-
dropping the best restaurants or by describing their latest visit to
one of the culinary paradises (France/Japan/China). Novel or
strange edibles are no longer scorned but prized, dinner-party fare
is judged according to its surprise value, and new types of ethnic
restaurants are opening in even the dullest suburb. Food, and
concern about it, has emerged as a new, crucial marker of social
grouping. The question is, why?

The general answer is affluence and its consequences. But the
particular form foodie-ism has taken varies slightly from country
to country. In the United States the burgeoning urban middle class
did not slavishly imitate the manners and tastes of their predecessors. Instead, buoyed up by affluence and prey to consumerism,
these products of the baby-boom made knowledge about food,
rather than about classical music or Renaissance art, into the

modern hallmark of social *savoir-faire*. To them, cooking was *the* art, the only form of pleasure worth discussing at length. The new standards they learnt to appreciate included freshness of ingredients, light sauces, undercooking, novel combinations of flavours, and the central importance of contrastive textures and colours on the same plate. T-bone steaks were out; fish was in. Ethnic cooking was revalued, new immigrant cuisines carefully assessed, and regional recipes resurrected. Thanks to the appearance of the food processor in the early 1970s, these upwardly mobile foodies could also start to prepare at home previously time-consuming and labour-intensive dishes like purées and mousses. Now the only effort needed to whisk, mince, or grate was pushing a finger against a button.

Though many foodies were influenced by the hippie ideals of experimentation and openness to novelty, they quickly forgot the flower children's notion of co-operation for the sake of a 'Me Generation' self-centredness. Generally, they were more concerned with cultivating their palate than with saving the planet. Becoming a foodie did not mean one had also to become a politicized wholefoodie. In fact, a few of the cuisines espoused by the new eating classes were blatantly anti-health, if not reactionary: Cajun cooking is rich in calories, fat, and salt; White Trash, the poor White counterpart of Soul Food, is strong on cholesterol, sugar, and processed foods; Neosquare celebrates the meals foodies' moms used to make out of packets and tins. For those who relish such cuisines, the sub-text seems to be, 'Why care about your heart so long as your stomach is happy?'

Foodies see themselves as individualists though they are, of course, members of a collective social movement, one of their own making. Close behind them come the trendies, those who wish to be in on the latest fashion though they may know as little about gastronomy as the Wild Boy of Aveyron. They do not go to an expensive foodie restaurant because of the chef, but because the place is in vogue. They go to see and be seen, and to be able to boast of the experience later. They are the sheep, led by the nose, and often paying through it as well.

Like the rise of French cuisine in the nineteenth century, the establishment of this culinary subculture is bolstered by a new breed of food journalists, ones keen to popularize and disseminate the emerging forms of gastronomy. The Big Four in the United

States have been Craig Clairborne, the late James Beard, Richard Olney, and, above all, Julia Childs. At the same time, restaurateurs like Alice Waters of Chez Panisse in Berkeley, California, see themselves as educators for ignorant but willing yuppies anxious to learn the guidelines of this new social game. These professional chefs are not scared of drawing from a wide range of different traditions to construct an innovative and winning style. Eclecticism, not classicism, rules.

In Britain, the first faint signs of a culinary culture arose in reaction to the post-war diet of rationed essentials, thin flavours, and substitute foods. The key actor in this scenario was a well-travelled, bookish cook with a literary bent called Elizabeth David. Her exhaustively researched tomes about Continental cuisines, with their polished but period style, provided a public starved of sensation with an almost encyclopaedic range of recipes. Though she started writing in the late 1940s, none of her works has been out of print for any length of time. Somewhat later, *A Book of Middle Eastern Food* and *Indian Cooking* by Claudia Roden and Madhur Jaffrey respectively were also highly influential in extending the tastes of British foodies. The work of these writers and their colleagues was complemented by the food journalism in the colour supplements of the quality Sunday newspapers, and by a still-continuing series of television programmes on cooking and the cuisines of different nations. Come the 1980s, no self-respecting British aspirant to social sophistication had any excuse for not knowing their way round the foodie's version of the world.

Continentals might have wondered what the fuss was about, for France, Italy, and Spain have long histories of appreciative and demanding publics who have always bothered about food. Ask any gastronome of the 1950s whether they would have preferred to eat in a grand London hotel or in the kitchen of a Mediterranean peasant cook, and the answer is rarely in doubt. The people of these countries were, in a sense, foodies *avant la lettre*. They did not need to be taught about food; they already cared about it deeply. *Nouvelle cuisine*, the much-touted 'revolution' in French cooking, was, in truth, simply the latest in a long series of culinary clarifications. It was yet another Return-To-Basics after a period of excess. *Nouvelle cuisine* has come, it has had its effect, and today it is no longer mentioned. Perhaps the only real change effected by the rise of affluence in these countries has been an increase in the number of people who can choose to vary and enrich their diet; who, thanks to air transport, can now try fresh, but previously unseen, exotic foods. And for those who *have* fallen prey to fast foods and the pace of modern business life, Italian and French chefs have launched an international 'Slow Food' movement, dedicated to the promotion of traditional local cuisine and of the two-hour lunch break. Founded in 1989, it already has chapters in twenty-six countries.

For foodies, dining out is a central activity. Going to a restaurant used to be merely part of having a night on the town. Where one went to eat was primarily determined by the role one wanted to play: thoughtful spouse, impassioned lover, supportive companion, entertaining friend, indulgent parent, or dutiful son or daughter to one's aged parents. Today's budding gastronomes can still perform any of these tired parts, but they do so through the medium of food. The meal itself is no longer an excuse for spending time together. It has now come close to being the main point of going out, and thus the key way of expressing the role one wishes to act. Foodies can still try to seduce or entertain, but these days the dishes they choose are as important as the conversation they make.

This new demand for novel cuisines and exciting tastes has generated, in turn, a market for new foods and hitherto unknown types of cooking. In an ambience of competitive consumption food has become fashion, and none of the aspiring classes wishes to be seen falling behind. Old varieties of familiar fruits, such as apples, are revived and foodies, unconsciously imitating the Victorians, can pass happy hours discussing their relative merits: the rich, dry, nuttiness of an Egremont Russet, the crisp, mildly sweet flavour of a Lord Lambourne, the strawberry hint of a Discovery, the pear-like quality of a St Edmunds Pippin, the sharp mushiness of a Savoury James Grieve, etc. (As you can see, it is all too easy to become a Foodie Bore.) At the same time prosaic staples are replaced by 'designer foods', upmarket and high-quality equivalents of the same old edibles. Instead of serving a ragout with spaghetti, you can now impress your guests with a bolognese of bison meat over *marille* – a beta-shaped form of pasta created by an industrial designer that is smooth on the outside but ribbed on the inside, so as to hold the sauce all the better. Rather than bore your diners with celeriac, parsnip, or potatoes, you can surprise them with skirret, rocket, turnip-rooted parsley, variegated endive, or balisier comestible.

The purest of foodies pride themselves on discovering obscure but surprisingly good recipes from neglected cuisines. Cookbooks now often specialize in the foods of highly specific regions or particular ethnic groups, their authors priding themselves on setting the cuisine firmly in its cultural context and on giving recipes which include hard-to-obtain ingredients. At the dinner-parties of the learned, it is as though the dishes come to the table each with its own footnotes, references, and bibliography. Guests are not meant to snigger at such academicism but to hum with flattered appreciation at the rare delicacies laid before them.

As foodies become more knowledgeable, the distinctions they make become ever finer. The more fashion-conscious stop patronizing Indian restaurants and start to seek out those that promise Balti, Bengali, or Kashmiri cooking, while Middle Eastern restaurants have been superseded by Lebanese, Iranian, or Afghan establishments. The archetypal foodie – who is, by definition, socially competitive – must keep abreast of all these trends or lose face and friends. For as soon as a food or a cuisine begins to shift downmarket, it is time to move your taste-buds on.

You do not want to be the last one in your circle still serving kiwi fruit.

26

THE LAST BITE?

The United States has the largest supermarkets in the world. With their aircraft-hangar size and their 50-metre long aisles (each devoted to a single type of food), they seem to embody everything the country stands for. The very sight of one, like a mirage taunting the eyes, would be enough to make a semi-starved Third Worlder cry. Which is just what Boris Yeltsin did when he entered one for the first time.

In Britain land is more expensive than in the United States, so supermarkets tend to be smaller. Yet they still come out as the most profitable in the world. How do they manage it?

One reason is that the Big Four food retailers in the country effectively control the market. But another, crucial factor is the amount of money they spend on research. Thanks to the psychologists who have worked for them, they can exactly predict and cunningly influence the behaviour of shoppers as if they were conditioned rats. Customers may *think* they know what they want to buy, but store managers know better, as they adroitly guide their subjects away from low-profit items towards more expensive, 'value-added' ones. The aim is to empty people's pockets fast, and to do it so skilfully they will keep on coming back.

It does not matter if customers get wise to some of the retailers' tricks, as harried buyers do not have the time to compensate for most of them. Supermarkets are constantly introducing so many new items (12,000 a year in the United States) that shoppers simply do not have the time to compare prices and check the nutritional information hidden away on the labels. By being offered so many different products in one store, customers are not spoiled for choice, they are confused by it – and so fall even easier prey to the manipulations of the supermarketeers. It may seem paradoxical, but, in this case, more choice means less.

Supermarketeers are not interested in propping up the social significance of food but in realizing its economic potential. If families stop eating together, then they can sell more individual microwave meals. And once these packaged products are glamorously advertised on television, children can pester their parents until the harassed adults agree to buy them. That way children can eat independently of their parents and learn to cultivate their food preferences from an early age. There is nothing sweeter for a supermarketeer than a population of choosy individuals, especially when he is choosing what they want.

Sales of fast food and frozen 'gourmet' meals continue to rise. According to a recent American survey, a quarter of adult consumers can now be classed as 'chase-and-grabbits' who 'have effectively said goodbye to their kitchens', while only 15 per cent of the adult population are 'Happy Cookers', that is, people who provide three meals a day, mostly made from basic ingredients. It is as though McDonald's and the microwave have spelt the end to anything that can be considered 'cooking'. Women might think ready-made meals mean an end to slaving at the stove, but all they are really doing is handing their chains over to a different master. A supermarketeer might seem less demanding on their time than a stove, but he wants more money.

If you wish to follow him all the way to the bank, follow these rules:

1. Place the entrance to your supermarket on the left-hand side of the building because people, when they enter a closed space, naturally look to the left and then start to move their eyes towards the right.

2. Place fruit, vegetables, flowers, and houseplants immediately after the entrance. That way you create an impression of freshness, healthy living, and natural growth, while masking the fact that most of the food on sale in your store is frozen, tinned, or preserved.

3. Paint the store green. It is restful on the eye and, again, suggests freshness, healthy living, and even environmental concern.

4. Hide staple groceries (tea, coffee, bread, etc.) at the back of the store so that people have to pass through aisles stocked with higher-margin items in order to get there.

5. From time to time rearrange the layout of foodstuffs in order to prevent regular customers from going straight to what they want and ignoring everything else. Remember, if shoppers do

not know where some item is, they have to scan the aisles
(and thus view many tempting new products) before they
find it.

6. Stack the low-profit items on the higher shelves in the
   narrower aisles. In these stretches of the store, shoppers push
   their trolleys that much faster as they speed ahead, lunging
   for what they want.

7. Put high-margin foods in the widest aisles. In these sections
   shoppers automatically slow down, start browsing, and,
   almost inevitably, buying.

8. Charge manufacturers extra if they want their foods posi-
   tioned at the end of aisles or on shelves at eye-level. Nothing
   sells as well as corner items seen by shoppers as they turn into
   the next aisle, while items they can eyeball directly are easier
   to spot than those higher up, or nearer the floor.

   For the same reasons place food otherwise difficult to sell
   – dented tins and items past their sell-by date – in dump bins
   at the end of each aisle, and position chiller cabinets containing ready-meals and other prepared high-margin foods at
   eye-level.

   Remember, 'Eye-level is buy-level.'

9. Put on the shelves as much as possible of each foodstuff. The
   rule here is, 'The more you display, the more you sell.'
   Customers like an atmosphere of super-abundance and will
   buy more from a fully stocked shop than from a half-empty
   one. In the same way, a 6-metre display of cornflakes is more
   tempting to buyers than a 3-metre one.

10. Pile confectionery at the checkout, at infant eye-level. For
    parents, put up magazines, a metre higher.

11. Keep your store clean, bright, and attractive. Do the job well
    enough and, you never know, it might end up like some of
    those in San Francisco, which function as unofficial pick-up
    joints on Wednesday nights.

    Is it every tired female shopper's dream to have a tall, dark
    stranger sidle his trolley up to hers and say, 'Excuse me, but
    do you know what the difference is between cider vinegar
    and balsamic?'

*

It would be nice to think that the future of our consuming culture lies with the wholefoodies. But it is more likely that the organic end of the market will remain a minority option for some time to come. Blitzed by so much conflicting nutritional advice, many of the public throw their hands into the air and surrender to the high-fat, sugar-rich foods they have always loved anyway. As far as they are concerned, the subtitle to their *kamikaze* behaviour reads, 'If you can't be sure what's good for you, why not just enjoy yourself anyway?' Especially if your cholesterol- and preservative-filled life is going to be a chemically fore-shortened one.

In this modern context of supermarketed conditioning, infor-mation overload, and fatalistic bingeing, the real consumers' motto of our day is not 'You are what you eat', rather 'You are what you are made to eat'.

Notes

INTRODUCTION
Bringeus (1975), pp. 251–73; Farb and Armelagos (1980), p. 161; Fischler (1980), p. 937; Parry (1982), pp. 74–110; Gow (1989), pp. 567–82.

1 THE CALL OF THE WILD
Zingg (1940), pp. 487–517; Singh and Zingg (1942); Curtiss (1977); Lane (1977); Malson (1972); Maclean (1977); Shattuck (1980).

2 CULTURE vs NATURE
Turnbull (1964), pp. 165–70; Mackay (1971), pp. 67–92; Wilson (1973); Wilson (1977), pp. 320–35; Grivetti (1978), pp. 171–7; De Garine (1979), pp. 70–92; Lee (1979), ch. 6 and 8; Farb and Armelagos, p. 224; Fischler (1980), pp. 937–53; Fieldhouse (1986), p. 41.

3 DESERT ISLAND DISHES
Rozin (1976); King (1980), pp. 75–6; Rozin and Schiller (1980), pp. 77–101; Root and de Rochemont (1976), p. 439; Rozin and Rozin (1981), pp. 243–52; Fieldhouse (1986), p. 207; 'Spanish Butter Wouldn't Melt in their Mouths', *Independent*, 25 January 1988; Chantree (1989), pp. 24–5; Schweid (1989); Ackerman (1990), pp. 169–70; *Independent*, 3 November 1990; the Cajun woman is quoted in Schweid (1989); the Marmite quote is from Marshall (1990); the food personality quotes are from King (1980), pp. 75–6.

4 OF LIFE, RICE AND REGULARITY
Fletcher (1899, 1903, 1914); Miles (1900, 1904); Hanks (1964, 1972); Avery (1984); Meigs (1984); Green (1985), p. 98; Manderson (1986a), p. 7; Coward (1989), pp. 144–6; Sobal (1990); the quote from Crowninshield (1909), p. 40, is cited in Levenstein (1988), p. 95; the *Green Farm* and 'the three times a day' quotes are both cited in Coward (1989), p. 145, and the naturopathy quote (Benjamin [1982]) on p. 49; the section on Fletcher is indebted to Levenstein (1988), pp. 87–95.

5 TABOO OR NOT TABOO
Holt (1885); Jacobi (1912), pp. 224–6; Angyal (1941), pp. 393–412; Bodenheimer (1951), pp. 10, 34–7; Gandhi (1954), quoted in Simoons (1979), p. 476; Douglas (1971), p. 1; Sutherland (1975), pp. 255–87; Taylor (1975), ch. 2. Diener and Robkin (1978), pp. 493–540; Jani (1979); Schwabe (1979), pp. 365–83; Simoons (1979), pp. 467–93; Feeley-Harnik (1981); Theodoratus (1981), p. 316; Okely (1983); Carroll (1985); Harris (1985), pp.

47–50; Reynell (1985), pp. 20–33; Cooper (1987); Isaacs (1987), pp. 175–6, 189–94; Arnold (1989), p. 54; *Guardian*, 22 November 1990; Rozin (1990); Cottam Ellis (1991), pp. 88–94; Eyton (1991), p. 16; Rebeyrol (1991); Reynell (1991), p. 55 fn. 2; Banks (1992); Gault and Millau are quoted in Root and de Rochemont (1976), p. 438; the 'crayfish' quote is from Gutierrez (1984), p. 177.

6 NO FOOD

Salisbury (1969), pp. 376–89, 413, 475–9; Omolulu (1971), pp. 165–8; Ellis (1976), pp. 125–33; Colson (1979), pp. 18–29; Winick (1979); Farb and Armelagos (1980), p. 26; Minns (1980), pp. 91, 99, 112; Neuman (1980), p. 32; Salzman (1982), pp. 14–18; Driver (1983), pp. 21–2, 32; Strang and Toomre (1985); Widdowson (1985), pp. 97–103; Chalker (1987); Levenstein (1988), p. vii; De Waal (1989); the Seamen's survival kit is from Black (1989); the Woolton pie recipe from Chalker (1987), p. 65; the tulip recipe from Holthius (1984), pp. 61–2.

7 MOVABLE FEASTS

Menagier de Paris (*c.* 1393), pp. 236–8, 264; Burnett (1966); Clark (1975), p. 40; Katona-Apte (1975), pp. 315–26; Murcott (1982), pp. 677–96; Palmer (1984); Mennell (1985), pp. 79, 150; Mintz (1985), p. 205; Kahn (1986), p. 46; Levenstein (1988), pp. 15, 167; Weismantel (1988), pp. 108–9, 127–30, 155–6, 177; Gow (1989), p. 569; Hendry (1990), pp. 57–62; Leeming (1991), pp. 154–5; information on India, M. Banks pers. comm., on the Tharu, C. MacDonaugh pers. comm., and on the Mambila, D. Zeitlyn pers. comm.; the section on the historical course is indebted to Tannahill (1988), pp. 38–40, 184–7, 296–303; the Bemba quote (from Richards [1939], pp. 46–9) is cited in Mintz (1985), pp. 9–10; the Jorai material comes directly from Downes (1977), pp. 161–4; the Homestead diet (from Byington [1910], pp. 63–4) is quoted in Levenstein (1988), pp. 101–2; the 'cooked dinner' and 'gravy' quotes are from Murcott (1982), pp. 677–96; the lists of English meal contents are from Burnett (1966) and Palmer (1984); the Scottish meals are from Lerche (1975), pp. 384–95; the Zumbagua meals are from Weismantel (1988).

8 SQUEEZE MY LEMON

Warner (1917), p. 136; Lévi-Strauss (1966), p. 105; Chagnon (1968), p. 47; Brillat-Savarin (1970), pp. 165–6; Millum (1972), pp. 167, 172; Downes (1977), p. 163; Tuzin (1978), p. 92, n. 4; Sillitoe (1979), pp. 77–97; Barer-Smith (1979), p. 170; Gregor (1985), pp. 70–5; Kahn (1986), pp. 72–3; Charles and Kerr (1988), pp. 64–7; Field (1989), p. 24; Schweid (1989), p. 130; Allan and Burridge (1991), pp. 99–100; the Baltimore quote is cited in Mintz (1985), p. 244; the extramarital and lesbian mealtimes quotes are from Cline (1990), pp. 61–3; the 'baby-bun' quotes are from Gelis (1984), pp. 122–3, 130–1, 152–5; 'The Pleasures of the Table' relies on Barr and Levy (1984), p. 20.

9 LOVIN' SPOONFULS

The key reference is to Farb and Armelagos (1980), pp. 84–7. Also Davenport (1869), p. 17; Wedeck (1962); Taberner (1985); Fussell (1989); Lake (1989); McLaren (1989), pp. 49–50; Stoddart (1990); *Merry Wives of Windsor*, v.v. 18–22.

10 ASKING FOR IT

Anell and Lagercrantz (1958); Trethowan and Coulon (1965), pp. 57–66; Dickens and Trethowan (1971), pp. 259–68; Barnes (1974), p. 146; Rivere (1974), pp. 423–35; Hook (1978), pp. 1355–62; Simon and Johnson (1978), pp. 41–49; Farb and Armelagos (1980), pp. 72–3; Cosminsky (1982), p. 212; Gelis (1984), pp. 122–3, 152–5; Bogren (1985); Fieldhouse (1986), pp. 221–2; Charles and Kerr (1988), p. 151; Murcott (1988), pp. 733–64.

11 REVOLUTION AT TABLE

The opening passages of this chapter are directly based on Greer's lecture, 'Sex and Food', attended by the author; Raum (1940), p. 213; Opie (1959); James (1979), pp. 83–95; Mead (1980); Reichel (1980), p. 46; Widdowson (1981), pp. 377–89; Murcott (1983b), p. 2; Spencer (1989), p. 11.

12 KID'S STUFF

Radcliffe-Brown (1922), pp. 94–101, 283, 304–5; C. Hugh-Jones (1979), pp. 114–123; Farb and Armelagos (1980), p. 79; Avery (1984), pp. xi–xiii; Mennell (1985), pp. 294–300; Levenstein (1988), p. 15; Freeman (1989), pp. 211–225; for other examples of juvenile food taboos, see Seligman (1910, p. 86), Fox (1924, p. 179), and Schieffelin (1976, p. 66); the Awa quote is cited in Newman and Boyd (1982), p. 247.

13 HOW TO MAKE FRIENDS

Richards (1932), p. 190; Bossard (1943), pp. 295–301; Evans-Pritchard (1951), pp. 55, 102; Fischer (1964), pp. 60–71; Holmberg (1969), p. 85; Barthes (1979), p. 172; Levi (1979), p. 166; Danforth (1982); Mintz (1982), p. 167; Coxon (1983), p. 176; Kalcik (1984), p. 49; Mintz (1985), pp. 204–5; Fieldhouse (1986), p. 86; Levy (1986), pp. 171–3; Charles and Kerr (1988), pp. 17–38, 207–224; *Sun*, 26 March 1990; Alison James (1991), pp. 30–33; Marshall (1991a), p. 35; the 'Christmas' quote is from Charles and Kerr (1988), p. 27; the Inuit quote is from Freuchen (1961), p. 154, cited in Farb and Armelagos (1980), p. 155; the Siriono quote is from Holmberg (1969), p. 85.

14 HOW TO MAKE ENEMIES

Brillat-Savarin (1970), pp. 165–6; Young (1971); D'Arms (1984), p. 346; Farb and Armelagos (1980), pp. 191–2; Levenstein (1988), p. 11; Weismantel (1988), pp. 110, 139; Jeanneret (1991); Willes (1991); the Benedictine comment is from Dom Daniel Rees, OSB; the Cicero quote (*ab fam.* 9.24.3) is cited in D'Arms (1984), p. 344; the Toklas quote is from Tannahill (1988), p. 80.

15 A CLASS ACT
LePatourel (1937), p. 79; Burnett (1966), ch. 4; Granet (1973); Befu (1974), pp. 196–203; Elias (1978), pp. 100–26; Cooper (1979), p. 202; S. Hugh-Jones (1979), p. 202, fn. 10; Sass (1981), pp. 253–60; Barr and York (1982), p. 63; Bourdieu (1984), pp. 177–200; Fussell (1984), pp. 97–107; Mennell (1985); pp. 208–11; Mintz (1985); Laurioux (1986), pp. 43–76; Witteveen (1986), pp. 22–31; Dumas (1987), pp. 270, 275; Charles and Kerr (1988), pp. 189–201; Tannahill (1988), pp. 187–92; MAFF (1989); Magomedkhan and Luguev (1989); OPCS (1990); *Sun*, 26 March 1990; Weber (1991), pp. 3–4; plus information kindly supplied by the Henley Centre and A. C. Nielson Co. Ltd; the 'cheap chips' quote is from Charles and Kerr (1988), p. 192.

16 RECIPES OF POWER
Graubard (1943), quoted in Kalcik (1984), p. 54; Castillo (1968), p. 7; Clark (1975), pp. 32–42; Zeldin (1977), pp. 724–55; Barthes (1979), pp. 169–70; Mintz (1982), p. 167; Mennell (1985), pp. 134–65; Mintz (1985), p. 209; Atkinson (1986), p. 37; Levy (1986), p. 100; Santona (1987), p. viii; Levenstein (1988), p. 146; the information on Futurism is from Marinetti (1989) and that on the British Raj from Brennan (1990); the 'Chinese Dinner' comes from Morgan (1979), p. 24, quoted in Doerper (1989).

17 JUST DESSERTS?
Much of the early part of this chapter is based on Charles and Kerr (1988) – the quotes are from page 46 – and Ellis (1983). Also Hirschon (1978), p. 83; Orbach (1978); Murcott (1983); Caskey (1981); Coward (1984), pp. 87–91, 101–5; Bynum (1987); Cooper (1987); Edwards (1987); Fursland (1987); Barthel (1989); Cline (1990); *Guardian*, 12 April 1991; James (1990); Orbach (1991); Lawson (1991); the chips quote is from Cline (1990), p. 167; the chocoholic quotes are from *Chocolate!*, screened on BBC2 in January 1991; the aggrieved Ecuadorian wife is from Weismantel (1988), p. 181.

18 MEAT AND VEG TOO
Sahlins (1976), p. 176; Farb and Armelagos (1980), p. 3; King (1980), p. 73; Schwabe (1981); Twigg (1983), pp. 18–30; Moran (1985); Fieldhouse (1986), pp. 140–3; Levenstein (1988), p. 199; Bramwell (1989), p. 196; Visser (1989), pp. 136–43; Adams (1990); Mellis and Davidson (1990); James (1990), p. 686 fn. 6; Eyton (1991), pp. 6, 63; Fiddes (1991) *passim*; the 'steak tartare' and the 'fox' quotes are from Fiddes (1991), ch. 6, and the 'gay dog' quote from ch. 10; the mice, bear, and rat recipes are from Schwabe (1981), pp. 204, 208, 210; the Cameroonian recipe is from Grimaldi and Bikia (1985).The 'if God's a chicken' quote is from Eyton (1991), p. 12.

19 OFFAL!
Wallis (1918), pp. 362–76; Moore (1957), pp. 77–82; Ayrton (1974); Root (1980), pp. 227, 520; Schwabe (1981); Abrahams (1984), p. 32; Kalcik (1984), p. 50; Mennell (1985), pp. 310–316; Arnold (1987), pp. 27–34; Brown (1987), pp. 60–4; Kirschenblatt-Gimblett (1987), pp. 7–16; Escoffier

(1989), pp. 309–10; Slatta (1990), p. 113; Mackie (1991), p. 125; the udder recipe is from Brown (1987); the geed recipe is from Kirschenblatt-Gimblett (1987); the ox tongue recipe is from David (1970), p. 176; the 'tongue' quote is from Welsch (1981), p. 369; the 'mountain men' quote is from Arnold (1987), p. 28.

20 FIRST CATCH YOUR MAN
Russell (1954), pp. 233–40; Read (1974); Arens (1979); Porter Poole (1983), pp. 6–32; Gillison (1983), pp. 33–50; Tuzin (1983), pp. 61–71; Sahlins (1983), pp. 72–93; Padel (1987); Price (1989), pp. 131; Camporesi (1991), pp. 162–88; the long final quote is from Johnson (1922) and the final line from Hastings (1918).

21 UNMENTIONABLE CUISINE
Gade (1976); Sahlins (1976); Schwabe (1981), pp. 157–76; Fitzgibbon (1982), p. 124 (quoted in Driver [1983], p. 32); Thomas (1983); Kalcik (1984), p. 37; Powers and Powers (1985); Harris (1985); Kraig (1985); Levy (1986), pp. 39, 97–100; *Daily Star*, 20 November 1989; Lake (1989), p. 13; Olowo (1990); the dogflesh menu comes from Levy (1986), pp. 98–9, the dog recipe is from Grimaldi and Bikia (1985), the cat recipe from Castillo (1983) p. 66 and the doggerel is quoted in Fort (1990).

22 GOBBLE, GULP AND GO
I do not want to be misunderstood: I have only focused on McDonald's in this chapter because it is the largest, and most intensively studied, fast-food chain. Many of my comments also apply to other chains. Kottak (1978), pp. 75–82; Law (1984), pp. 171–96; Edelman (1987), pp. 541–61; Love (1987); Gabriel (1988), pp. 93–6, 125–7; Lobstein (1988a), p. 72, (1988b), pp. 19, 71–89; Weismantel (1988), pp. 120–2; Visser (1989), pp. 117–19; Fiddes (1991), ch. 6; Marshall (1992); O'Shaughnessy (1992); the final quote is from Fiddes (1991), ch. 6; the M40 recipe and the caveat are adapted from Maynard and Scheller (1989); the hamburger recipe is from Lobstein (1988b), p. 19.

23 THE WHOLE TRUTH? NATURALLY!
The key reference for the first part of this chapter is Coward (1989), chs 1 and 5; also Atkinson (1980), pp. 79–89; Draper (1986); Gremier (1987); Cannon (1988), pp. 148, 205, 290; Lobstein (1988a), pp. 16, 109–20; '"Natural" is Misleading', *The Food Magazine*, London Food Commission, spring 1988, pp. 6–7; Belasco (1989); Robbins (1989); Visser (1989), pp. 219–20; Fellows and Voichick (1990); Gussow (1990), pp. 10–18; Heasman (1990); Ho (1990); Rudd (1990); *Guardian*, 25 June 1991, p. 2; Marshall (1991b), p. 32; the C. W. Post quote is cited in Fieldhouse (1986), p. 12; the examples for 'Believe It or Not' are from Tannahill (1988), pp. 354–5; the 'Guide to Good Nutrition' is based on 'Feeding Frenzy', *Newsweek*, 27 May 1991; part of the list of advertisers' terms is from 'It's Natural! It's Organic! Or Is It?', *Consumer Reports*, July 1980, pp. 410–15, quoted in Belasco (1989), p. 186; the 'Gastronomic Guidelines' are also adapted from Belasco (ibid).

24 EATING THE OTHER
Lo (1972), p. 83; Root and de Rochemont (1976), pp. 276–8; Driver (1983), pp. 73–96; Lockwood and Lockwood (1983), pp. 84–94; Szathmary (1983), pp. 137–43; Goode *et al* (1984), pp. 66–88; Kalcik (1984), pp. 37–65; Mars (1984), pp. 144–6; Messer (1984), p. 228; Zelinsky (1985), pp. 51–72; Mars and Mars (1988); Belasco (1989), pp. 229–36; Staub (1989), pp. 109, 129, 161.

25 HOW TO WORSHIP FOOD
Barr and Levy (1984); Du Cann (1985); Mickler (1986); Belasco (1989); Finkelstein (1989); Hawke (1989), pp. 221–38; Davidson (1990), p. 41; Glancey and Fergusson (1990), p. 36; Sinden (1990), p. 18; Smith (1990), p. 177; Bedford (1991), p. 18.

26 THE LAST BITE?
The supermarketeer's guide to making money is heavily indebted to Martin (1990), pp. 25–36; Belasco (1989), p. 247; Gussow (1990), pp. 10–18; on San Francisco supermarkets, check out 'Love and the Proper Shopper' in Armistead Maupin's *Tales of the City*, Corgi, 1980.

Bibliography

Abrahams, R. (1984). 'Equal Opportunity Eating: A Structural Excursus on Things of the Mouth', in Brown and Mussell, op. cit., pp. 19–36.

Adams, C. J. (1990). *The Sexual Politics of Meat. A Feminist-Vegetarian Critical Theory*, Cambridge: Polity.

Allan, K. and Burridge, K. (1991). *Euphemism and Dysphemism. Language as Shield and Weapon*, New York: Oxford University Press.

Anell, B. and Lagercrantz, S. (1958). *Geophagical Customs*, Studia Ethnographica Upsaliensia XVII, Uppsala.

Angyal, A. (1941). 'Disgust and Related Aversions', *Journal of Abnormal and Social Psychology 36* , pp. 393–412.

Arens, W. (1979). *The Man-Eating Myth: Anthropology and Anthropophagy*, New York: Oxford University Press.

Arnold, S. (1987). 'Food and Drink of the Mountain Men', *PPC 25* , pp. 27–34.

Arnold, Sue (1989). 'Hot on the Scent', *Observer* Magazine, 29 October, p. 54.

Arnott, M. L. (ed.) (1975), *Gastronomy. The Anthropology of Food and Food Habits*, The Hague: Mouton.

Atkinson, P. (1980). 'The Symbolic Significance of Health Foods', in M. Turner, op. cit., pp. 79–89.

Atkinson, S. J. (1986). 'Adolescent Nutrition and Diets', unpublished M.Sc. thesis, University College, London.

Avery, G. (1984). 'Children's Corner', *New Society*, 20/27 December, pp. xi–xiii.

Ayrton, E. (1974). *The Cookery of England*, London: Andre Deutsch.

Banks, M. *Organizing Jainism in India and England*, Oxford: Oxford University Press (in press).

Barer-Smith, T. (1979). *You Are What You Eat. A Study of Ethnic Food Traditions*, Toronto: McClelland and Stewart.

Barnes, R. H. (1974). *Kedang. A Study of the Collective Thought of an Eastern Indonesian People*, Oxford: Clarendon Press.

Barr, A. and York, P. (1982). *The Official Sloane Ranger Handbook*, London: Methuen.

Barr, A. and Levy, P. (1984). *The Official Foodie Handbook*, London: Ebury.

Barthel, D. (1989). 'Modernism and Marketing: The Chocolate Box Revisited', *Theory, Culture and Society 6*, pp. 424–38.

Barthes, R. (1979). 'Towards a Psychosociology of Contemporary Food Consumption', in *Food and Drink in History. Selections from the Annales. Economies, Societes, Civilisations 5*, edited by R. Forster and O. Rarum (originally published in *Annales. Economies ... 16*, pp. 977–86), Baltimore: Johns Hopkins University Press, 1961.

225

Bedford, H. (1991). 'Sluggish Reaction to the Fast Life', *Guardian*, 13 April, p. 18.

Befu, H. (1974). 'An Ethnography of Dinner Entertainment in Japan', *Arctic Anthropology XI* , Supplement, pp. 196–203.

Belasco, W. J. (1989). *Appetite for Change. How the Counterculture Took on the Food Industry (1966–1988)*, New York: Pantheon.

Benjamin, H. (1982). *Everybody's Guide to Nature Cure*, North Hollywood, Ca: Newcastle Publications.

Birnbach, L. (ed.) (1981). *The Official Preppy Handbook*, London: Ebury.

Black, M. (1989).'Survival Kit (Sixteenth-Century Seamen's Fare)', in *Staple Foods*, Oxford Food Symposium, London: Prospect Books.

Bodenheimer, F. S. (1951). *Insects as Human Food. A Chapter of the Ecology of Man*, The Hague: Junk.

Bogren, L. (1985). *The Couvade Syndrome and Side Preference in Child Holding*, Linkoping University, Sweden: Linkoping University Medical Dissertations No. 194.

Bossard, J. H. S. (1943). 'Family Table-talk – An Area for Sociological Study', *American Sociological Review VIII*, pp. 295–301.

Bourdieu, P. (1984). *Distinction. A Social Critique of the Judgement of Taste*, London: Routledge and Kegan Paul.

Bramwell, A. (1989). *Ecology in the Twentieth Century. A History*, New Haven: Yale University Press.

Brennan, J. (1990). *Curries and Bugles. A cookbook of the British Raj*, London: Viking.

Brillat-Savarin, J-A. (1970). *The Philosopher in the Kitchen*, Harmondsworth: Penguin (originally published 1825).

Bringeus, N-A. (1975). 'Food and Folk Beliefs: On Boiling Blood Sausage', in Arnott, op. cit., pp. 251–73.

Brown, L. (1987). 'Elder: "A Good Udder to Dinner"', *PPC 26*, pp. 60–4.

Brown, L. K. and Mussell, K. (eds.) (1984). *Ethnic and Regional Foodways in the United States. The Performance of Group Identity*, Knoxville: University of Tennessee Press.

Burnett, J. (1966). *Plenty and Want. A Social History of Diet in England from 1815 to the Present Day*, London: Nelson.

Byington, M. (1910). *Homestead. The Households of a Mill Town*, New York: Charities Publication Committee.

Bynum, C. W. (1987). *Holy Feast and Holy Fast. The Religious Significance of Food to Medieval Women*, Berkeley: University of California Press.

Camporesi, P. (1991). *The Fear of Hell. Images of Damnation and Salvation in Early Modern Europe*, Cambridge: Polity.

Cannon, G. (1988). *The Politics of Food*, London: Century.

Carrithers, M. and Humphrey, C. (eds.) (1991). *The Assembly of Listeners,* Cambridge: Cambridge University Press.

Carroll, M. P. (1985). 'One More Time: Leviticus Revisited', in *Anthropological Approaches to the Old Testament*, edited by B. Lang, London: SPCK.

Caskey, N. (1981). 'Interpreting Anorexia Nervosa', in *The Female Body in Western Culture*, edited by S. R. Suleiman, Cambridge, Mass: Harvard

University Press.

Castillo, J. (1968). *El manual de la cocina economica vasca*, San Sebastian: Txertoa.

—— (1983). *Recetas de cocina de abuelas vascas. Tomo 1. Alava-navarra*, Fuenterabbia.

Chagnon, N. (1968). *Yanomami. The Fierce People*, New York: Holt, Rinehart and Winston.

Chalker, B. (1987). *Cook-ups of World War Two*, Bristol: Redcliffe.

Chantree, P. (1989). 'Death Fish', *Taste*, August, pp. 24–5.

Chapman, M. and Macbeth, H. (eds.) (1990). *Food for Humanity. Cross-Disciplinary Readings*, Oxford: Oxford Polytechnic.

Charles, N. and Kerr, M. (1988). *Women, Food and Families*, Manchester: Manchester University Press.

Clark, P. P. (1975). 'Thoughts for Food, I: French Cuisine and French Culture', *French Review XLIX*, pp. 32–42.

Cline, S. (1990). *Just Desserts. Women and Food*, London: Deutsch.

Colson, E. (1979). 'In Good Year and Bad: Food Strategies of Self-Reliant Societies', *Journal of Anthropological Research 35*, pp. 18–29.

Cooper, J. (1979). *Class. A View from Middle England*, London: Methuen.

Cooper, S. (1987). 'The Laws of Mixture: An Anthropological Study in Halakhah', in *Judaism. Viewed from Within and from Without*, edited by H. E. Goldberg, New York: SUNY Press.

Cooper, T. (1987). 'Anorexia and Bulimia: The Political and the Personal', in Lawrence, pp. 175–92.

Cosminsky, S. (1982). 'Childbirth and Change: A Guatemalan Study', in *Ethnography of Fertility and Birth*, edited by C. P. MacCormack, London: Academic Press, pp. 205–29.

Cottam Ellis, C. M. (1991). 'Jain Merchant Castes of Rajasthan', in Carrithers and Humphrey, op. cit., pp. 75–107.

Coward, R. (1984). *Female Desire: Women's Sexuality Today*, London: Paladin.

—— (1989). *The Whole Truth. The Myth of Alternative Health*, London: Faber.

Coxon, T. (1983). 'Men in the Kitchen: Notes from a Cookery Class', in Murcott, op. cit., pp. 165–77.

Crowninshield, F. (1909). *Manners for the Metropolis*, New York: Appleton.

Curtiss, S. (1977). *Genie: A Psycholinguistic Study of a Modern Day 'Wild Child'*, New York: Academic Press.

Danforth, L. (1982). *The Death Rituals of Rural Greece*, Princeton: Princeton University Press.

D'Arms, J. H. (1984). 'Control, Companionship and *Clientela*: Some Social Functions of the Roman Communal Meal', *Echos du Monde Classique (Classical Views)*, XXVIII, N.S. 3.

Davenport, J. (1869). *Aphrodisiacs and Anti-Aphrodisiacs*, London.

David, E. (1970). *Spices, Salt and Aromatics in the English Kitchen*, Harmondsworth: Penguin.

Davidson, A. (1983). *Oxford Symposium (1983). Food In Motion. The Migration of Foodstuffs and Cookery Techniques*, Leeds: Prospect Books.

—— (1990). 'Picking the crops of the future', *Independent*, 31 March, p. 41.

Davis, J. (1909). *Travels of Four Years and a Half in the United States of America during 1798, 1799, 1800 and 1802*, New York.

Dickens, G. and Trethowan, W. H. (1971). 'Cravings and Aversions during Pregnancy', *Journal of Psychosomatic Research 15*, pp. 259–68.

Diener, P. and Robkin, E. E. (1978). 'Ecology, Evolution, and the Search for Cultural Origins: The Question of the Islamic Pig Prohibition', *Current Anthropology 19*, pp. 493–540.

Doerper, J. (1989). 'Staple Foods of the American West Coast (A Semi-Historical Perspective; or, Culture Change in Action)', in *Staple Foods*, Oxford Food Symposium, London: Prospect Books.

Douglas M. (1966). *Purity and Danger: An Analysis of Concepts of Pollution and Taboo*, London: Routledge and Kegan Paul.

—— (1971). 'Deciphering a Meal', *Daedalus 101*, p. 1.

Downes, J. (1977). 'Time and Menu', in *The Anthropologists' Cookbook*, edited by J. Kuper, London: Routledge and Kegan Paul, pp. 161–4.

Draper, A. (1986). 'What's in a Health Food? An Analysis of Food Choice with Reference to the Contemporary Obsession for Health', unpublished M.Sc. thesis, University College, London.

Driver, C. (1983). *The British at Table 1940–1980*, London: Chatto and Windus.

Du Cann, C. (1985). *Offal and the New Brutalism*, London: Heinemann.

Dumas, A. (1987). *Dumas on Food: Recipes and Anecdotes from the Classic Grand Dictionnaire de Cuisine*, translated by A. and J. Davidson, Oxford: Oxford University Press.

Edelman, M. (1987). 'From Costa Rican Pasture to North American Hamburger', in *Food and Evolution. Toward a Theory of Human Food Habits*, edited by M. Harris and E. B. Ross, Philadelphia: Temple University Press, pp. 541–61.

Edwards, G. (1987). 'Anorexia and the Family', in Lawrence, op. cit.

Elias, N. (1978). *The Civilizing Process. Vol. 1. The History of Manners*, Oxford: Blackwell.

Ellis, J. (1976). *Eye-Deep in Hell. The Western Front 1914–18*, London: Croom Helm.

Ellis, R. (1983). 'On Domestic Violence'; 'The Way to a Man's Heart: Food in the Violent Home', in Murcott, op. cit., pp. 164–71.

Escoffier, A. (1989). *Ma Cuisine*, originally published 1934, London: Hamlyn.

Evans-Pritchard, E. E. (1951). *Kinship and Marriage among the Nuer*, Oxford: Clarendon Press.

Eyton, A. (1991). *The Kind Food Guide*, Harmondsworth: Penguin.

Farb, P. and Armelagos, G. (1980). *Consuming Passions. The Anthropology of Eating*, Boston: Houghton Mifflin.

Feeley-Harnik, G. (1981). *The Lord's Table. Eucharist and Passover in Early Christianity*, Philadelphia: University of Pennsylvania Press.

Fenton, A. and Owen, T. M. (eds.) (1981). *Food in Perspective. Proceedings of the Third International Conference on Ethnological Food Research*, Edinburgh: John Donald.

Fellows, B. and Voichick, J. (1990). 'Minority and White Low-Income Homemakers' Views on Dietary Fat and Cancer', paper given at the Fourth

Annual Conference of the Association for the Study of Food and Society, Philadelphia.

Fiddes, N. (1991). *Meat. A Natural Symbol*, London: Routledge.

Field, C. (1989). *The Italian Baker*, New York: Harper and Row.

Fieldhouse, P. (1986). *Food and Nutrition: Customs and Culture*, London: Croom Helm.

Fildes, V. A. (1986). *Breasts, Bottles and Babies. A History of Infant Feeding*, Edinburgh: Edinburgh University Press.

—— (1988). *Wet Nursing. A History from Antiquity to the Present*, Oxford: Basil Blackwell.

Fink, A. (1985). 'Nutrition, Lactation and Fertility in Two Mexican Rural Communities', *Social Science and Medicine 20*, pp. 1295–1305.

Finkelstein, J. (1989). *Dining Out. A Sociology of Modern Manners*, Cambridge: Polity.

Fischer, H. (1964). 'The Clothes of the Naked Nuer', *International Archives of Ethnography 50*, pp. 60–71.

Fischler, C. (1980). 'Food Habits, Social Change, and the Nature/Culture Dilemma', *Social Science Information 19: 6*, pp. 937–53.

Fitzgibbon, T. (1982). *With Love: An Autobiography 1938–1946*, London.

Fletcher, H. (1899). *The Glutton or Epicure*, Chicago: Stone.

—— (1903). *The New Glutton or Epicure*, London: Grant Richards.

—— (1914). *Fletcherism, What It Is, or How I Became Young at Sixty*, London: Ewart, Seymour.

Fort, M. (1990). 'Horses for Courses', *Weekend Guardian, Guardian*, 30 June, pp. 18–19.

Fox, C. E. (1924). *The Threshold of the Pacific. An Account of the Social Organization, Magic and Religion of the People of San Cristoval in the Solomon Islands*, London: Kegan Paul, Trench and Trubner.

Freeman, S. (1989). *Mutton and Oysters. The Victorians and Their Food*, London: Gollancz.

Freuchen, P. (1961). *Book of the Eskimo*, Cleveland: World.

Fulford, R. (ed.). (1968). *Dearest Mama: Letters between Queen Victoria and the Crown Princess of Prussia 1861–64*, London.

Fursland, A. (1987). 'Eve Was Framed: Food and Sex and Women's Shame', in Lawrence, op. cit., pp. 15–26.

Fussell, P. (1984). *Caste Marks. Style and Status in the USA*, London: Heinemann.

—— (1989). *Wartime. Understanding and Behaviour in the Second World War*, Oxford: Oxford University Press.

Gabriel, Y. (1988). *Working Lives in Catering*, London: Routledge and Kegan Paul.

Gade, D. W. (1976). 'Horsemeat as Human Food in France', *Ecology of Food and Nutrition 5*, pp. 1–11.

Gandhi, M. K. (1954). *How to Serve the Cow*, Ahmedabad: Navajivan.

Garine, I. De. (1979). 'Culture et nutrition', *Communications 31*, pp. 70–92.

Gault, H. and Millau, C. (1967). *Guide de New York, Boston, Chicago, Los Angeles, New Orleans, San Francisco et Montreal*, Paris: Juillard.

Gelis, J. (1984). *L'arbre et le fruit. La naissance dans l'Occident moderne XVIe–XIXe siecle*, Paris: Fayard.

Gillison, G. (1983). 'Cannibalism among Women in the Eastern Highlands of Papua New Guinea', in Tuzin and Brown, op. cit.

Glancey, J. and Fergusson, J. J. (1990). 'Love, Whim, Science and Pasta', *Independent*, 20 January, p. 36.

Goode, J., Theophano, J. and Curtis, K. (1984). 'A Framework for the Analysis of Continuity and Change in Shared Sociocultural Rules for Food Use: The Italian-American Pattern', in Brown and Mussell, op. cit., pp. 66–88.

Gow, P. (1989). 'The Perverse Child: Desire in a Native American Subsistence Economy', *Man 24: 3*, pp. 567–82.

Granet, M. (1973). 'Right and Left in China', in *Right and Left. Essays on Dual Symbolic Classification*, edited by Rodney Needham, Chicago: University of Chicago Press.

Graubard, M. (1943). *Man's Food, Its Rhyme and Reason*, New York: Macmillan.

Green, S. (1985). 'My Own Message to the Streets', *Sunday Times* Magazine, 10 June, p. 98.

Gregor, T. (1985). *Anxious Pleasures. The Sexual Lives of an Amazonian People*, Chicago: Chicago University Press.

Gremier, S. R. (1987). 'Food Faddism', unpublished M.Sc. thesis, University College, London.

Grimaldi, J. and Bikia, A. (1985). *La grand livre de la cuisine camerounaise*, Yaounde, Cameroon: SOPECAM.

Grivetti, L. E. (1978). 'Culture, Diet, and Nutrition: Selected Themes and Topics', *Bioscience 28: 3*, pp. 171–7.

Gussow, J. D. (1990). 'Dazed in the Supermarket: Is This Free Choice?', ASFS Newsletter, November, pp. 10–18.

Gutierrez, C. P. (1984). 'The Social and Symbolic Uses of Ethnic/Regional Foodways: Cajuns and Crawfish in South Louisiana', in Brown and Mussell, op. cit., pp. 169–82.

Hanks, L. M. (1964). 'Reflections on the Ontology of Rice', in *Primitive Views of the World*, edited by S. Diamond, Columbia: Columbia University Press, pp.151–4.

—— (1972). *Rice and Man: Agricultural Ecology in Southeast Asia*, Chicago: Aldine Atherton.

Hardyment, C. (1983). *Dream Babies. Child Care from Locke to Spock*, Oxford: Oxford University Press.

Harris, M. (1985). *The Sacred Cow and the Abominable Pig. Riddles of Food and Culture*, originally published as *Good to Eat*, New York: Simon and Schuster.

Hastings, J. (ed.) (1918). *Encyclopaedia of Religion and Ethics*, 13 vols., New York.

Hawke, R. (1989). 'Mass Media and Lifestyle Differentiation: An Analysis of the Public Discourse about Food', *Communication 11*, pp. 221–38.

Heasman, M. (1990). 'The Development and Market for 'Lite' Products in the UK and its Nutritional Significance', paper given at the Fourth Annual Conference of the Association for the Study of Food and Society,

Philadelphia.

Hendry, J. (1990). 'Food as Social Metaphor: The Japanese Case', in Chapman and Macbeth, op. cit., pp. 57–62.

Herdt, G. H. (1982). 'Fetish and Fantasy in Sambia Initiation', in *Rituals of Manhood. Male Initiation in Papua New Guinea*, edited by G. H. Herdt, Berkeley: University of California Press, pp. 44–98.

—— (1984). 'Semen Transactions in Sambia Culture', in *Ritualized Homosexuality in Melanesia*, edited by G. H. Herdt, Berkeley: University of California Press, pp. 167–210.

Hirschon, R. (1978). 'Open Body/Closed Space: The Transformation of Female Sexuality', in *Defining Females. The Nature of Women in Society*, edited by S. Ardener, London: Croom Helm.

Ho, E .E., Lamborn, K., Fujikawa, M., and Gribble, M. (1990). 'Developing Measures and Consumer Profiles on Dietary Behaviours Related to Cancer Risk Reduction', paper given at the Fourth Annual Conference of the Association for the Study of Food and Society, Philadelphia.

Holmberg, A. R. (1969). *Nomads of the Long Bow. The Siriono of Eastern Bolivia*, New York: Natural History Press.

Holt, V. M. (1885). *Why Not Eat Insects?*, London: Field and Tuer.

Holthuis, L. B. (1984). 'Food in Wartime Netherlands', *PPC 18*, pp. 61–2.

Hook, E. B. (1978). 'Dietary Cravings and Aversions During Pregnancy', *American Journal of Clinical Nutrition 31*, pp. 1355–62.

Hugh-Jones, C. (1979). *From the Milk River: Spatial and Temporal Processes in Northwest Amazonia*, Cambridge: Cambridge University Press.

Hugh-Jones, S. (1979). *The Palm and the Pleiades: Initiation and Cosmology in Northwest Amazonia*, Cambridge: Cambridge University Press.

Hunter, L. (1991). 'Illusion and Illustration in English Cookery Books since the 1940s', in *The Appetite and the Eye. Visual Aspects of Food and Its Presentation Within Their Historical Context*, edited by C. A. Wilson, Edinburgh: Edinburgh University Press, pp. 141–60.

Isaacs, J. (1987). *Bush Food. Aboriginal Food and Herbal Medicine*, Sydney: Weldon.

Jacobi, H. (1912). 'Cow (Hindu)', in Hastings, vol. 2, op. cit., pp. 224–6.

James, A. (1979). 'Confections, Concoctions, and Conceptions', *JASO X*, pp. 83–95.

—— (1990). 'The Good, the Bad and the Delicious: The Role of Confectionery in British Society', *Sociological Review 38*, November, pp. 666–88 .

James, Alison, (1991). 'What's for Executive Lunch?', *Inflight*, February.

Jani, P. S. (1979). *The Jaina Path of Purification*, Berkeley: University of California Press.

Jeanneret, M. (1991). *A Feast of Words. Banquets and Table Talk in the Renaissance*, Cambridge: Polity.

Johnson, M. (1922). *Cannibal Land*, Chicago.

Kahn, M. (1986). *Always Hungry, Never Greedy. Food and the Expression of Gender in a Melanesian Society*, Cambridge: Cambridge University Press.

Kalcik, S. (1984). 'Ethnic Foodways in America: Symbolism and the

Performance of Identity', in Brown and Mussell, op. cit., pp. 37–65.

Katona-Apte, J. K. (1975). 'Dietary Aspects of Acculturation: Meals, Feasts, and Fasts in a Minority Community in South India', in Arnott, op. cit., pp. 315–26.

King, S. (1980). 'Presentation and the Choice of Food', in Turner, op. cit., pp. 67–78.

Kirshenblatt-Gimblett, B. (1987). 'Udder and Other Extremities: Recipes from the Jews of the Yemen', *PPC 27*, pp. 7–16.

Kortlandt, A. (1984). 'Habitat Richness, Foraging Range and Diet in Chimps and Some Primates', in *Food Acquisition and Processing in Primates*, edited by D. J. Chivers, B. A. Wood, and A. Bilsborough, New York: Plenum.

Kottak, C. P. (1978). 'Rituals at McDonald's', *Natural History Magazine 87*, pp. 75–82.

Kraig, J. n. d. (1985). 'Cynophagy: A Western Food Taboo', paper presented to the Oxford Food Symposium.

Lake, M. (1989). *Scents and Sexuality. The Essence of Excitement*, London: John Murray.

Lane, H. (1977). *The Wild Boy of Aveyron*, London: George Allen and Unwin.

Laurioux, B. (1986). 'Spices in the Medieval Diet', *Food and Foodways 1* No. 1, pp. 43–76.

Law, J. (1984). 'How Much of Society can the Sociologist Digest at one Sitting? The "Macro" and the "Micro" Revisited for the Case of fast Food', *Studies in Symbolic Interaction 5* (1984), pp. 171–96.

Lawrence, M. (ed.). (1987). *Fed Up and Hungry. Women, Oppression and Food*, London: Women's Press.

Lawson, N. (1991). 'Hey, Fat People! Wanna Change Your Life?', *Independent*, 16 March, p. 35.

Lee, R. B. (1979). *The !Kung San. Men, Women, and Work in a Foraging Society*, Cambridge: Cambridge University Press.

Leeming, M. (1991). *A History of Food. From Manna to Microwave*, London: BBC.

Leonardi, S. J. (1989). 'Recipes for Reading: Summer Pasta, Lobster à la Riseholme, and Key Lime Pie', *Proceedings of the Modern Language Association 104* No. 3, pp. 340–7.

LePatourel, J. H. (1937). *The Medieval Administration of the Channel Islands*, Oxford: Oxford University Press.

Lerche, G. (1975). 'Notes on Different Types of "Bread" in North Scotland: Bannocks, Oatcakes, Scones, and Pancakes', in Arnott, op. cit., pp. 384–95.

Levenstein, H. (1988). *Revolution at the Table. The Transformation of the American Diet*, New York: Oxford University Press.

Levi, P. (1979). *If This Is a Man*, Harmondsworth: Penguin.

Lévi-Strauss, C. (1966). *The Savage Mind*, London: Weidenfeld and Nicolson.

Levy, P. (1986). *Out to Lunch*, London: Chatto and Windus.

Lo, K. (1972). *Chinese Food*, Harmondsworth: Penguin.

Lobstein, T. (1988a). *Children's Food. The Good, the Bad and the Useless*, London: Unwin.

—— (1988b). *Fast Food Facts. A Compendium of Hidden Secrets of Fast Food Catering*, London: Camden Press.

Lockwood, W. G. and Lockwood, Y. R. (1983). 'The Cornish Pasty in Northern Michigan', in Davidson, op. cit, pp. 84–94.

London, A. and Kahn Bishov, B. (1983). *The Complete Jewish Cookbook*, London: W. H. Allen.

Love, J. F. (1987). *McDonald's. Behind the Arches*, New York: Bantam.

Mackay, D. A. (1971). 'Food, Illness and Folk Medicine: Insights from Ulu Trengganu, West Malaysia', *Ecology of Food and Nutrition 1: 1*, pp. 67–92.

Mackie, C. (1991). *Life and Food in the Caribbean*, London: Weidenfeld and Nicolson.

Maclean, C. (1977). *The Wolf Children*, London: Allen Lane.

MAFF (Ministry of Agriculture, Food, and Fisheries) (1989). *Household Food Consumption and Expenditure: 1988. Annual Report of the National Food Survey Committee*, London: HMSO.

Magomedkhan, M. and Luguev, S. (1989). 'Traditional Table Manners in Dagestan', in *Staple Foods*, Oxford Food Symposium, London: Prospect Books.

Malson, L. (1972). *Wolf Children*, London: New Left Books.

Manderson, L. (1986a). 'Introduction', in Manderson (1986b), op. cit.

Manderson, L. (1986b). *Shared Wealth and Symbol. Food, Culture, and Society in Oceania and Southeast Asia*, Cambridge: Cambridge University Press.

Marinetti, F. P. (1989). *The Futurist Cookbook*, translated by S. Brill, edited with an introduction by L. Chamberlain, London: Trefoil.

Mars, V. (1983). 'Spaghetti – But not on Toast! Italian Food in London,' in Davidson (1983), op. cit., pp. 144–6.

Mars, V. and Mars, G. (1988). 'Cracking the Airline Food Code: How a New Cuisine has Arisen from the Old', in *Proceedings of the First International Food Congress Turkey*, edited by F. Halki, Ankara: Nurol Matbaacilik.

Marshall, J. (1990). 'Marmite Thrives, but Trouble's Brewing', *Independent*, 3 October.

—— (1991a). 'The Family That No Longer Eats Together', *Independent*, 16 February, p. 35.

—— (1991b). 'Free to Range? Don't You Believe It', *Guardian*, 13 July, p. 32.

—— (1992). 'Big Mac Is Not So Fat', *Independent*, 1 February, p. 34.

Martin, P. (1990). 'Trolley Fodder. How Supermarkets Make a Meal of You', *Sunday Times* Magazine, 4 November, pp. 25–36.

Maynard, C. and Scheller, B. (1989). *Manifold Destiny. The One! The Only! Guide to Cooking on Your Car Engine*, New York: Villard.

McLaren, A. (1990). *A History of Contraception: From Antiquity to the Present Day*, Oxford: Blackwell.

Mead, M. (1980). 'A Perspective on Food Patterns', in *Issues in Nutrition for the 1980s*, edited by L. A. Tobias and P. J. Thompson, Monterey.

Meigs, A. S. (1984). *Food, Sex, and Pollution. A New Guinea Religion*, New Brunswick: Rutgers University Press.

Mellis, S. and Davidson, B. (1990). *The Born-Again Carnivore. The Real Meat Guide*, London: Macdonald Optima.

Menagier de Paris (*c.* 1393). Published as *The Goodman of Paris*, translated and introduced by E. Powers (1928), London: Routledge.

Mennell, S. (1985). *All Manners of Food. Eating and Taste in England and France from the Middle Ages to the Present*, Oxford: Blackwell.

Messer, E. (1984). 'Anthropological Perspectives on Diet', *Annual Review of Anthropology 1984*, Annual Reviews Inc., pp. 205–49.

Mickler, E. M. (1986). *White Trash Cooking*, Berkeley: Ten Speed.

Miles, E. (1900). *Muscle, Brain, and Diet. A Plea for Simpler Foods*, London: Sonnenschein.

—— (1904). *A Boy's Control and Self-Expression*, Cambridge.

Millum, T. (1972). *Images of Women. Advertising in Women's Magazines*, London: Chatto and Windus.

Minns, R. (1980). *Bombers and Mash. The Domestic Front 1939–45*, London: Virago.

Mintz, S. (1982). 'Choice and Occasion: Sweet Moments', in *The Biology of Human Food Selection*, edited by L. M. Barker, Chichester: Ellis Horwood.

—— (1985). *Sweetness and Power: The Place of Sugar in Modern History*, New York: Viking.

Moore, H. B. (1957). 'The Meaning of Food', *American Journal of Clinical Nutrition 5*, pp. 77–82.

Moran, V. (1985). *Compassion. The Ultimate Ethic*, Wellingborough: Thorson.

Morgan, M. (1979). *Puget's Sound: A Narrative of Early Tacoma and the Southern Sound*, Seattle: University of Washington Press.

Murcott, A. (1982). 'On the Social Significance of the "Cooked Dinner" in South Wales', *Social Science Information 21*, pp. 677–96.

—— (1983a). 'It's a Pleasure to Cook for Him': Food, Mealtimes and Gender in some South Wales Households', in *The Public and the Private*, edited by E. Garmanikov *et al*, London: Heinemann, pp. 78–90.

—— (ed.) (1983b). *The Sociology of Food and Eating*, Aldershot: Gower.

—— (1988). 'On the Altered Appetites of Pregnancy: Conceptions of Food, Body and Person', *Sociological Review*, pp. 733–64.

Newman, J. L. (1980). 'Dimensions of Sandawe Diet', in Robson, op. cit.

Newman, P. L. and Boyd, D. J. (1982). 'The Making of Men: Ritual and Meaning in Awa Male Initiation', in Herdt (1982), op. cit., pp. 239–285.

Office of Population Censuses and Surveys (1990). *The Dietary and Nutritional Survey of British Adults*, London: HMSO.

Okely, J. (1983). *Traveller Gypsies*. Cambridge: Cambridge University Press.

Olowo Ojoade, J. (1990). 'Nigerian Cultural Attitudes to the Dog', in *Signifying Animals. Human Meaning in the Natural World*, edited by R. G. Willis, *One World Archaeology 16*, London: Unwin Hyman, pp. 215–21.

Omolulu, A. (1971). 'Changing Food Habits in Africa', *EFN 1*, pp. 165–8.

Opie, I. and P. (1959). *The Lore and Language of Schoolchildren*, Oxford: Oxford University Press.

Orbach, S. (1978). *Fat is a Feminist Issue*, London: Paddington.

—— (1991). 'Food Fads Fixed', *Weekend Guardian, Guardian*, 18 May, p. 10.

O'Shaughnessy, H. (1992). 'Is There Honey Still For Tea?', *Observer*, 16 February, p. 65.

Padel, F. (1987). 'British Rule and the Konds of Orissa: A Study of Tribal Administration and its Legitimating Discourse', unpublished D.Phil. thesis, University of Oxford.

Palin, M., Chapman, G., Cleese J., Idle, E., Jones, T. and Gilliam, T. (1973). *The Brand New Monty Python Bok*, London: Eyre Methuen.

Palmer, A. (1984). *Movable Feasts. Changes in English Eating-Habits*, 2nd edn., originally published 1952, Oxford: Oxford University Press.

Parry, J. (1982). 'Sacrificial Death and the Necrophagous Ascetic', in *Death and the Regeneration of Life*, edited by M. Bloch and J. Parry, Cambridge: Cambridge University Press.

Pocock, D. (1984). 'Introduction' to Palmer, op. cit., pp. xi–xxxiv.

Porter Poole, F. J. (1983). 'Cannibals, Tricksters, and Witches: Anthropophagic Images among Bimim-Kuskusmin', in Tuzin and Brown, op. cit.

Powers, W. K. and Powers, M. M. N. (1984). 'Metaphysical Aspects of an Oglala Food System', in *Food in the Social Order: Studies of Food and Festivities in Three American Communities*, edited by M. Douglas, New York: Russell Sage Foundation.

Price, S. (1989). *Primitive Art in Civilized Places*, Chicago: University of Chicago Press.

Radcliffe-Brown, A. R. (1922). *The Andaman Islanders*, Cambridge: Cambridge University Press.

Raum, O. F. (1940). *Chaga Childhood*, London: International Institute of African Languages and Cultures.

Read, P. P. (1974). *Alive: The Story of the Andes Survivors*, London: Secker and Warburg.

Rebeyrol, Y. (1991). 'Fried Lice and Ant Pâté', *Le Monde*, 13 February.

Reichel, R. (1980). 'The Crunching of America', *Ms*, 8 February, p. 46.

Reynell, J. (1985). 'Renunciation and Ostentation: A Jain paradox', *Cambridge Anthropology 9: 3*, pp. 20–33

—— (1991). Women and the Reproduction of the Jain Community', in Carrithers and Humphrey, op. cit., pp. 41–65.

Richards, A. (1932). *Hunger and Work in a Savage Tribe. A Functional Study of Nutrition among the Southern Bantu*, London: Routledge.

—— (1939). *Land, Labour and Diet in North Rhodesia*, Oxford: Oxford University Press.

Riviere, P. G. (1974). 'The Couvade: A Problem Reborn', *Man 9*, pp. 423–35.

Robbins, C. (1989). '"Natural" Ain't Natural', paper given at ICAF conference, Oxford Polytechnic.

Robson, J. R. K. (ed.) (1980). *Food, Ecology and Culture. Readings in the Anthropology of Dietary Practices*, New York: Gordon and Breach.

Root, W. (1980). *Food*, New York: Simon and Schuster.

Root, W. and Rochemont, R. de. (1976). *Eating in America. A History*, New York: Ecco.

Rozin, P. (1976). 'The Selection of Food by Rats, Humans and Other Animals', in *Advances in the Study of Behaviour 6*, edited by J. Rosenblatt, R. A. Hinde, C. Beer and E. Shaw, New York: Academic Press.

—— (1990). 'Disgust and Ambivalence to Meat', paper given at the Fourth Annual Conference of the Association for the Study of Food and Society, Philadelphia.

Rozin, P. and Rozin, E. (1981). 'Some Surprisingly Unique Characteristics of Human Food Preferences', in Fenton and Owen, op. cit., pp. 243–52.

Rozin, P. and Schiller, D. (1980). 'The Nature and Acquisition of a Preference for Chilli Peppers by Humans', *Motivation and Emotion*.

Rudd, J. (1990). '"All I Wanted Was a Lite (Food)": Consumers and Food Label Descriptive Terms', paper given at the Fourth Annual Conference of the Association for the Study of Food and Society, Philadelphia.

Russell, Lord (of Liverpool) (1954). *The Knights of Bushido. A Short History of Japanese War Crimes*, London: Cassell.

Sahlins, M. (1976) *Culture and Practical Reason*, Chicago: University of Chicago Press.

—— (1983). 'Raw Women, Cooked Men, and Other "Great Things" of the Fiji Islands', in Tuzin and Brown, op. cit., pp. 72–93.

Salisbury, H. E. (1969). *The Siege of Leningrad*, London: Secker and Warburg.

Salzman, C. (1982). 'Food in the Netherlands during the Second World War', *PPC 12*, pp. 14–18.

Santich, B. (1989). 'Feed The Man Meat!', paper given at the Oxford Food Symposium.

Santona, H. (1987). 'Sobre la gastronomia navarra', *Navarra Hoy*, 21 August, p. viii.

Sass, L. J. (1981). 'The Preference for Sweets, Spices, and Almond Milk in Late Medieval English Cuisine', in Fenton and Owen, op. cit., pp. 253–60.

Schieffelin, E. L. (1976). *The Sorrow of the Lonely and the Burning of the Dancers*, New York: St Martin's Press.

Schwabe, C. W. (1981). *Unmentionable Cuisine*, Charlottesville, VA: University Press of Virginia.

Schweid, R. (1989). *Hot Peppers. Cajuns and Capsicums in New Iberia, Louisiana*, Berkeley, CA: Ten Speed Press.

Seligman, C. G. (1910). *The Melanesians of British New Guinea*, Cambridge: Cambridge University Press.

Shattuck, R. (1980). *The Forbidden Experiment: The Story of the Wild Boy of Aveyron*, London: Secker and Warburg.

Sillitoe, P. (1979). 'Man-Eating Women: Fears of Sexual Pollution in the Papua New Guinea Highlands', *Journal of the Polynesian Society 88*, pp. 77–97.

Simoons, F. J. (1979). 'Questions in the Sacred-Cow Controversy', *Current Anthropology 20:3*, pp. 467–93.

Simpson, A. W. B. (1984). *Cannibalism and the Common Law*, Chicago: Chicago University Press.

Sinden, N. (1990). 'The Apples Bite Back', *Food Magazine*, October, p. 18.

Singh, J. A. L. and Zingg, R. M. (1942). *Wolf Children and Feral Man*, New York: Harper and Row.

Smith, D. (1990). *Modern Cooking*, London: Sidgwick and Jackson.

Snow, L. F. and Johnson, S. M. (1978). 'Folklore, Food, Female Reproductive

Cycle', *Ecology of Food and Nutrition* 7, pp. 41–9.

Sobal, J. (1990). 'Public Beliefs about the Amount of Fiber in Foods', paper given at the Fourth Annual Conference of the Association for the Study of Food and Society, Philadelphia.

Spencer, C. (1989). 'Sex, Lies and Fed by Men', *Weekend Guardian, Guardian*, 4–5 November, p. 11.

Staub, S. (1989). *Yemenis in New York City. The Folklore of Ethnicity*, London: Associated Universities Press.

⟋ Stoddart, D. M. (1990). *The Scented Ape. The Biology and Culture of Human Odour*, Cambridge: Cambridge University Press.

Strang, J. and Toomre, J. (1985). 'Ireland Without the Potato: Short and Long-Term Solutions', paper given at the Oxford Food Symposium.

Sturgis, M. (1991). 'Wing or Leg?', *ES* (*Evening Standard* Magazine), July, p. 14.

Sutherland, A. (1975). *Gypsies. The Hidden Americans*, New York: Oxford University Press.

Szathmary, L. (1983). 'New Festive Foods of the Old World Became Commonplace in the New, or the American Perception of Hungarian Goulash', in Davidson (1983), op. cit., pp. 137–43.

Taberner, P. V. (1985). *Aphrodisiacs. The Science and the Myth*, London: Croom Helm.

Tannahill, R. (1988). *Food in History*, 2nd edn., Harmondsworth: Penguin.

Taylor, R. L. (1975). *Butterflies in My Stomach*, Santa Barbara, CA: Woodbridge Press.

Theodoratus, R. J. (1981). 'Greek-American Cuisine in America: Continuity and Change', in Fenton and Owen, op. cit., pp. 313–23.

Thomas, K. (1983). *Man in the Natural World. Changing Attitudes in England 1500–1800*, London: Allen Lane.

Trethowan, W. H. and Coulon, M. F. (1965). 'The Couvade Syndrome', *British Journal of Psychiatry 111*, pp. 57–66.

Turnbull, C. (1964). *Wayward Servants. The Two Worlds of the Mbuti Pygmies*, London: Eyre and Spottiswoode.

Turner, M. (ed.) (1980). *Nutrition and Lifestyles*, London: Applied Science Publishers.

Tuzin, D. F. (1978). 'Sex and Meat-Eating in Ilahita: A Symbolic Study', *Canberra Anthropology 1*, pp. 82–93.

—— (1983). 'Cannibalism and Arapesh Cosmology: A Wartime Incident with the Japanese', in Tuzin and Brown, op. cit.

Tuzin, D. F. and Brown, P. (eds.) (1983). *The Ethnography of Cannibalism*, Washington, DC: Society for Psychological Anthropology.

Twigg, J. (1983). 'Vegetarianism and the Meanings of Meat', in Murcott (1983), op. cit., pp. 18–30.

Visser, M. (1989). *Much Depends On Dinner. The Extraordinary History and Mythology, Allure and Obsessions, Perils and Taboos, of an Ordinary Meal*, Harmondsworth: Penguin.

Waal, A. De (1989). *Famine that Kills. Darfur, Sudan, 1984-1985*, Oxford: Clarendon.

Wallis, W. D. (1918). 'Prodigies and Portents', in Hastings, op. cit., vol. 10, pp. 362–76.

Warner, R. (1791). *Antiquitates Culinariae: Or Curious Tracts Relating to the Culinary Affairs of the Old English*, London: Blamire.

Weber, E. (1991). 'La Grande Bouffe. The Rise and Fall of the Gallic Gastronome', *The Times Literary Supplement*, 9 August, pp. 3–4.

Wedeck, H. E. (1962). *Dictionary of Aphrodisiacs*, London: Peter Owen.

Weismantel, M. J. (1988). *Food, Gender, and Poverty in the Ecuadorian Andes*, Philadelphia: University of Pennsylvania Press.

Welsch, R. L. (1981). 'An Interdependence of Foodways and Architecture: A Foodways Context on the American Plains', in Fenton and Owen, op. cit., pp. 365–76.

Widdowson, J. D .A. (1981). 'Food and Traditional Verbal Modes in the Social Control of Children', in Fenton and Owen, op. cit., pp. 377–89.

Widdowson, E. M. (1985). 'Responses to Deficits of Dietary Change', in *Nutritional Adaptation in Man*, edited by K. Blaxter and J. C. Waterlow, London: John Libbey.

Willes, M. (1991). 'Soop Meagre and Syllabub', *Oxford Today. The University Magazine*, Hilary Issue, pp. 24–5.

Wilson, C. S. (1973). 'Food Habits: A Selected Annotated Bibliography', *Journal of Nutritional Education 5*, Supplement 1.

Wilson, P. J. (1977). 'La Pensée Alimentaire: The Evolutionary Context of Rational Objective Thought', *Man 12*, pp. 320–35.

Winick, M. (ed.) (1979). *Hunger Diseases. Studies by the Jewish Physicians in the Warsaw Ghetto*, New York: John Wiley.

Witteveen, J. (1986). 'On Swans, Cranes, and Herons: Part 1, Swans', *PPC 24*, pp. 22–31.

Young, M. (1971). *Fighting with Food. Leadership, Values and Social Control in a Massim Society*, Cambridge: Cambridge University Press.

Zeldin, T. (1977). *France 1848–1945*, vol. 2. *Intellect, Taste and Anxiety*, Oxford: Clarendon Press.

Zelinsky, W. (1985). 'The Roving Palate: North America's Ethnic Restaurant Cuisines', *Geoforum 16*, pp. 51–72.

Zingg, R. (1940). 'Feral Man and Extreme Cases of Isolation', *American Journal of Psychology 53*, pp. 487–517.

Index